# Sword of the Demon Hunter

## KIJIN GENTŌSHŌ

KIJIN
GENTŌSHŌ

Motoo Nakanishi
Yu Satomi

5

TABLE OF CONTENTS:
# KIJIN GENTŌSHŌ 5

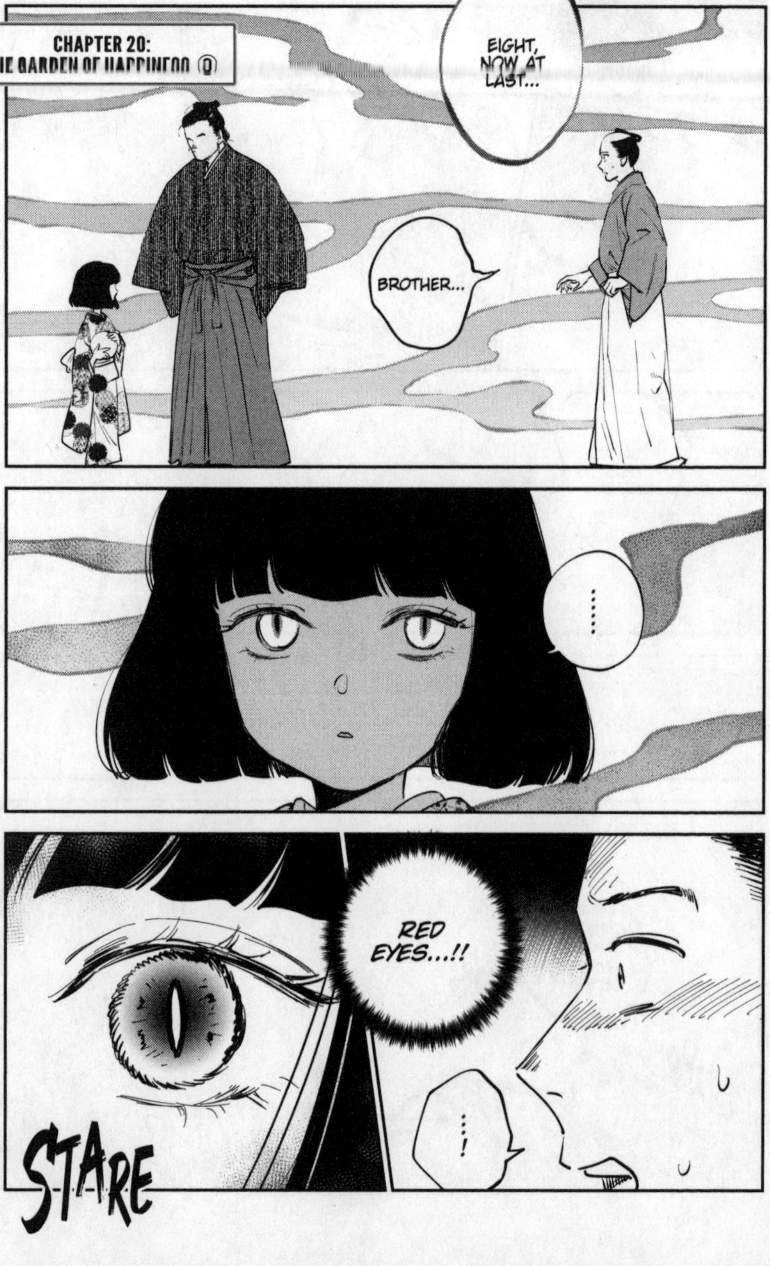
CHAPTER 20: THE GARDEN OF HAPPINESS ①
EIGHT, NOW AT LAST...
BROTHER...
......
RED EYES...!!
...!
STARE

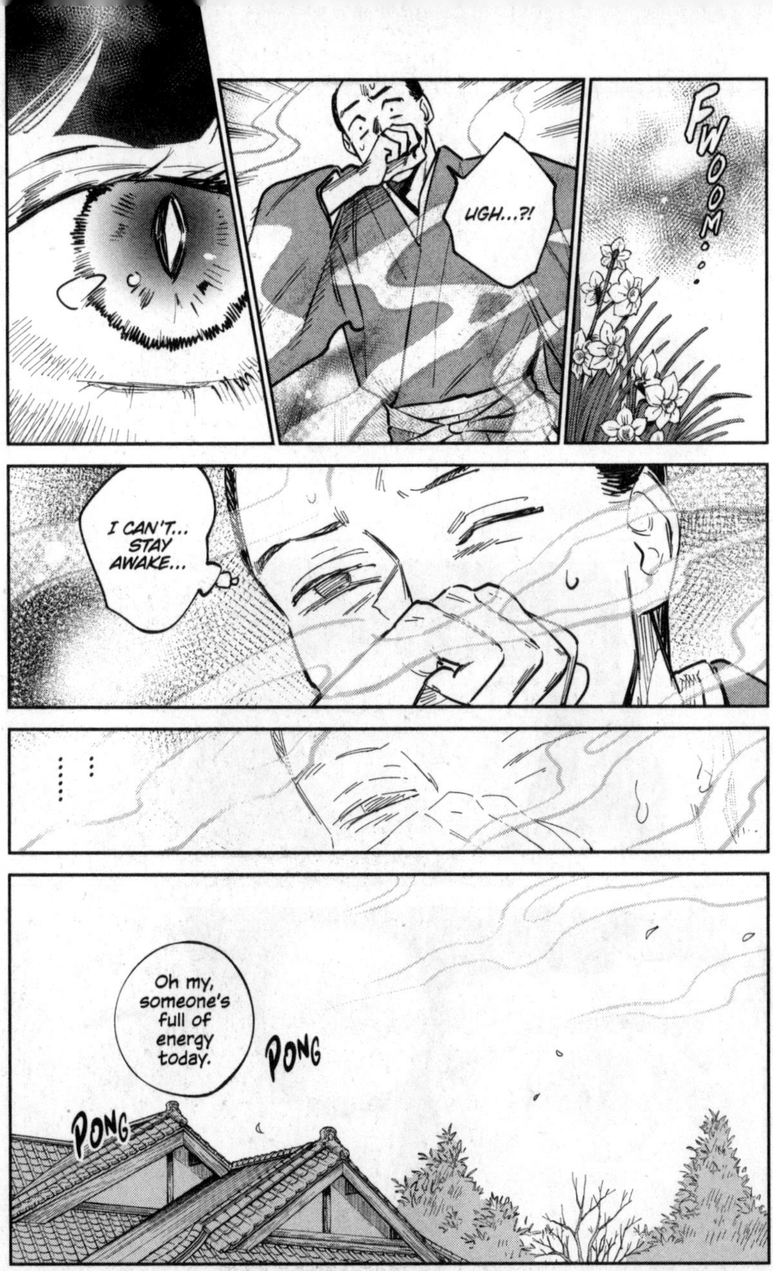
FWOOM...
UGH...?!
I CAN'T... STAY AWAKE...
......
Oh my, someone's full of energy today.
PONG
PONG

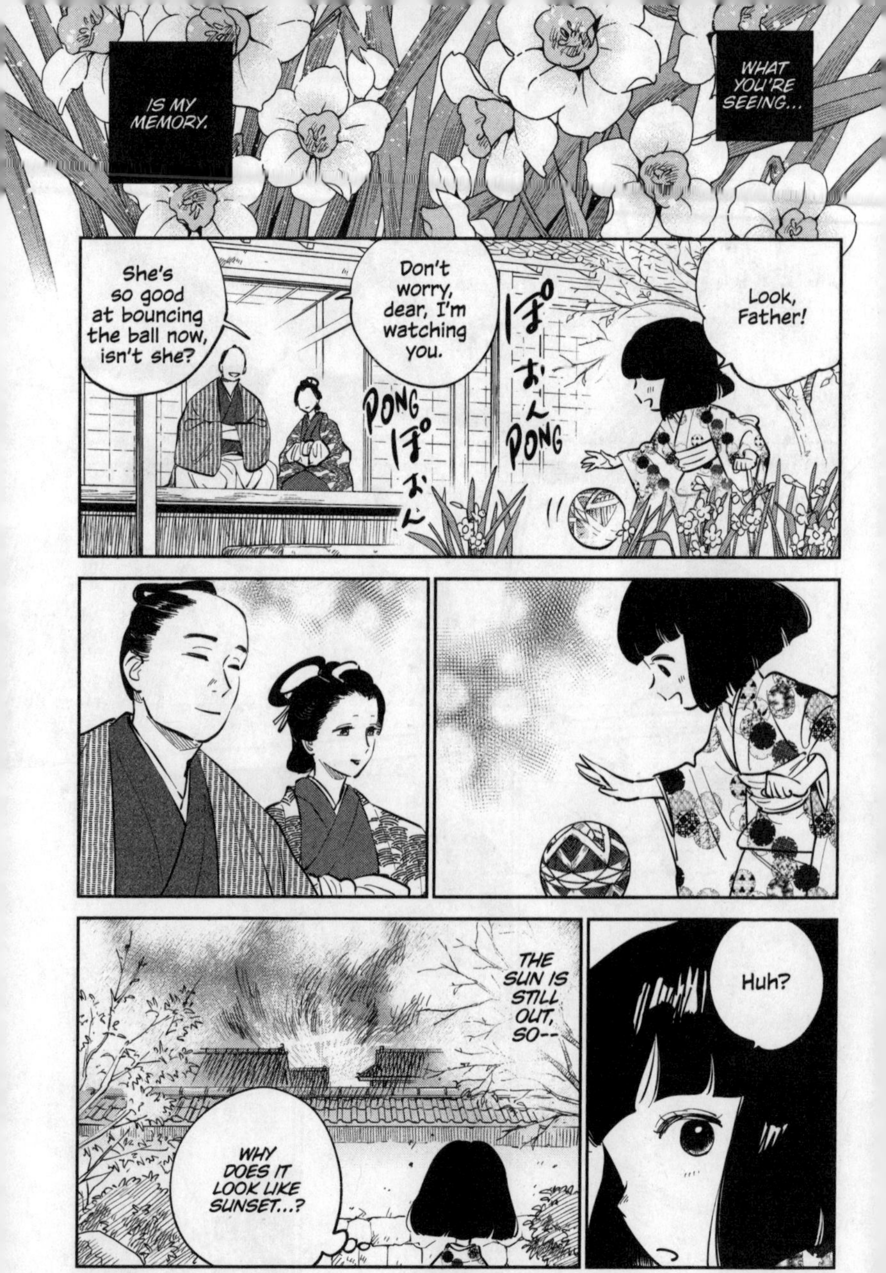
WHAT YOU'RE SEEING...
IS MY MEMORY.
Look, Father!
ぽおん PONG
Don't worry, dear, I'm watching you.
She's so good at bouncing the ball now, isn't she?
PONG ぽおん
Huh?
THE SUN IS STILL OUT, SO--
WHY DOES IT LOOK LIKE SUNSET...?

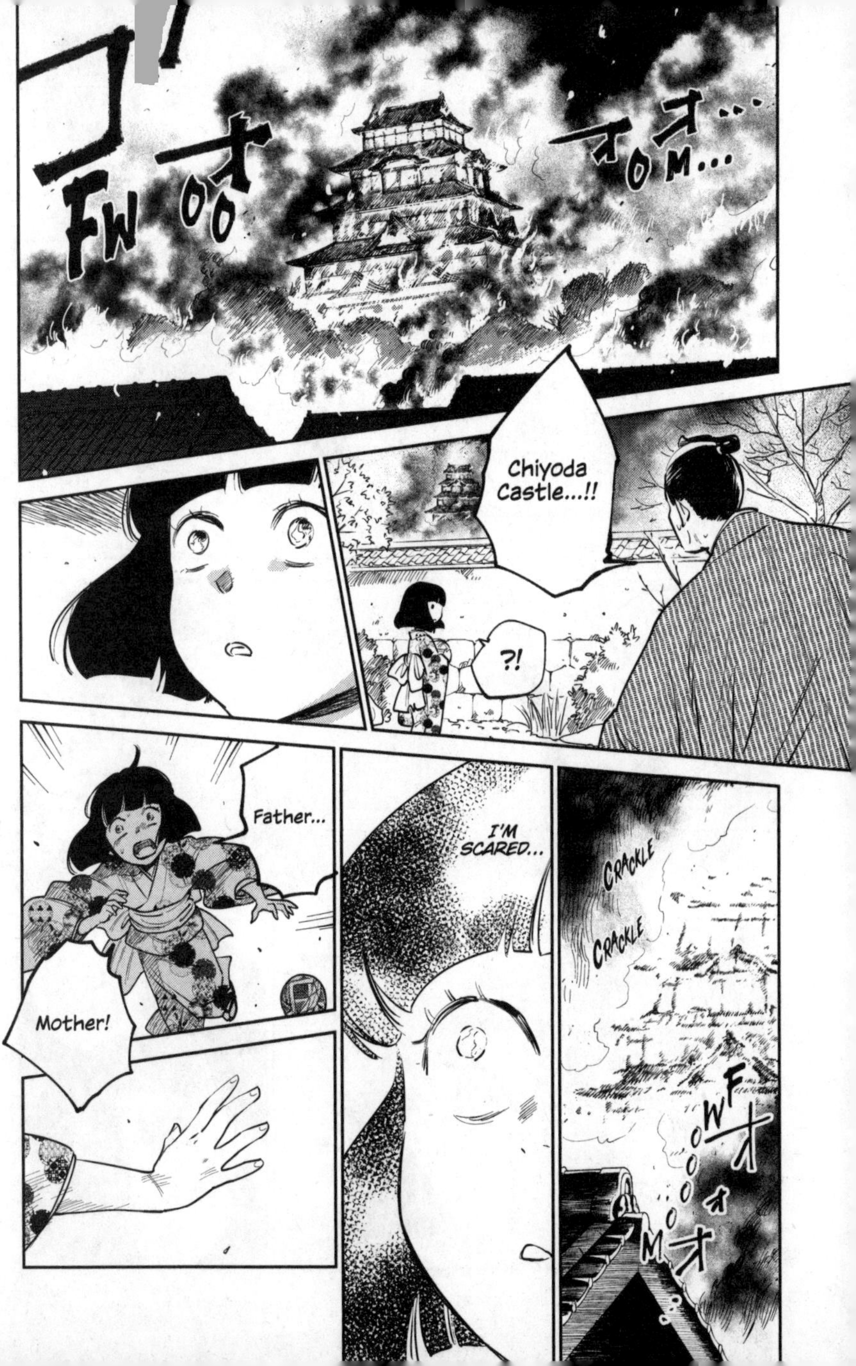

FW
OO
OM...
Chiyoda Castle...!!
?!
CRACKLE
CRACKLE
FWOOOOOM
I'M SCARED...
Father...
Mother!

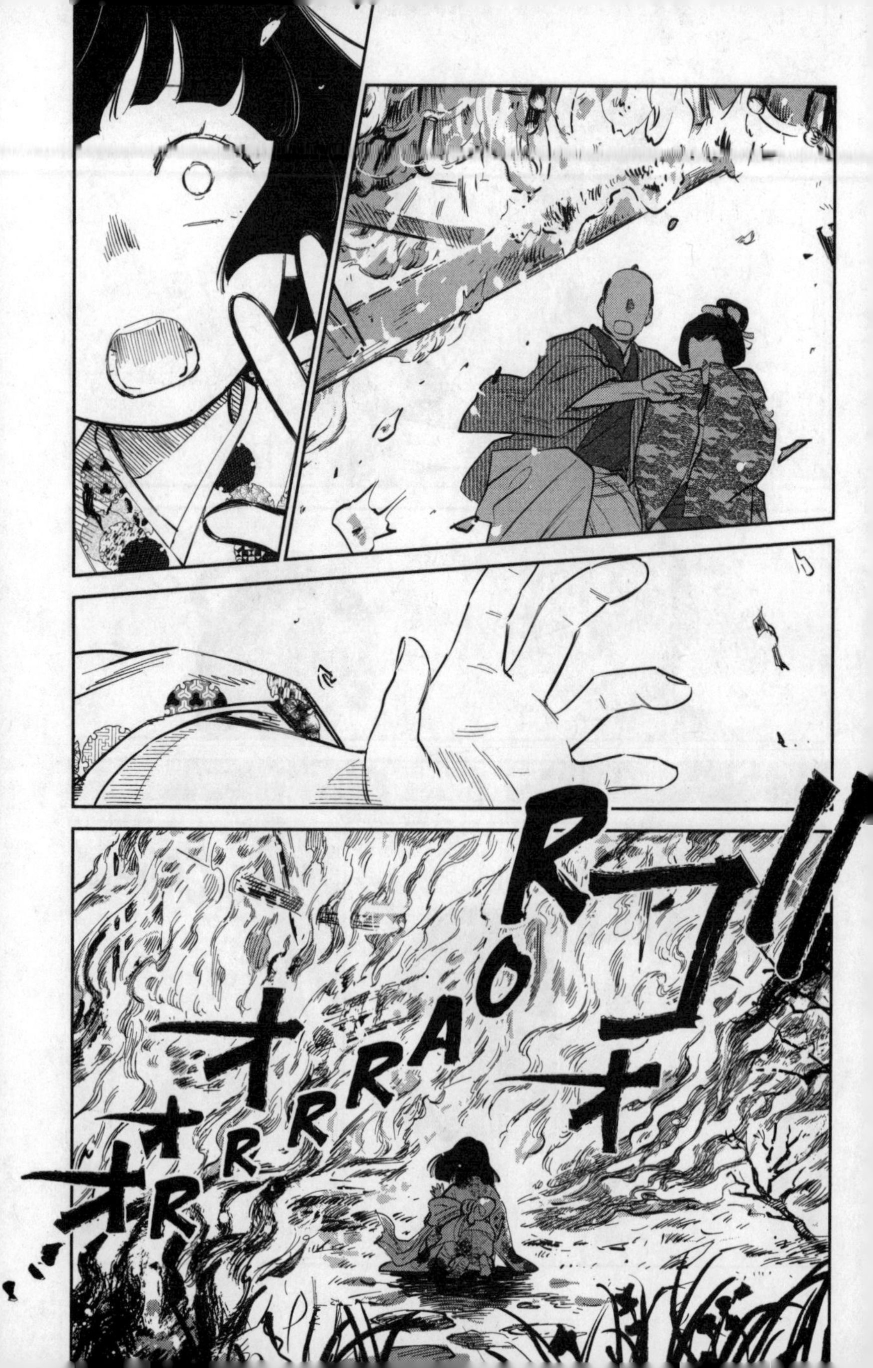

ゴーオオオオ
ROARRRR

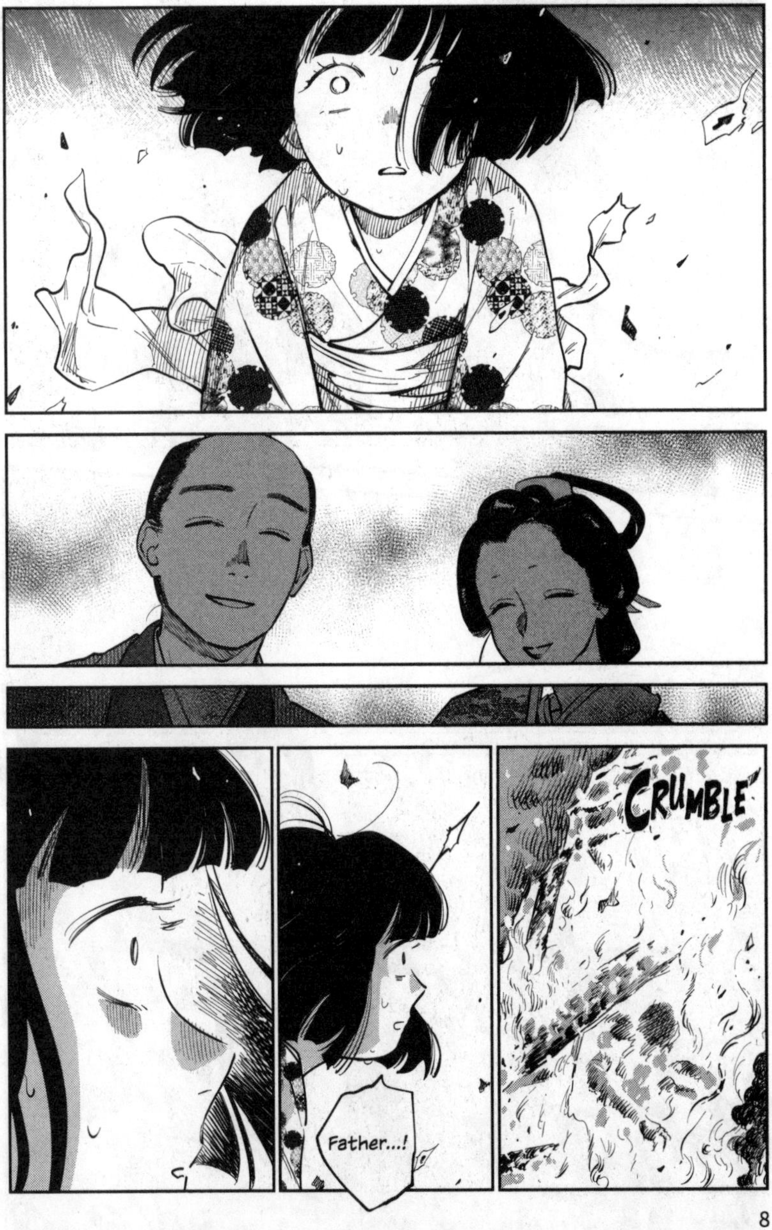
CRUMBLE
Father...!

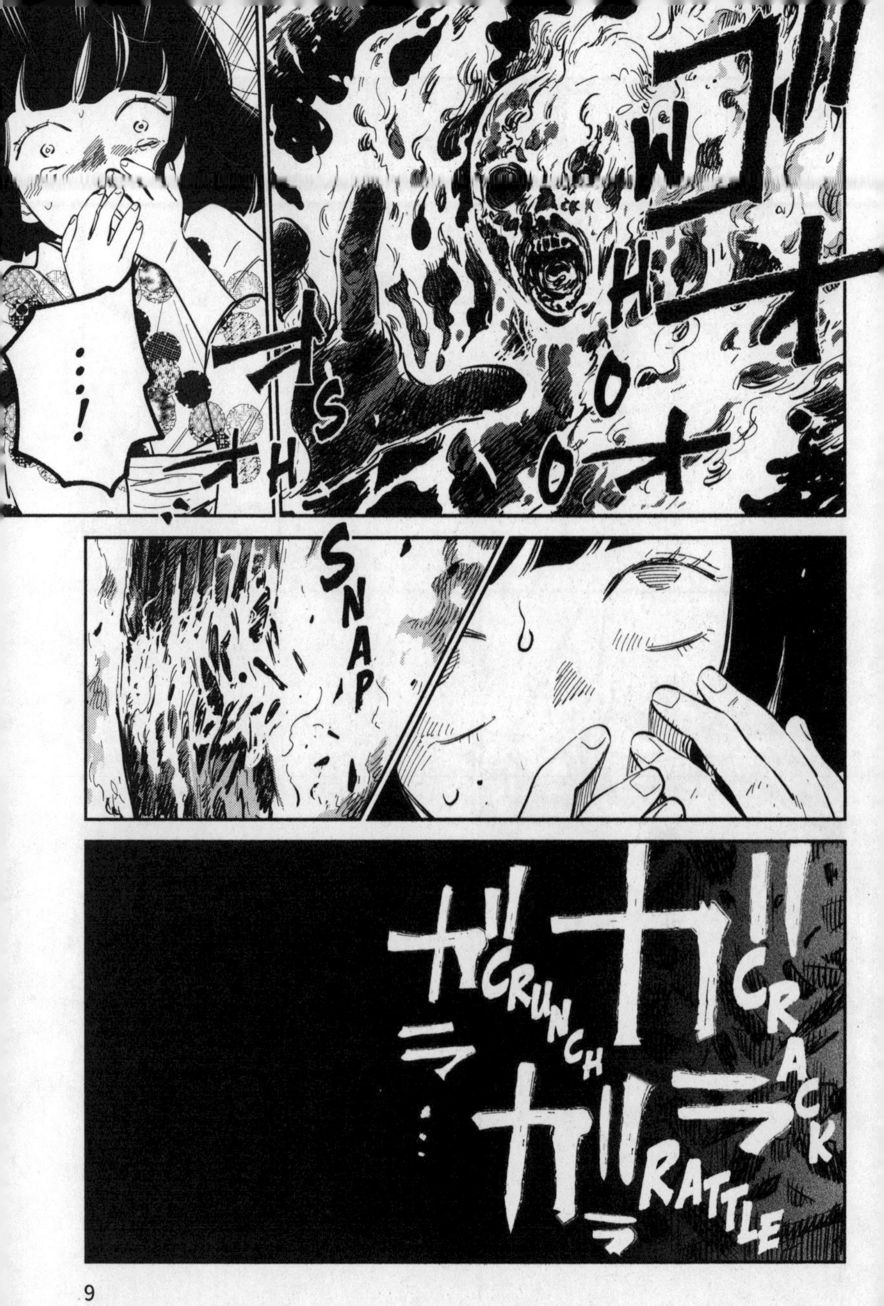
WHOOSH
...!
SNAP
CRACK
CRUNCH
RATTLE

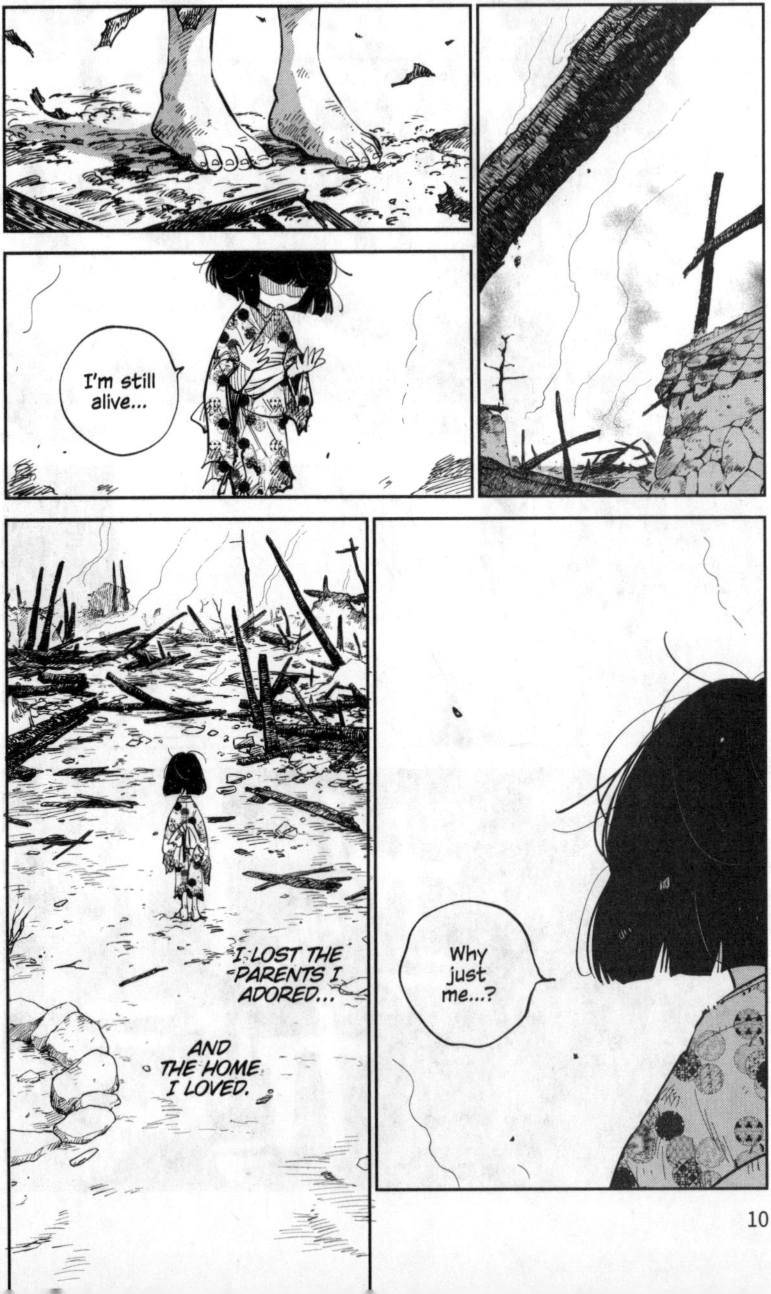
I'm still alive...
Why just me...?
I LOST THE PARENTS I ADORED...
AND THE HOME I LOVED.

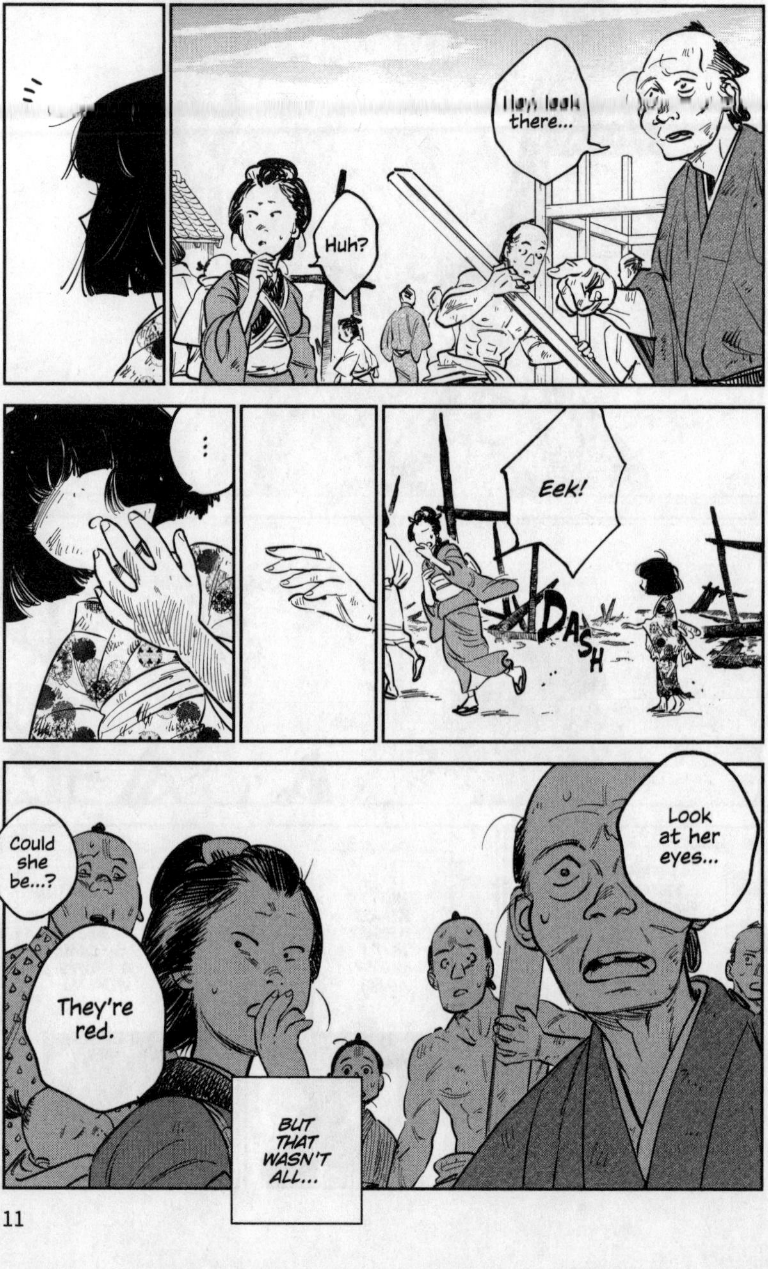
look there...
Huh?
Eek!
DASH
...
Look at her eyes...
Could she be...?
They're red.
BUT THAT WASN'T ALL...

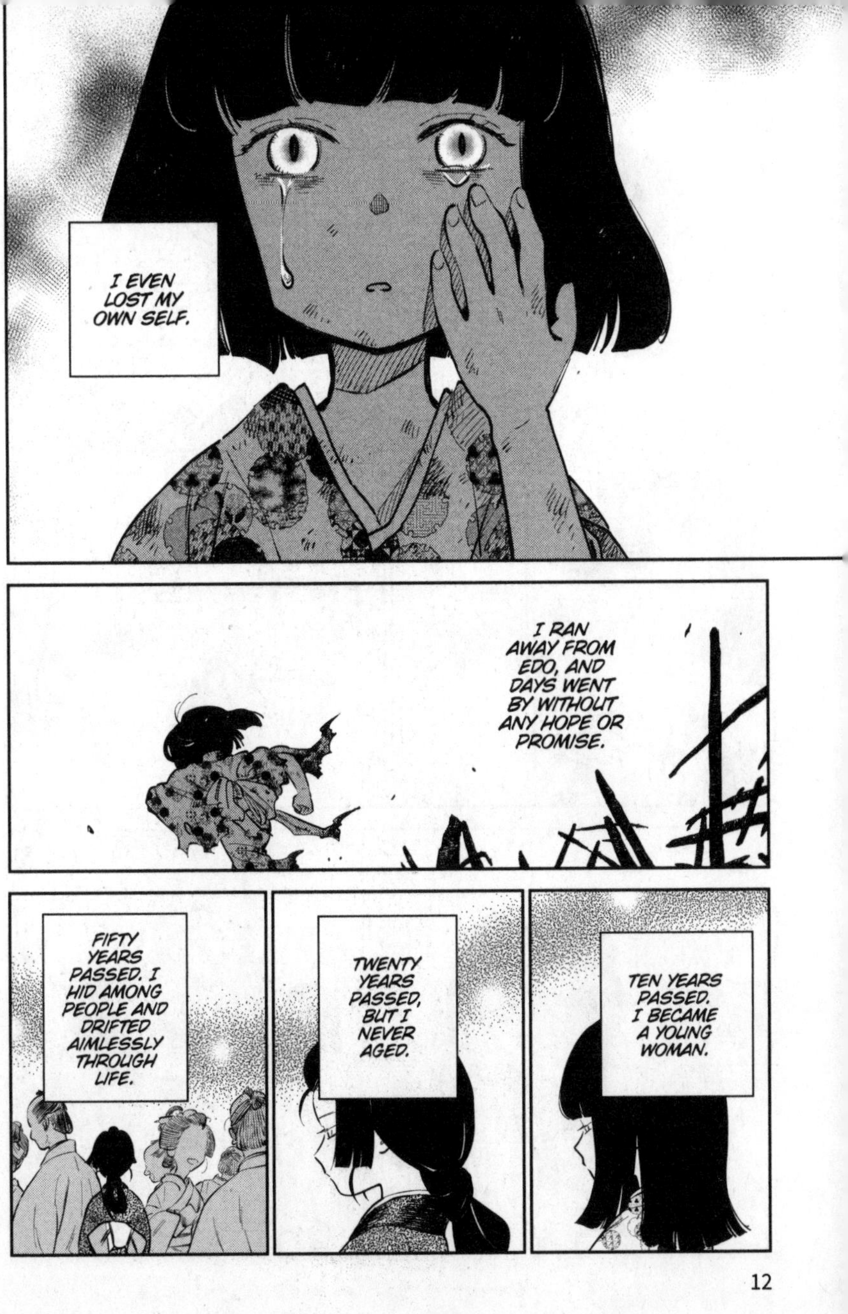
I EVEN LOST MY OWN SELF.
I RAN AWAY FROM EDO, AND DAYS WENT BY WITHOUT ANY HOPE OR PROMISE.
TEN YEARS PASSED. I BECAME A YOUNG WOMAN.
TWENTY YEARS PASSED, BUT I NEVER AGED.
FIFTY YEARS PASSED. I HID AMONG PEOPLE AND DRIFTED AIMLESSLY THROUGH LIFE.

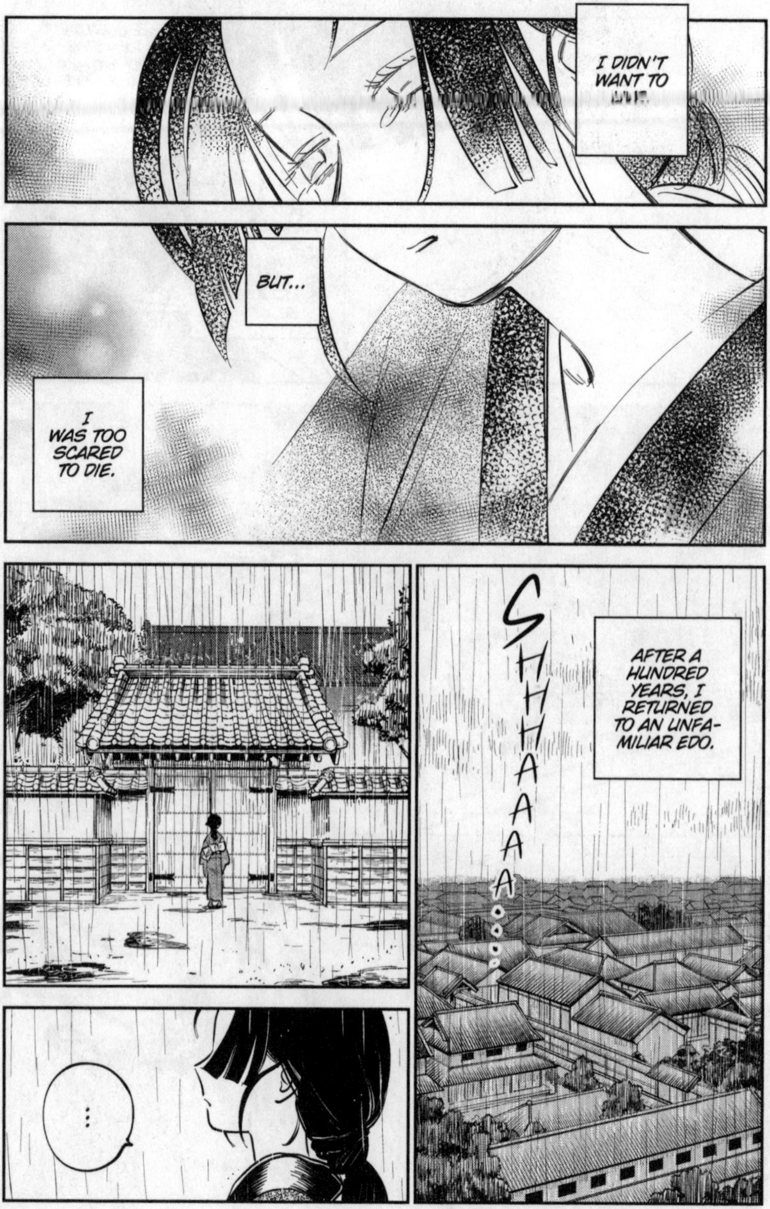

I DIDN'T WANT TO
BUT...
I WAS TOO SCARED TO DIE.
SHHHAAAA...
AFTER A HUNDRED YEARS, I RETURNED TO AN UNFAMILIAR EDO.
...

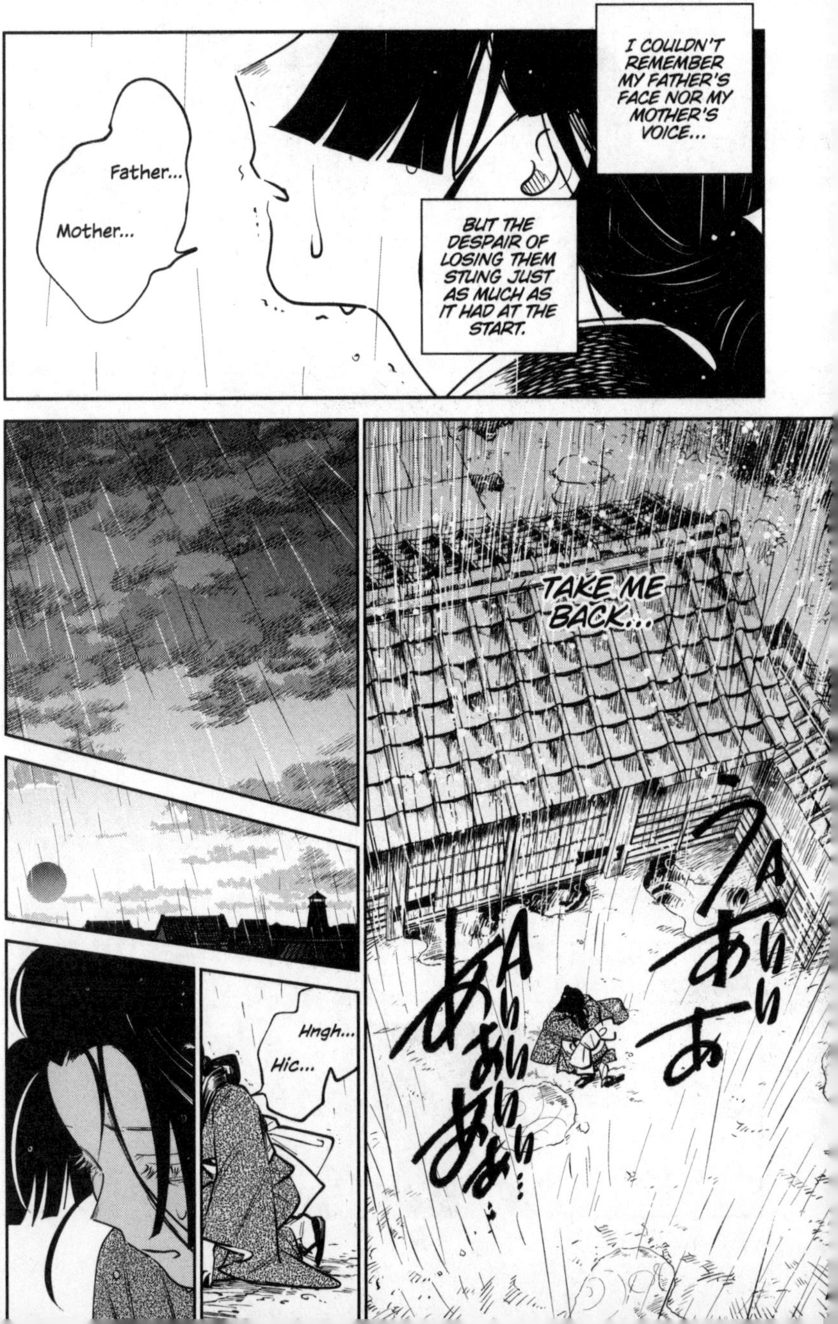
I COULDN'T REMEMBER MY FATHER'S FACE NOR MY MOTHER'S VOICE...
BUT THE DESPAIR OF LOSING THEM STUNG JUST AS MUCH AS IT HAD AT THE START.
Father... Mother...
TAKE ME BACK...
Hngh... Hic...

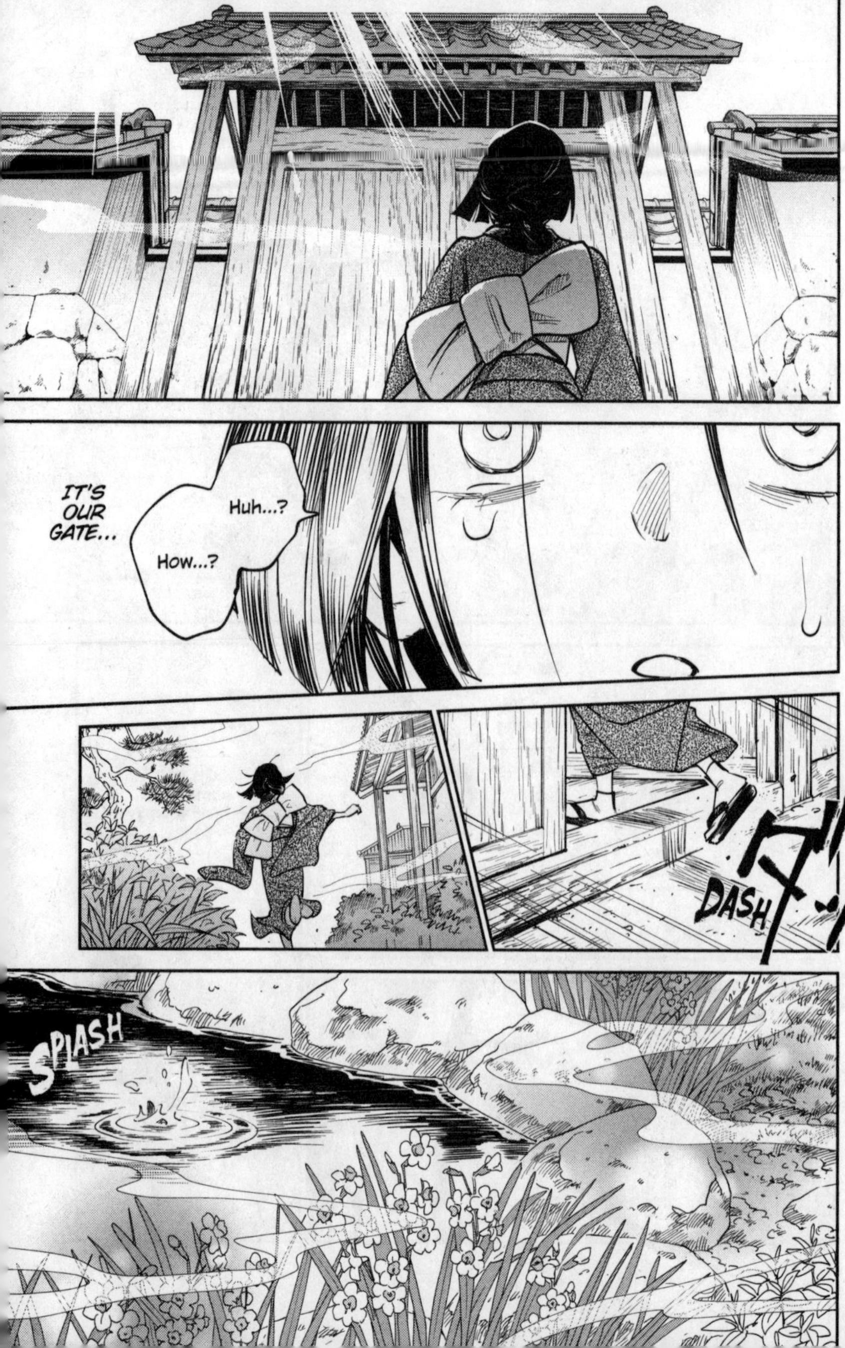
Huh...?
How...?
IT'S OUR GATE...
DASH
SPLASH

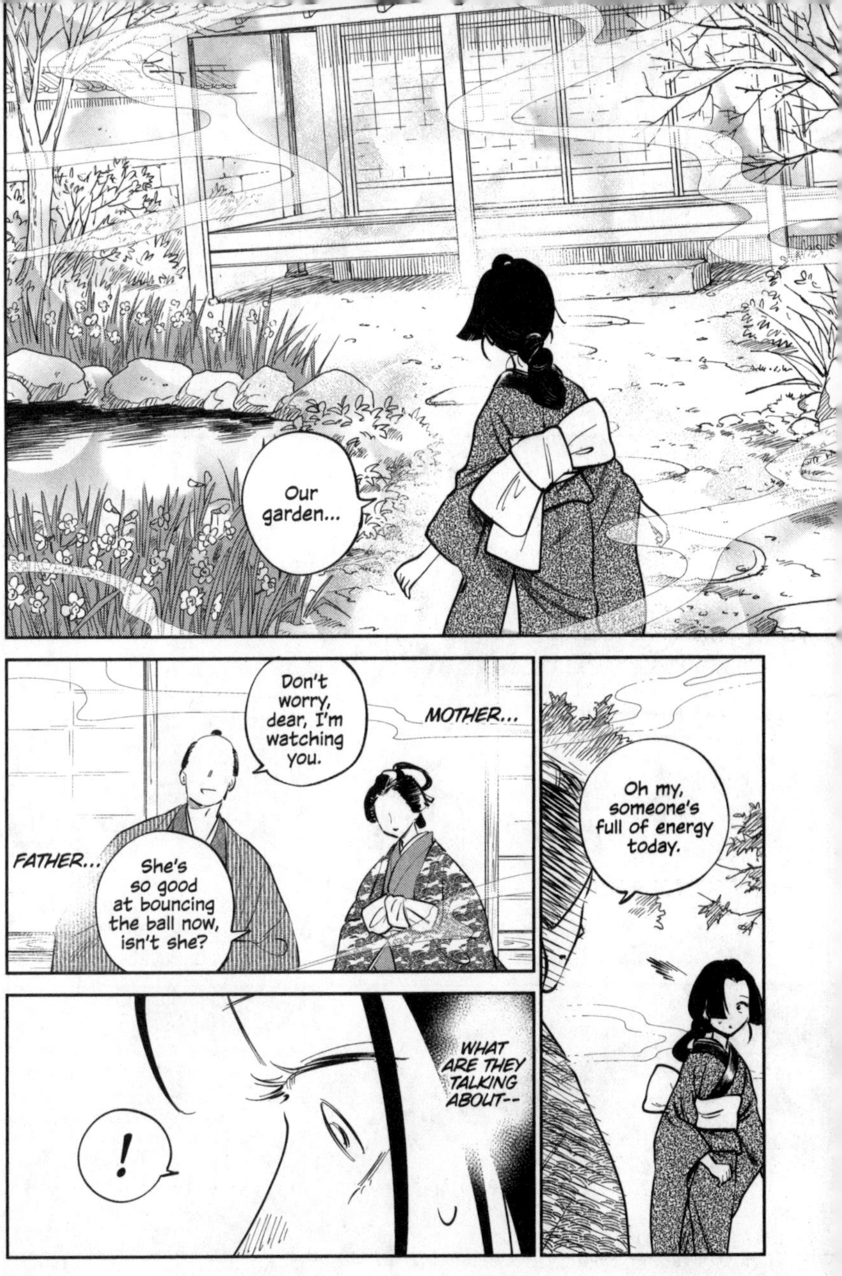
Our garden...
Oh my, someone's full of energy today.
MOTHER...
Don't worry, dear, I'm watching you.
FATHER...
She's so good at bouncing the ball now, isn't she?
WHAT ARE THEY TALKING ABOUT--
!

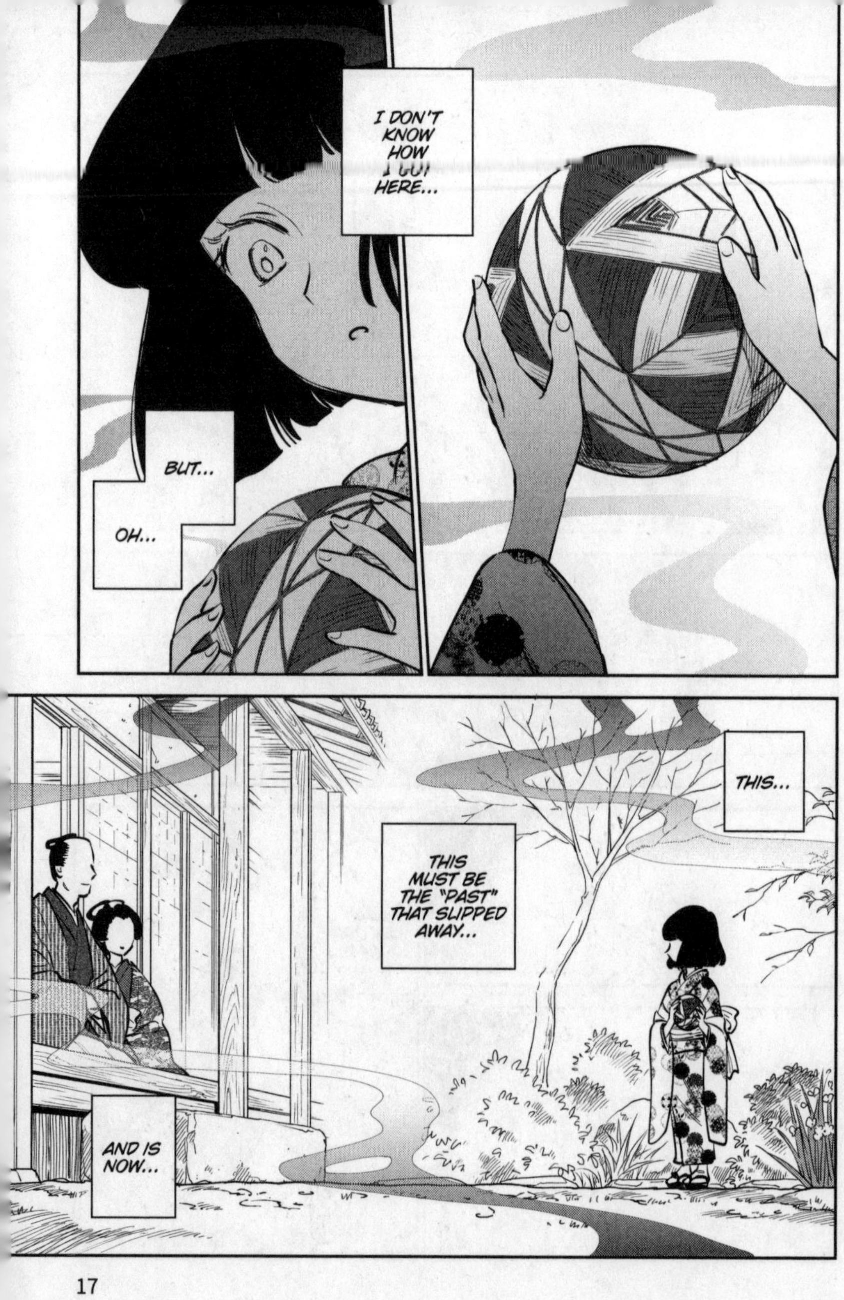
I DON'T KNOW HOW I GOT HERE...
BUT...
OH...
THIS...
THIS MUST BE THE "PAST" THAT SLIPPED AWAY...
AND IS NOW...

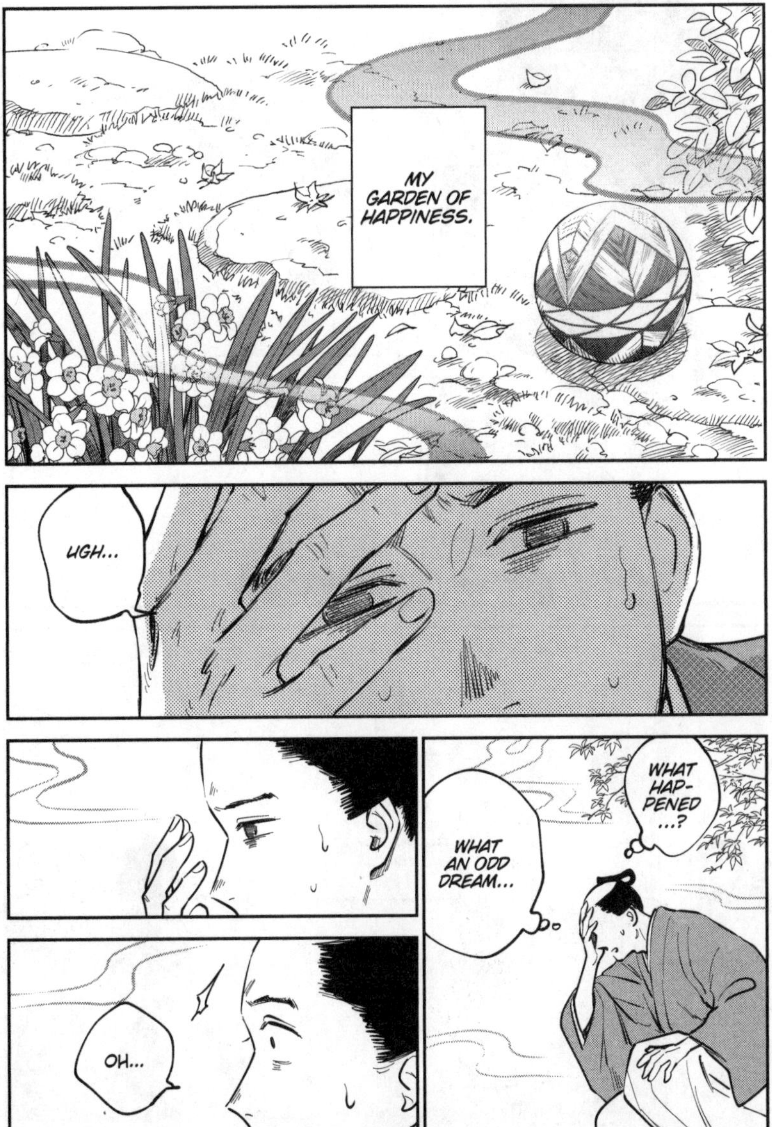
MY GARDEN OF HAPPINESS.
UGH...
WHAT HAP-PENED ...?
WHAT AN ODD DREAM...
OH...

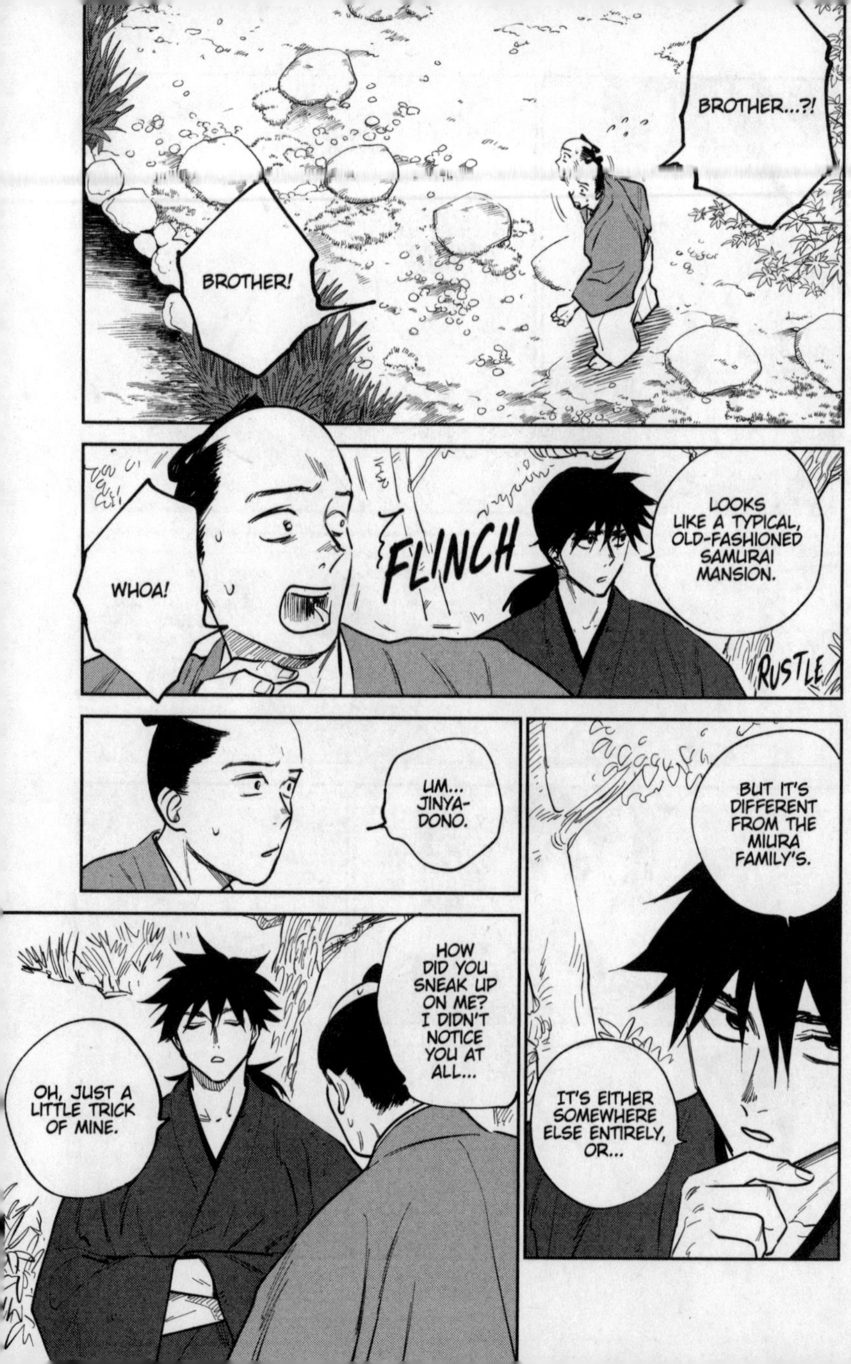
BROTHER...?!
BROTHER!
LOOKS LIKE A TYPICAL, OLD-FASHIONED SAMURAI MANSION.
FLINCH
WHOA!
RUSTLE
BUT IT'S DIFFERENT FROM THE MIURA FAMILY'S.
IT'S EITHER SOMEWHERE ELSE ENTIRELY, OR...
UM... JINYA-DONO.
HOW DID YOU SNEAK UP ON ME? I DIDN'T NOTICE YOU AT ALL...
OH, JUST A LITTLE TRICK OF MINE.

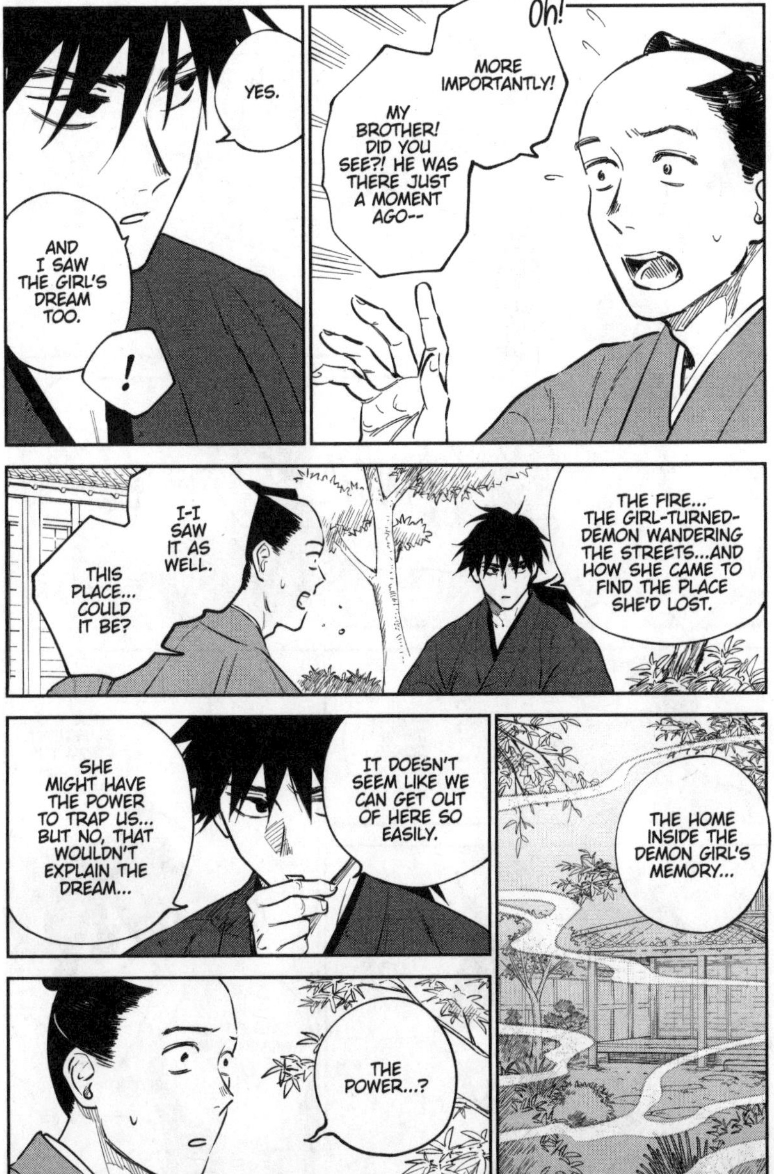
Oh!
MORE IMPORTANTLY!
MY BROTHER! DID YOU SEE?! HE WAS THERE JUST A MOMENT AGO--
YES.
AND I SAW THE GIRL'S DREAM TOO.
!
THE FIRE... THE GIRL-TURNED-DEMON WANDERING THE STREETS...AND HOW SHE CAME TO FIND THE PLACE SHE'D LOST.
I-I SAW IT AS WELL.
THIS PLACE... COULD IT BE?
THE HOME INSIDE THE DEMON GIRL'S MEMORY...
IT DOESN'T SEEM LIKE WE CAN GET OUT OF HERE SO EASILY.
SHE MIGHT HAVE THE POWER TO TRAP US... BUT NO, THAT WOULDN'T EXPLAIN THE DREAM...
THE POWER...?

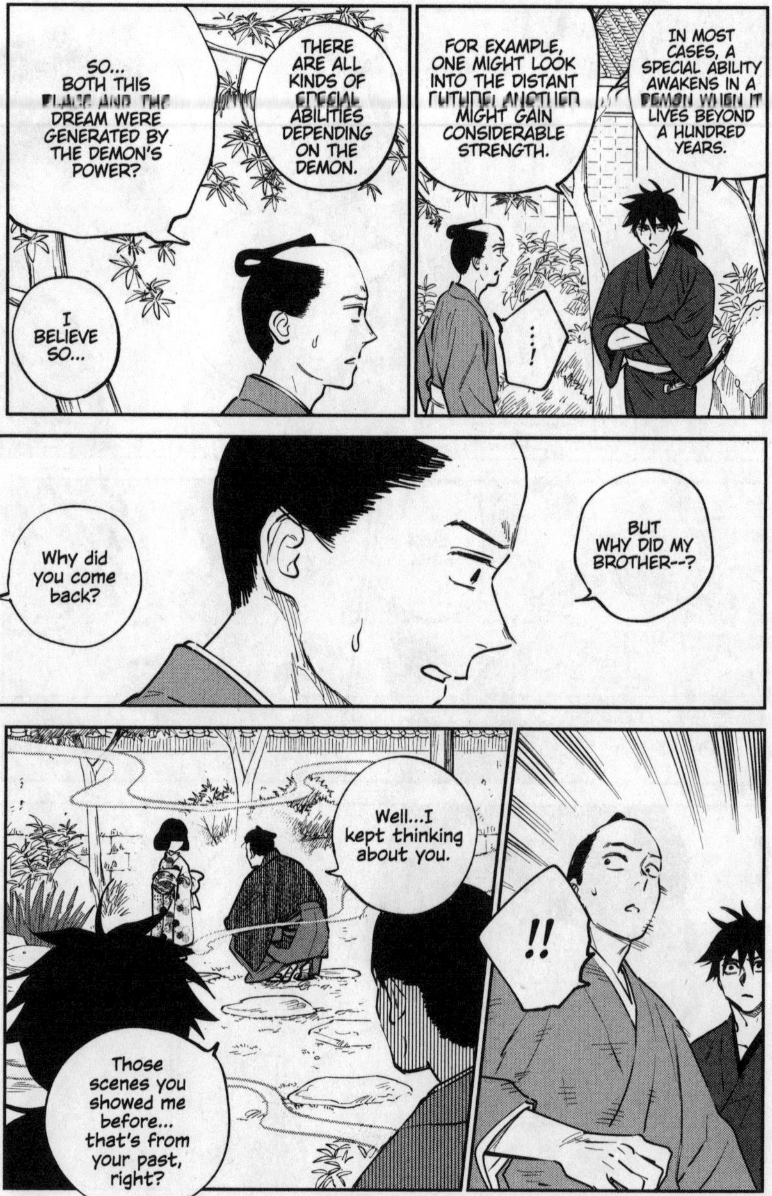

IN MOST CASES, A SPECIAL ABILITY AWAKENS IN A DEMON WHEN IT LIVES BEYOND A HUNDRED YEARS.
FOR EXAMPLE, ONE MIGHT LOOK INTO THE DISTANT FUTURE; ANOTHER MIGHT GAIN CONSIDERABLE STRENGTH.
...!
THERE ARE ALL KINDS OF SPECIAL ABILITIES DEPENDING ON THE DEMON.
SO... BOTH THIS PLACE AND THE DREAM WERE GENERATED BY THE DEMON'S POWER?
I BELIEVE SO...
BUT WHY DID MY BROTHER--?
Why did you come back?
!!
Well...I kept thinking about you.
Those scenes you showed me before... that's from your past, right?

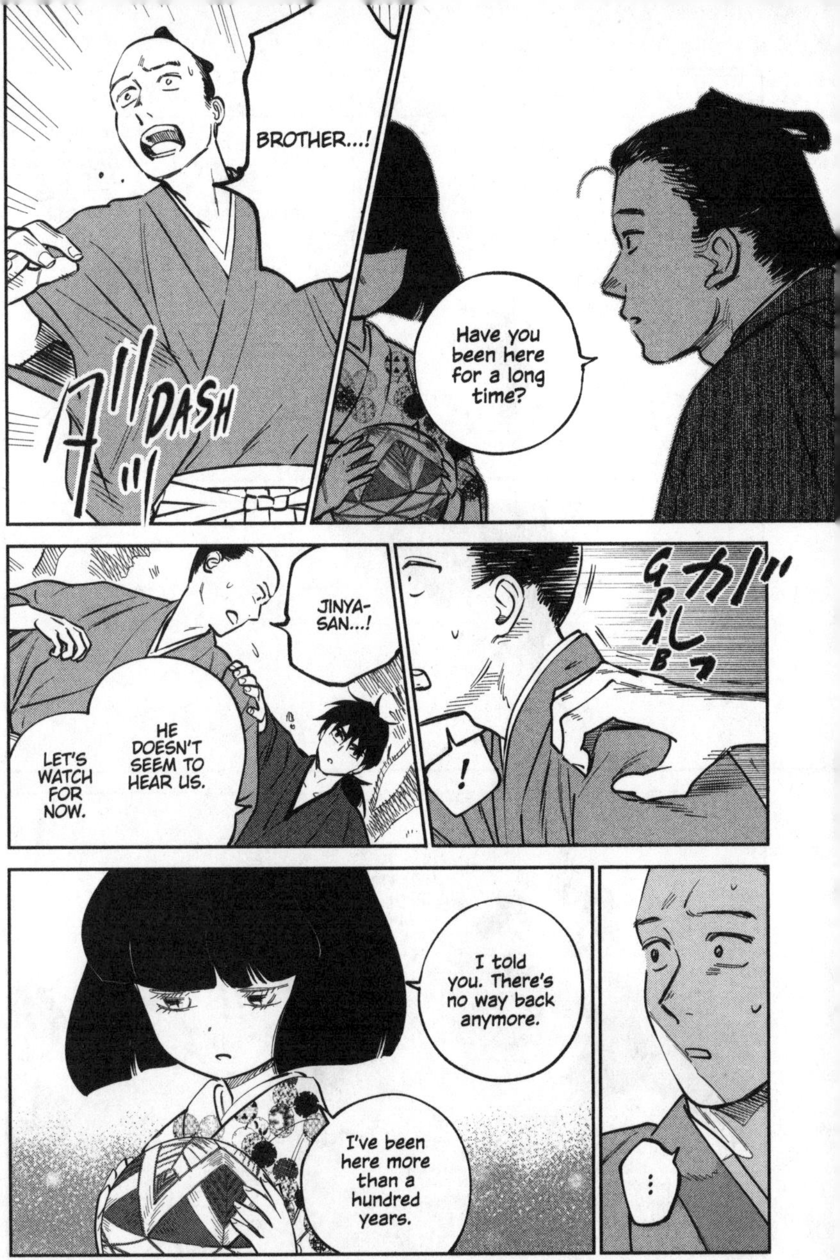
Have you been here for a long time?
BROTHER...!
DASH
GRAB
!
JINYA-SAN...!
HE DOESN'T SEEM TO HEAR US.
LET'S WATCH FOR NOW.
...
I told you. There's no way back anymore.
I've been here more than a hundred years.

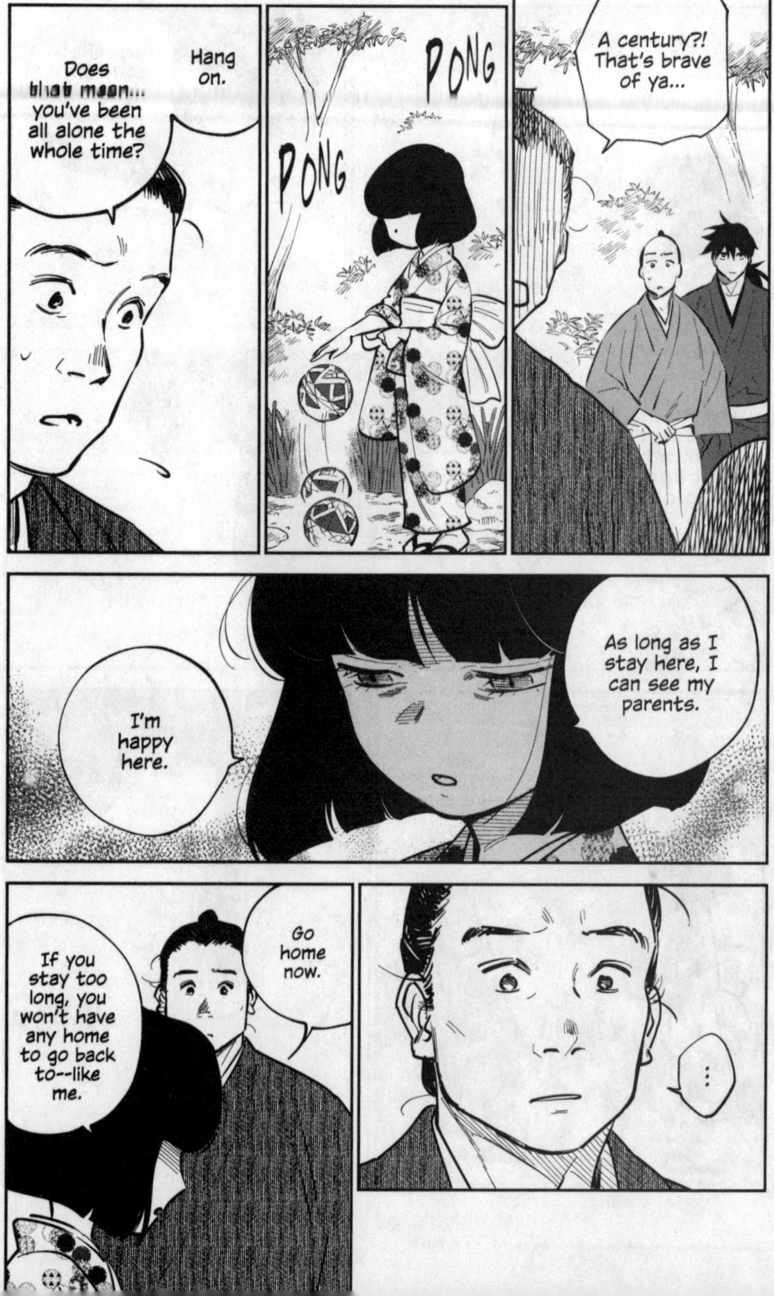
A century?! That's brave of ya...
PONG
PONG
Hang on.
Does that mean... you've been all alone the whole time?
As long as I stay here, I can see my parents.
I'm happy here.
...
Go home now.
If you stay too long, you won't have any home to go back to--like me.

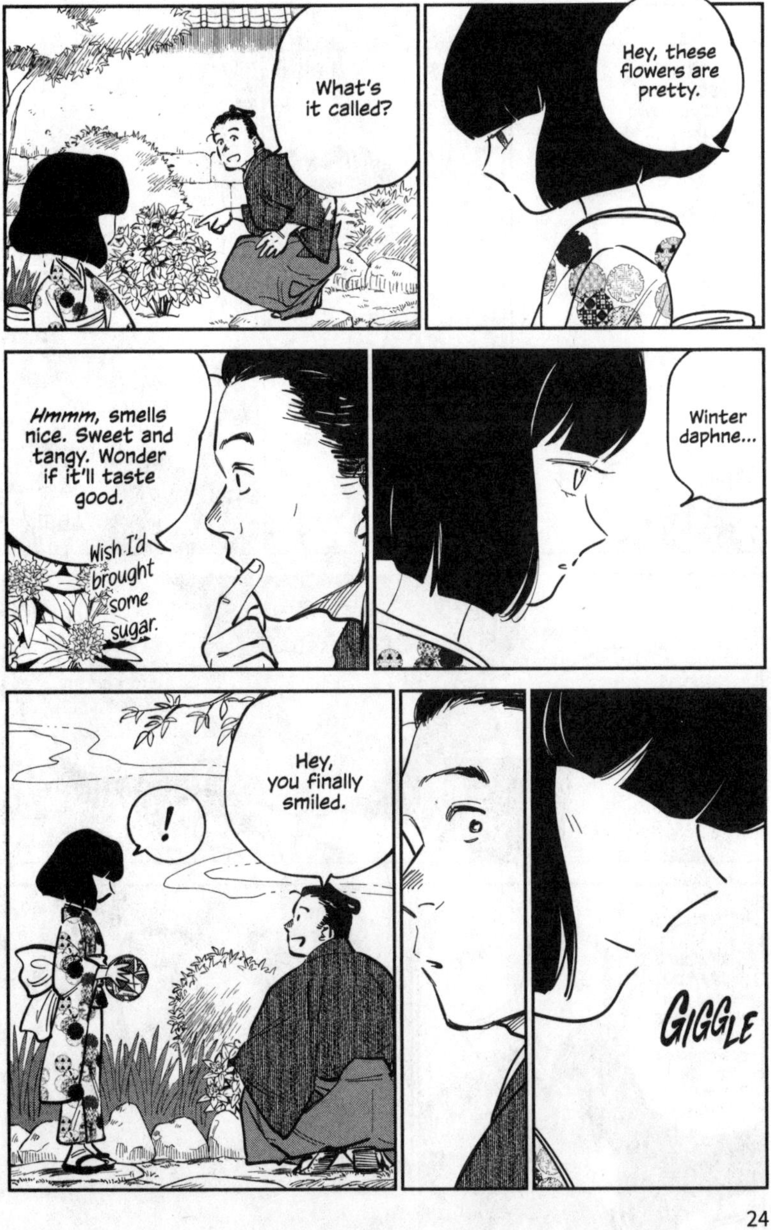
Hey, these flowers are pretty.
What's it called?
Winter daphne...
*Hmmm*, smells nice. Sweet and tangy. Wonder if it'll taste good.
Wish I'd brought some sugar.
GIGGLE
Hey, you finally smiled.
!

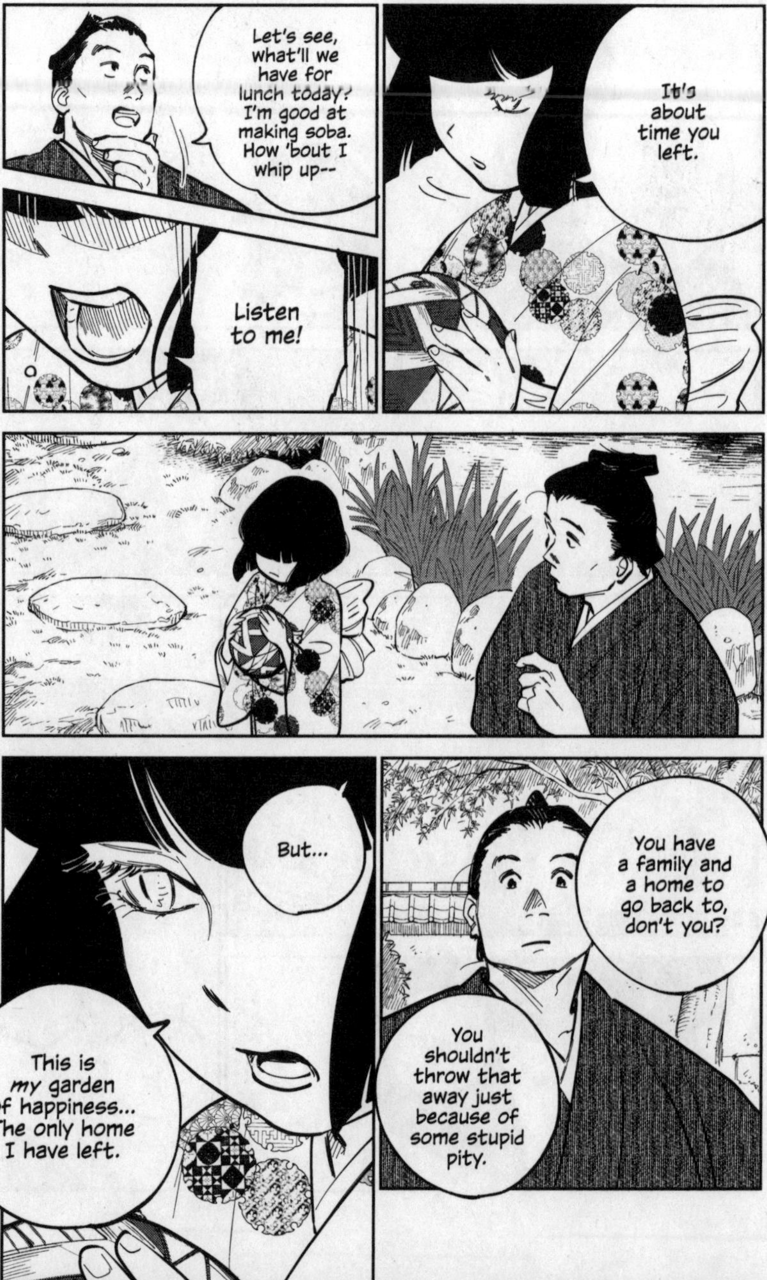
It's about time you left.
Let's see, what'll we have for lunch today? I'm good at making soba. How 'bout I whip up--
Listen to me!
You have a family and a home to go back to, don't you?
You shouldn't throw that away just because of some stupid pity.
But...
This is *my* garden of happiness... The only home I have left.

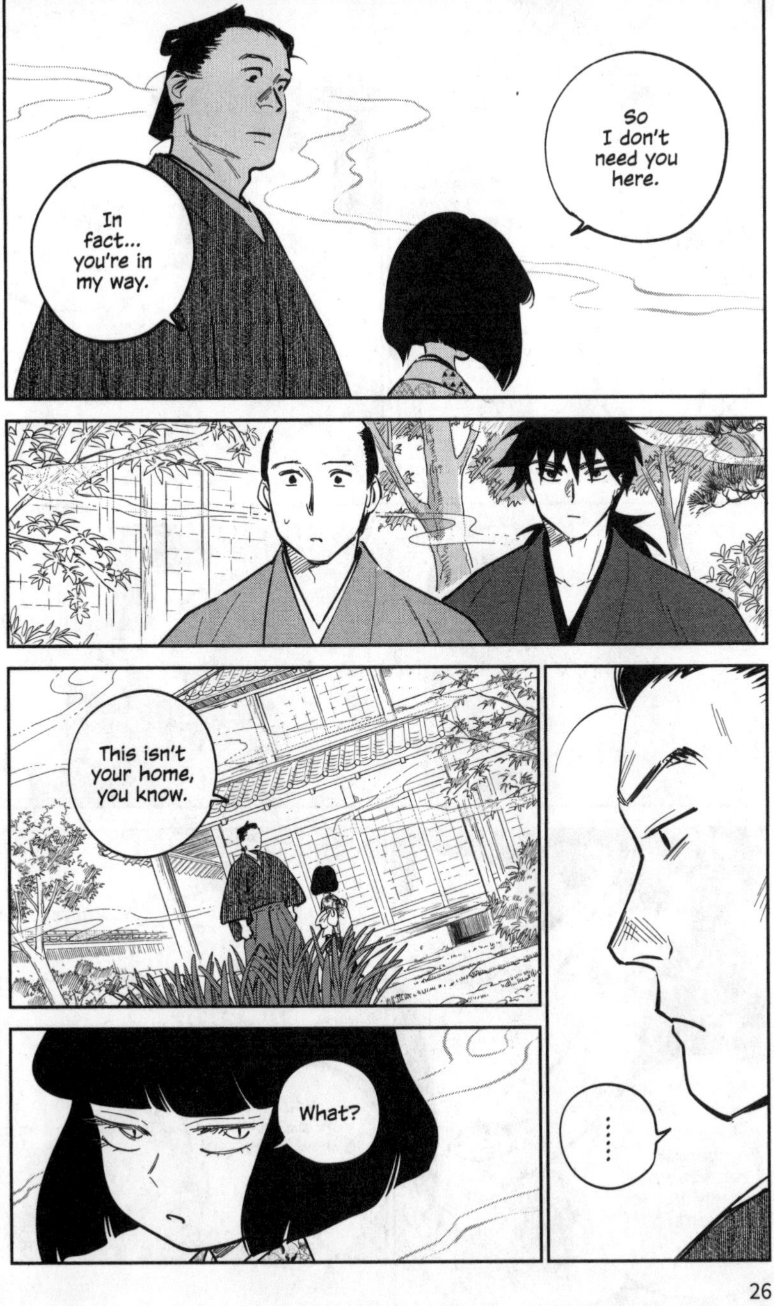
So I don't need you here.
In fact... you're in my way.
......
This isn't your home, you know.
What?

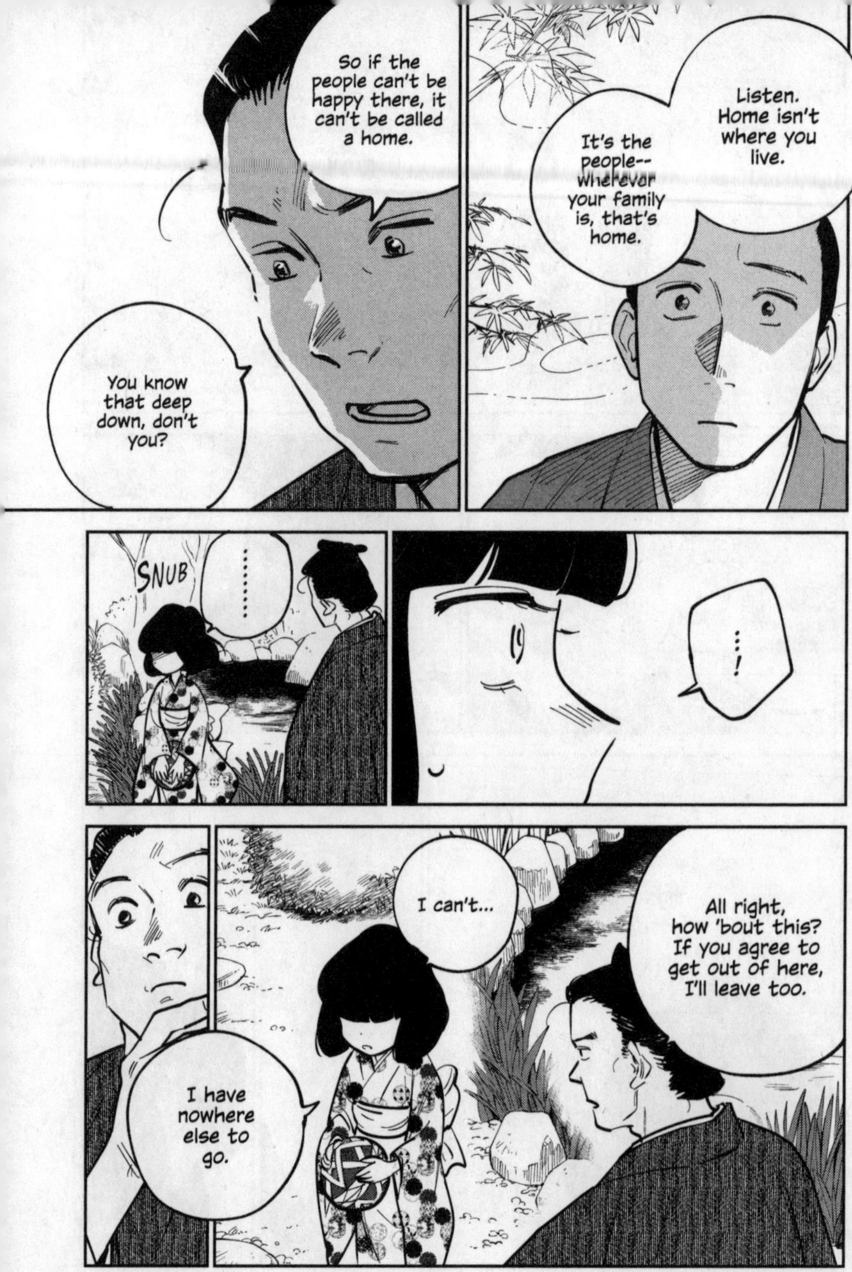
Listen. Home isn't where you live.
It's the people-- wherever your family is, that's home.
So if the people can't be happy there, it can't be called a home.
You know that deep down, don't you?
...!
SNUB
......
All right, how 'bout this? If you agree to get out of here, I'll leave too.
I can't...
I have nowhere else to go.

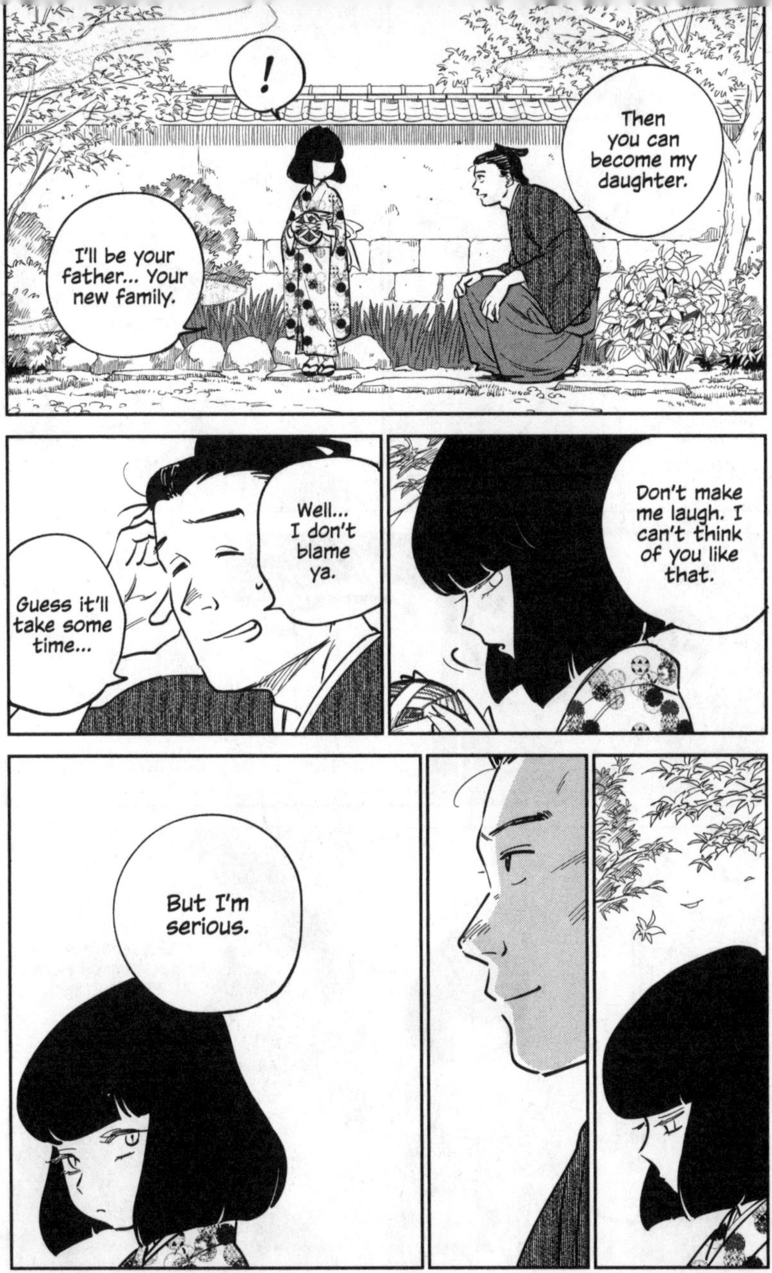
Then you can become my daughter.
!
I'll be your father... Your new family.
Don't make me laugh. I can't think of you like that.
Well... I don't blame ya.
Guess it'll take some time...
But I'm serious.

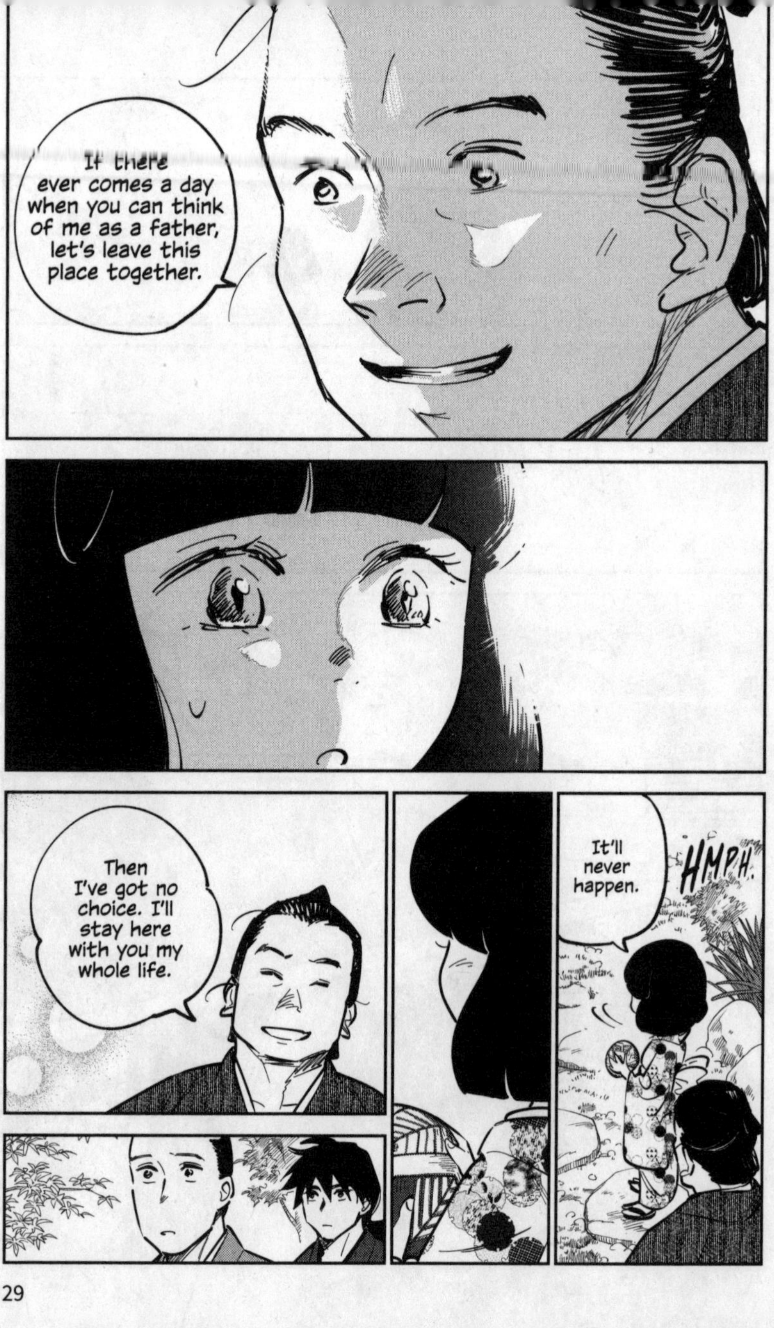
If there ever comes a day when you can think of me as a father, let's leave this place together.
It'll never happen.
HMPH.
Then I've got no choice. I'll stay here with you my whole life.

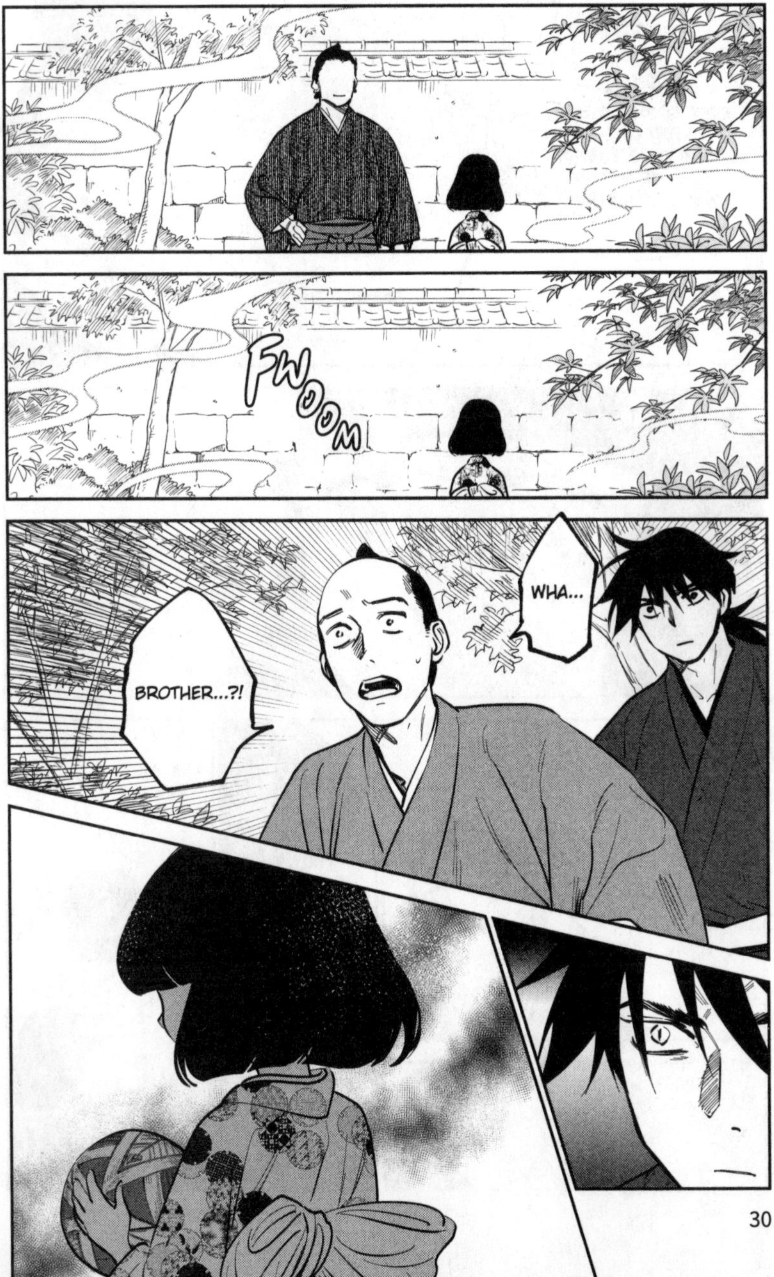
FWOOM
WHA...
BROTHER...?!

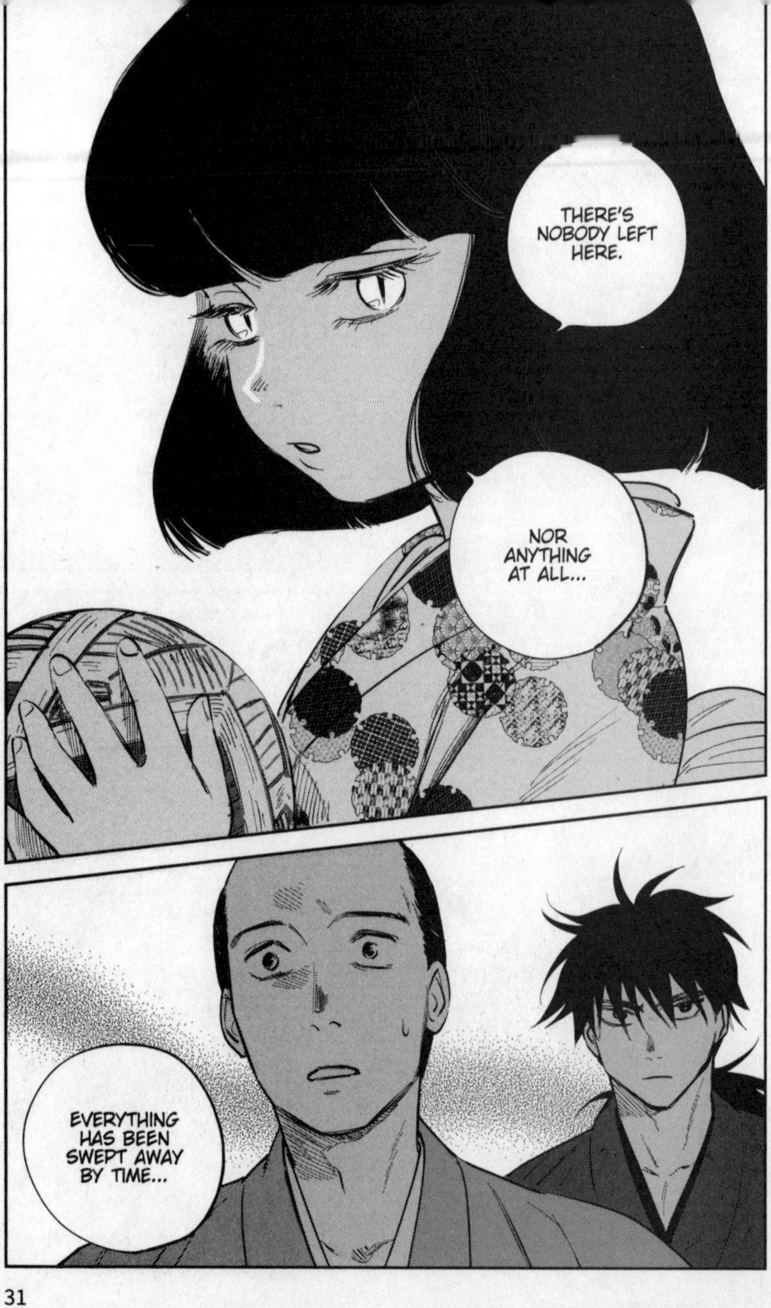
THERE'S NOBODY LEFT HERE.
NOR ANYTHING AT ALL...
EVERYTHING HAS BEEN SWEPT AWAY BY TIME...

Sword
of the Demon
Hunter KIJIN
GENTŌSHŌ

## CHAPTER 21: THE GARDEN OF HAPPINESS ④

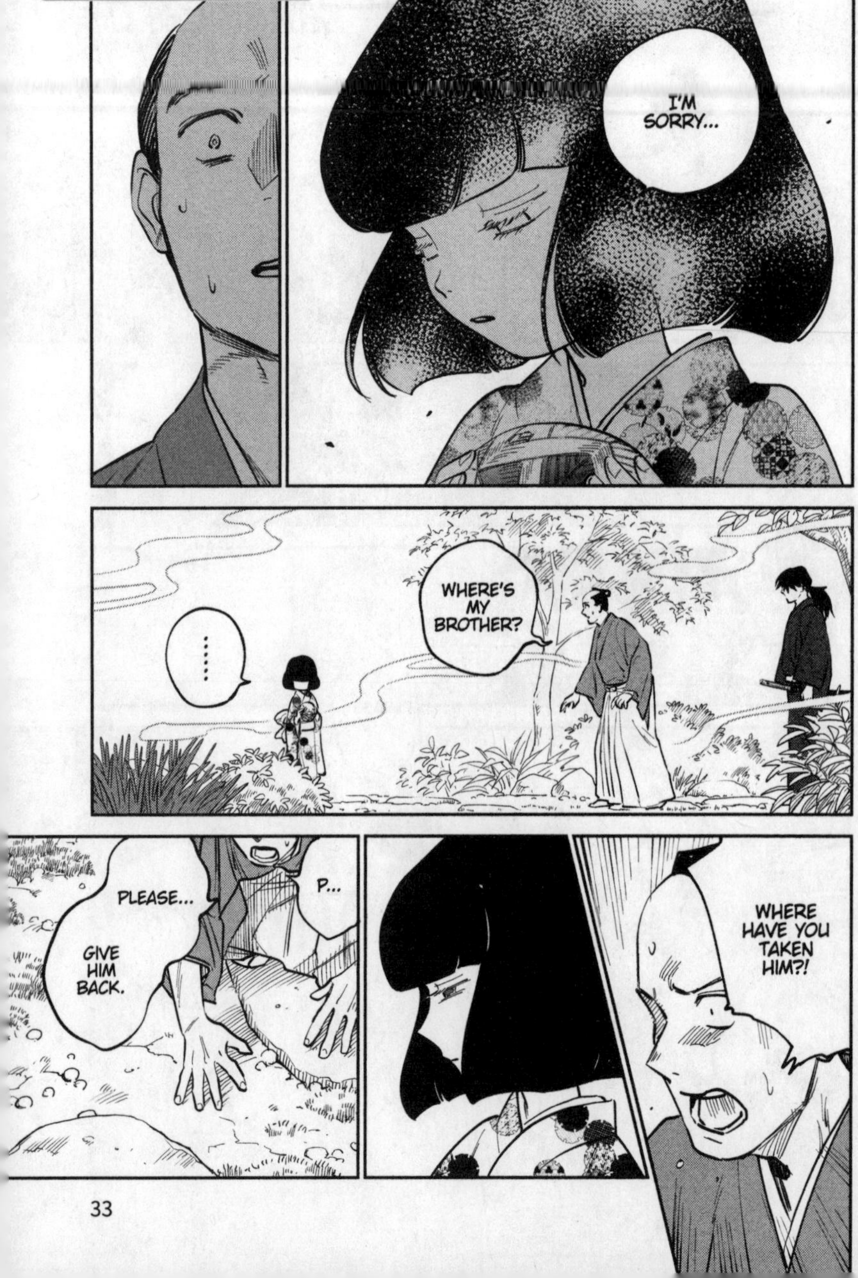

I'M SORRY...
WHERE'S MY BROTHER?
......
WHERE HAVE YOU TAKEN HIM?!
P...
PLEASE...
GIVE HIM BACK.

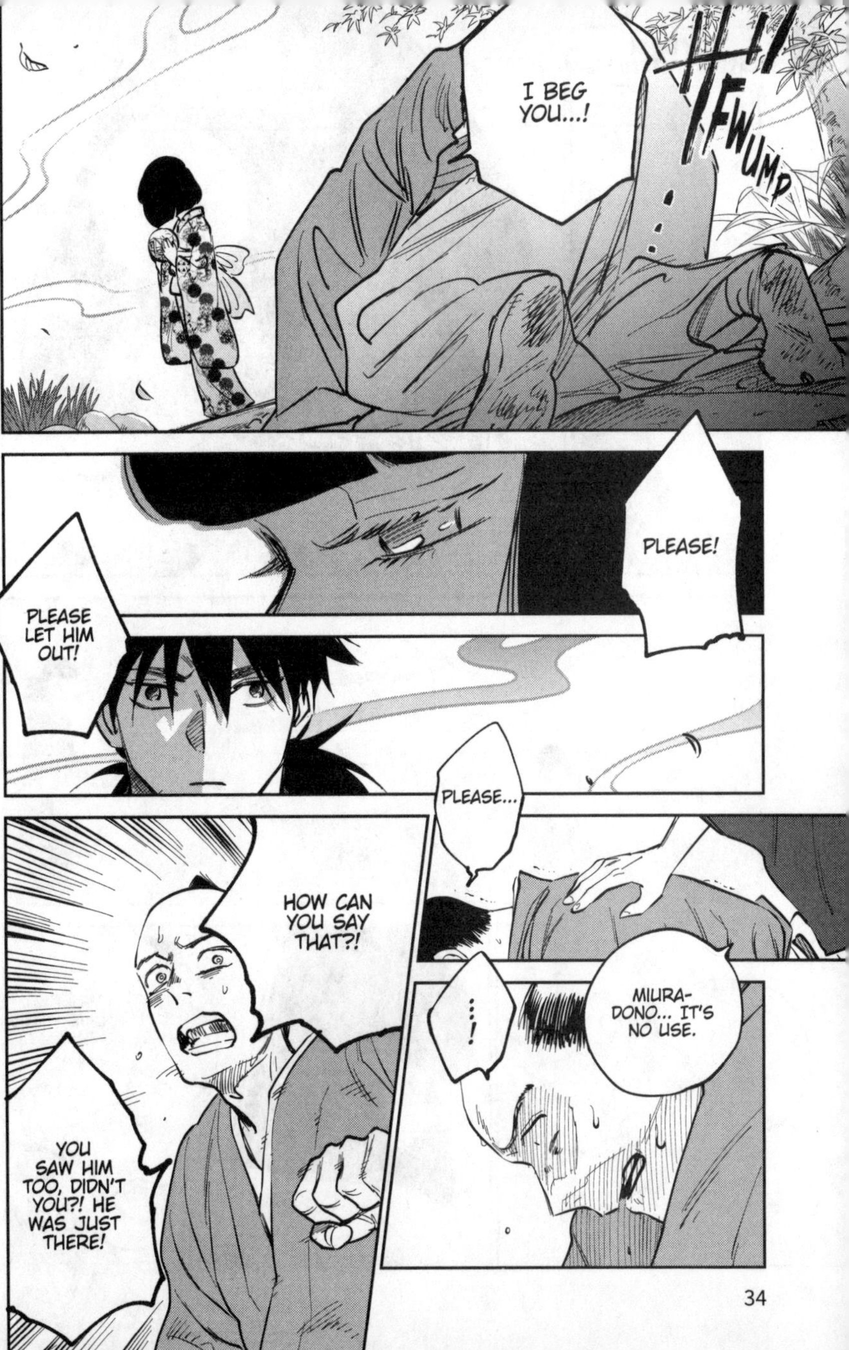
FWUMP
I BEG YOU...!
PLEASE!
PLEASE LET HIM OUT!
PLEASE...
MIURA-DONO... IT'S NO USE.
...!
HOW CAN YOU SAY THAT?!
YOU SAW HIM TOO, DIDN'T YOU?! HE WAS JUST THERE!

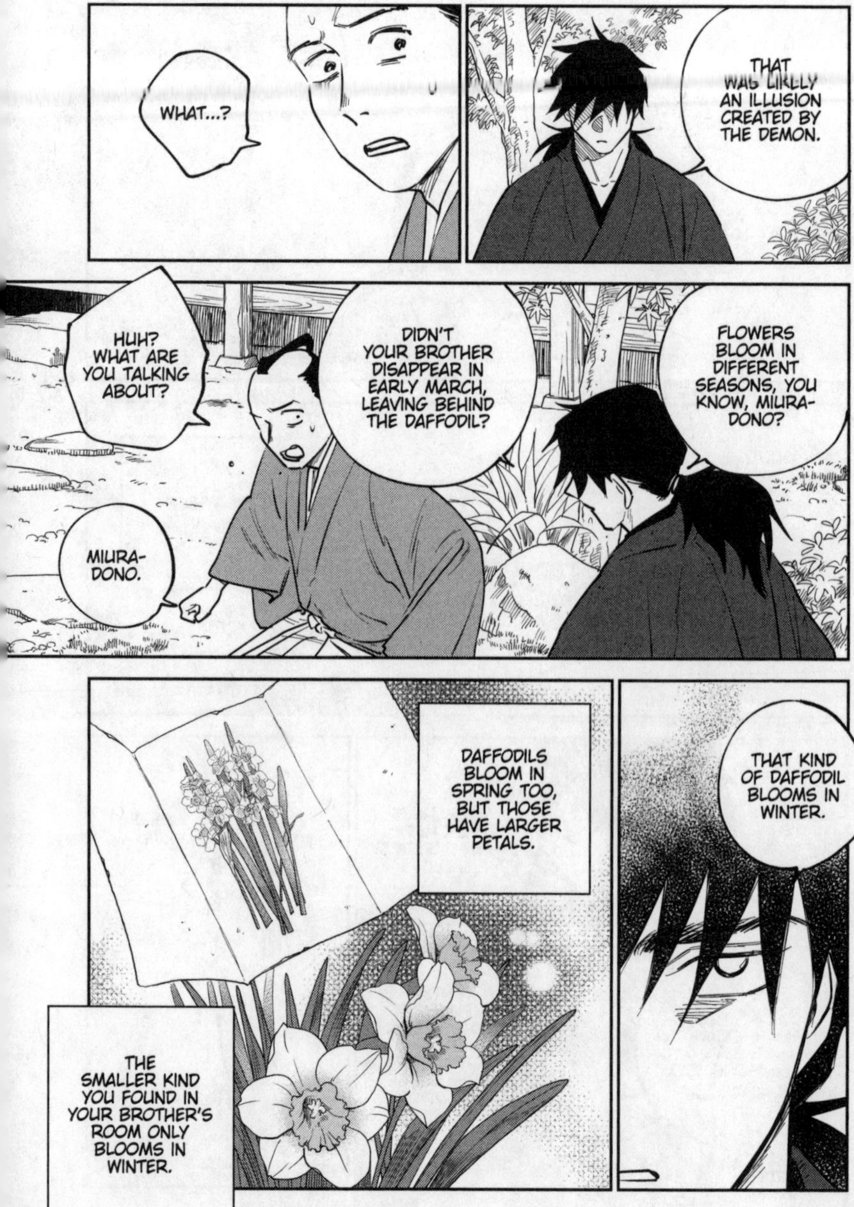
THAT WAS LIKELY AN ILLUSION CREATED BY THE DEMON.
WHAT...?
FLOWERS BLOOM IN DIFFERENT SEASONS, YOU KNOW, MIURA-DONO?
DIDN'T YOUR BROTHER DISAPPEAR IN EARLY MARCH, LEAVING BEHIND THE DAFFODIL?
HUH? WHAT ARE YOU TALKING ABOUT?
MIURA-DONO.
THAT KIND OF DAFFODIL BLOOMS IN WINTER.
DAFFODILS BLOOM IN SPRING TOO, BUT THOSE HAVE LARGER PETALS.
THE SMALLER KIND YOU FOUND IN YOUR BROTHER'S ROOM ONLY BLOOMS IN WINTER.

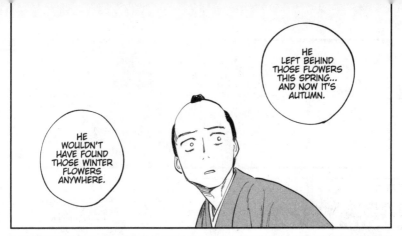

HE LEFT BEHIND THOSE FLOWERS THIS SPRING... AND NOW IT'S AUTUMN.

HE WOULDN'T HAVE FOUND THOSE WINTER FLOWERS ANYWHERE.

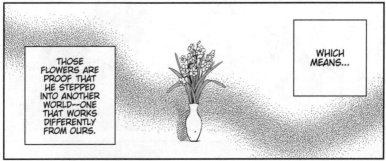

THOSE FLOWERS ARE PROOF THAT HE STEPPED INTO ANOTHER WORLD--ONE THAT WORKS DIFFERENTLY FROM OURS.

WHICH MEANS...

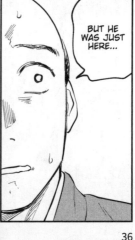

BUT HE WAS JUST HERE...

YES, HE MUST HAVE BEEN HERE BEFORE, AT LEAST.

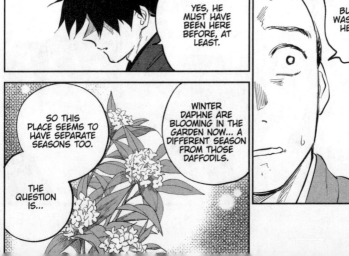

WINTER DAPHNE ARE BLOOMING IN THE GARDEN NOW... A DIFFERENT SEASON FROM THOSE DAFFODILS.

SO THIS PLACE SEEMS TO HAVE SEPARATE SEASONS TOO.

THE QUESTION IS...

36

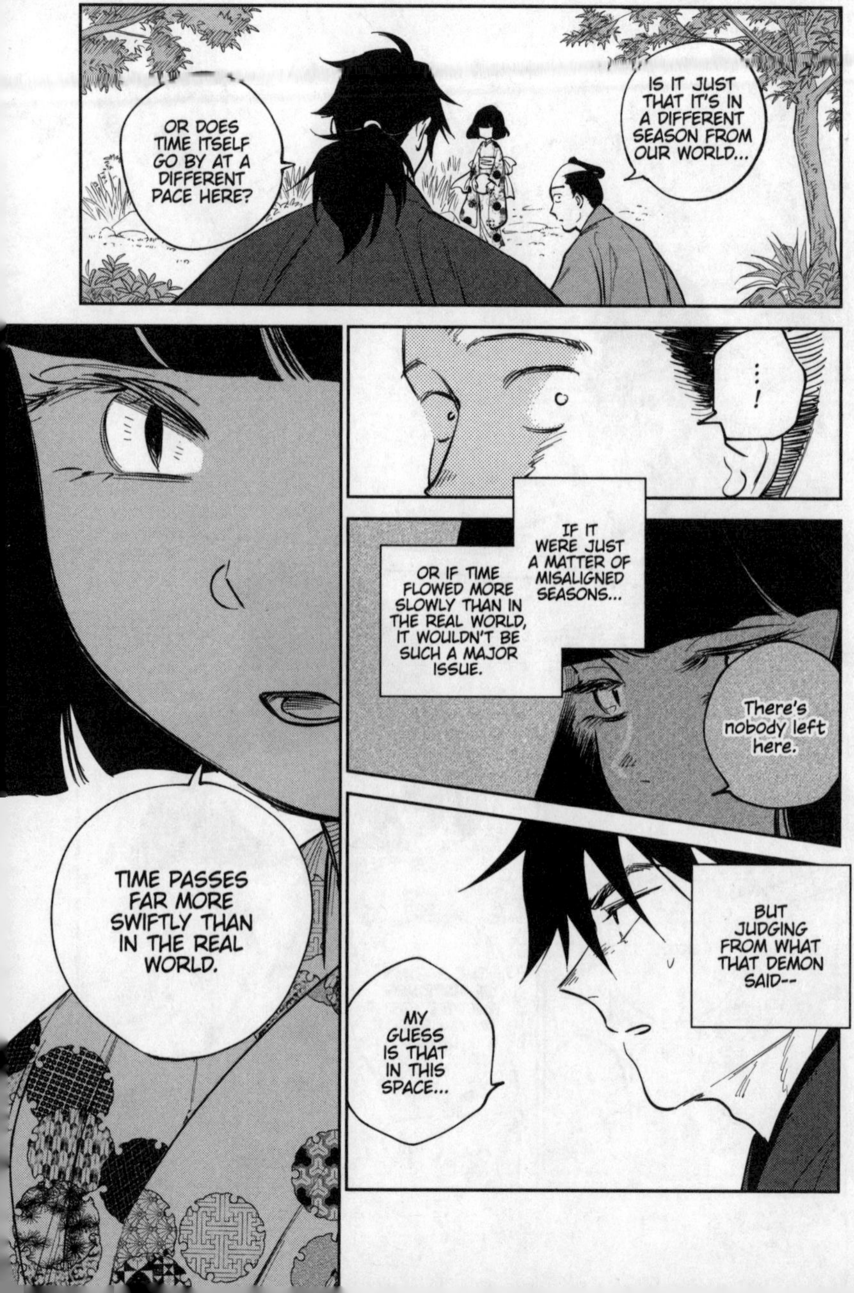
IS IT JUST THAT IT'S IN A DIFFERENT SEASON FROM OUR WORLD...
OR DOES TIME ITSELF GO BY AT A DIFFERENT PACE HERE?
...!
IF IT WERE JUST A MATTER OF MISALIGNED SEASONS...
OR IF TIME FLOWED MORE SLOWLY THAN IN THE REAL WORLD, IT WOULDN'T BE SUCH A MAJOR ISSUE.
There's nobody left here.
BUT JUDGING FROM WHAT THAT DEMON SAID--
MY GUESS IS THAT IN THIS SPACE...
TIME PASSES FAR MORE SWIFTLY THAN IN THE REAL WORLD.

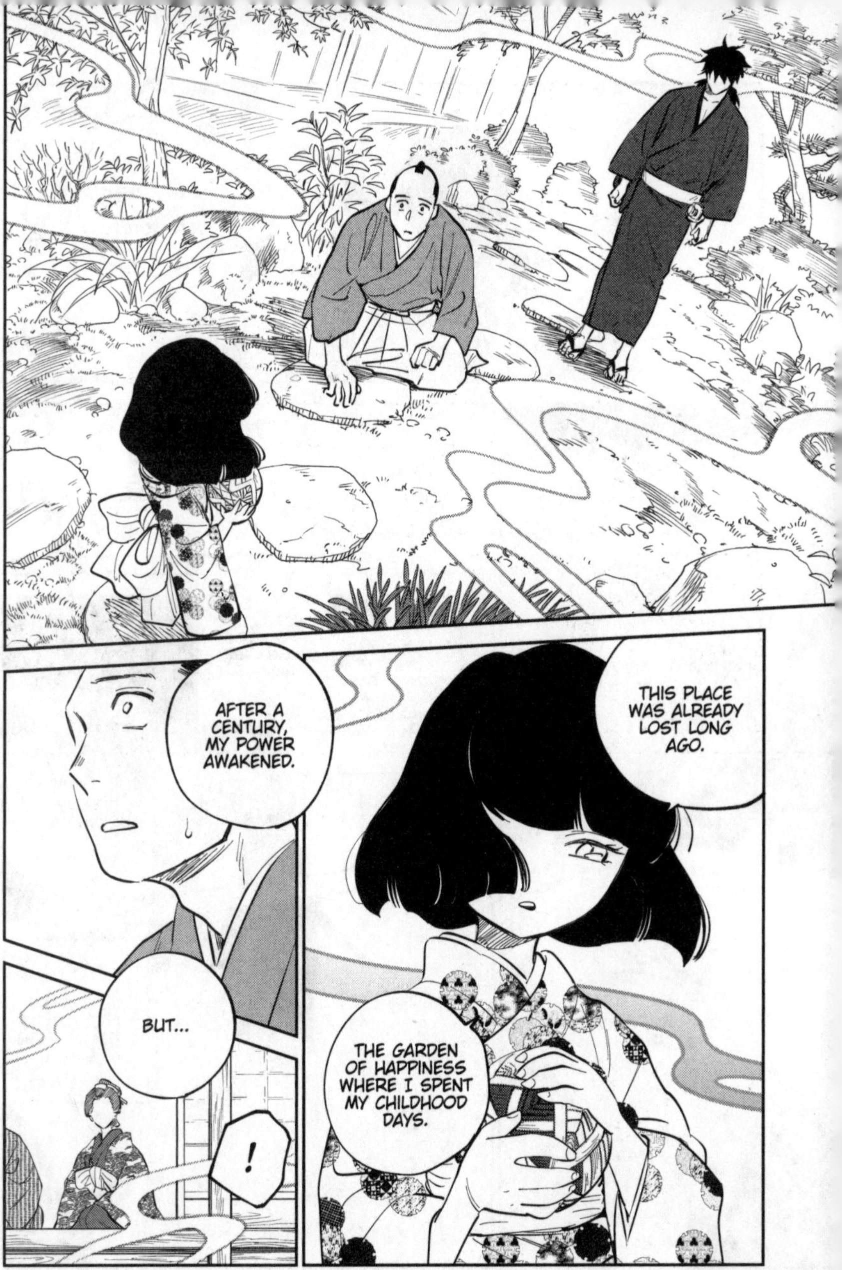
THIS PLACE WAS ALREADY LOST LONG AGO.
THE GARDEN OF HAPPINESS WHERE I SPENT MY CHILDHOOD DAYS.
AFTER A CENTURY, MY POWER AWAKENED.
BUT...
!

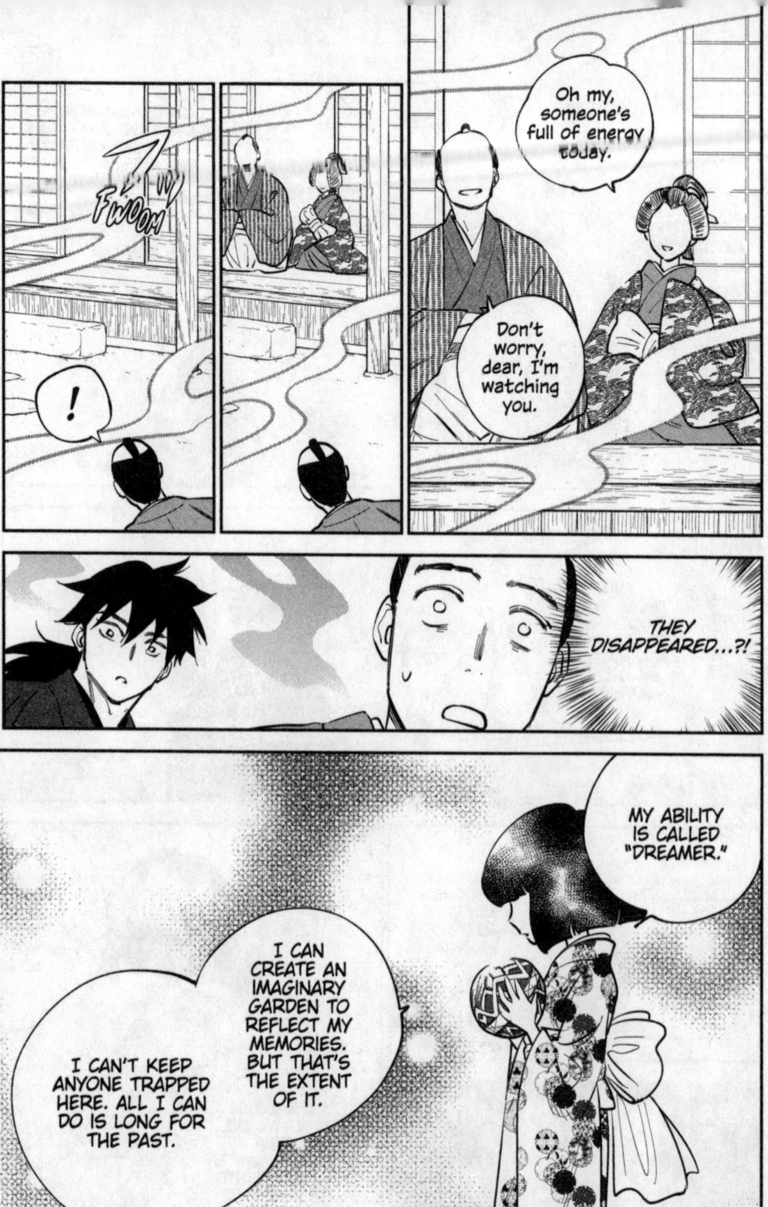
Oh my, someone's full of energy today.
Don't worry, dear, I'm watching you.
FWOOM
!
THEY DISAPPEARED...?!
MY ABILITY IS CALLED "DREAMER."
I CAN CREATE AN IMAGINARY GARDEN TO REFLECT MY MEMORIES. BUT THAT'S THE EXTENT OF IT.
I CAN'T KEEP ANYONE TRAPPED HERE. ALL I CAN DO IS LONG FOR THE PAST.

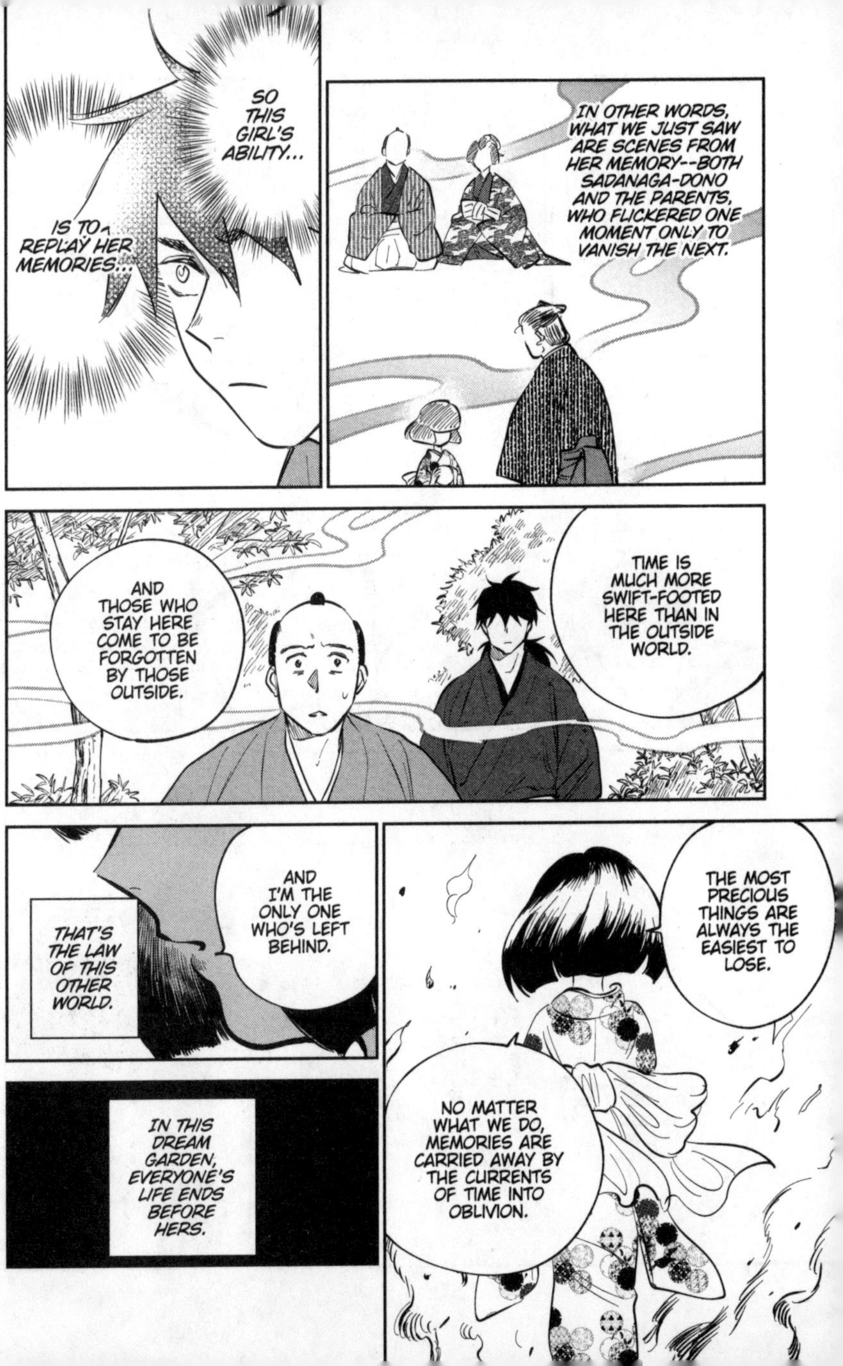
IN OTHER WORDS, WHAT WE JUST SAW ARE SCENES FROM HER MEMORY--BOTH SADANAGA-DONO AND THE PARENTS, WHO FLICKERED ONE MOMENT ONLY TO VANISH THE NEXT.
SO THIS GIRL'S ABILITY...
IS TO REPLAY HER MEMORIES...
TIME IS MUCH MORE SWIFT-FOOTED HERE THAN IN THE OUTSIDE WORLD.
AND THOSE WHO STAY HERE COME TO BE FORGOTTEN BY THOSE OUTSIDE.
THE MOST PRECIOUS THINGS ARE ALWAYS THE EASIEST TO LOSE.
NO MATTER WHAT WE DO, MEMORIES ARE CARRIED AWAY BY THE CURRENTS OF TIME INTO OBLIVION.
AND I'M THE ONLY ONE WHO'S LEFT BEHIND.
THAT'S THE LAW OF THIS OTHER WORLD.
IN THIS DREAM GARDEN, EVERYONE'S LIFE ENDS BEFORE HERS.

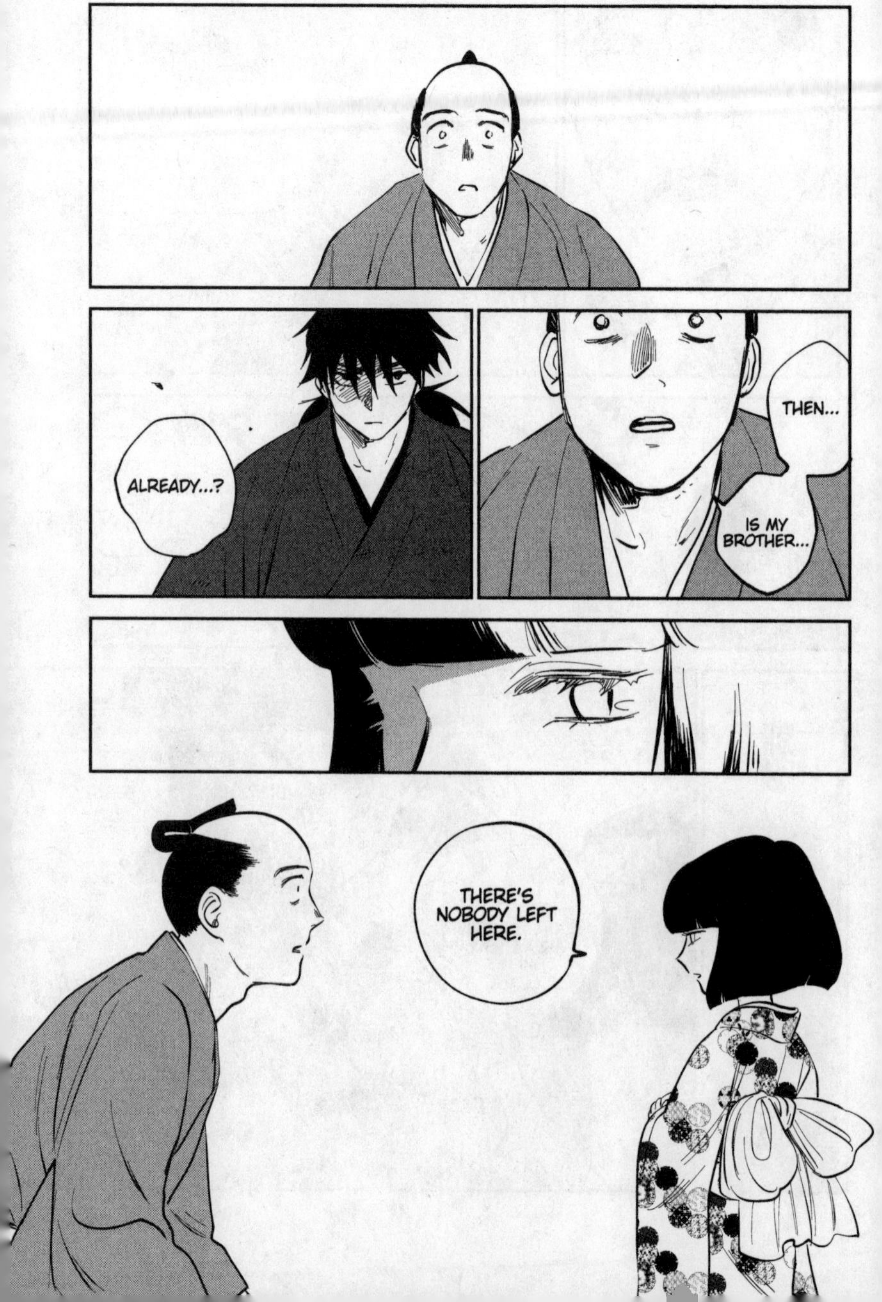
THEN...
IS MY BROTHER...
ALREADY...?
THERE'S NOBODY LEFT HERE.

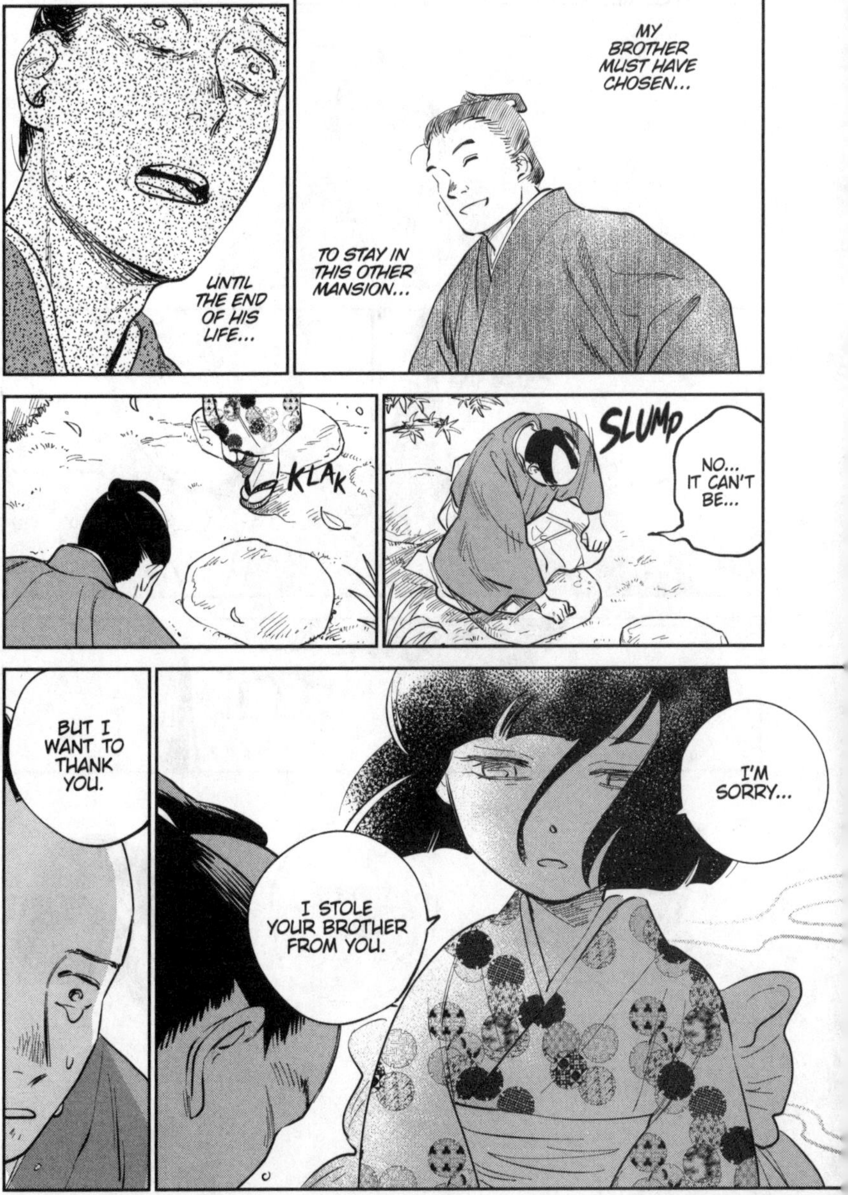
MY BROTHER MUST HAVE CHOSEN...
TO STAY IN THIS OTHER MANSION...
UNTIL THE END OF HIS LIFE...
SLUMP
NO... IT CAN'T BE...
KLAK
I'M SORRY...
I STOLE YOUR BROTHER FROM YOU.
BUT I WANT TO THANK YOU.

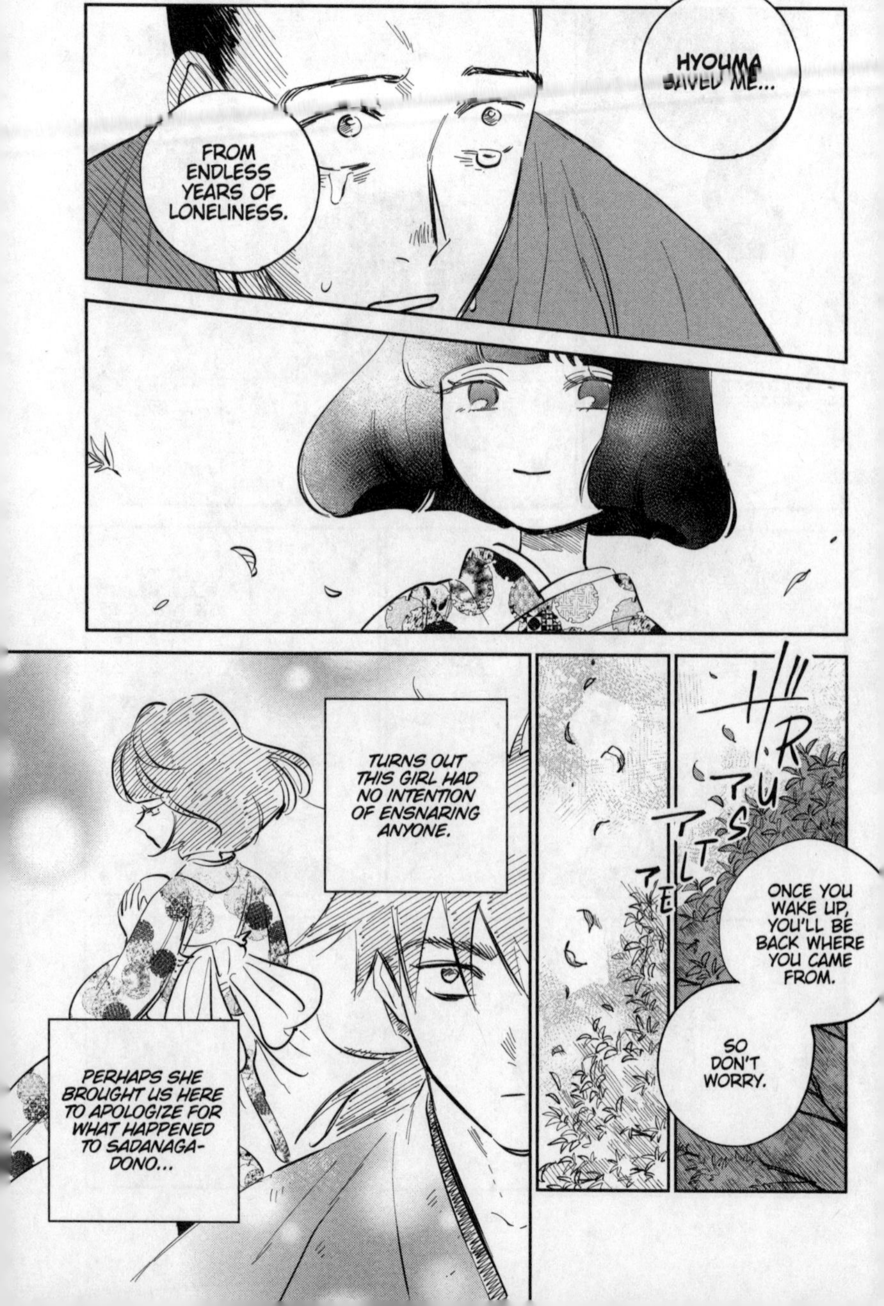
HYOUMA SAVED ME...
FROM ENDLESS YEARS OF LONELINESS.
RUSTLE
ONCE YOU WAKE UP, YOU'LL BE BACK WHERE YOU CAME FROM.
SO DON'T WORRY.
TURNS OUT THIS GIRL HAD NO INTENTION OF ENSNARING ANYONE.
PERHAPS SHE BROUGHT US HERE TO APOLOGIZE FOR WHAT HAPPENED TO SADANAGA-DONO...

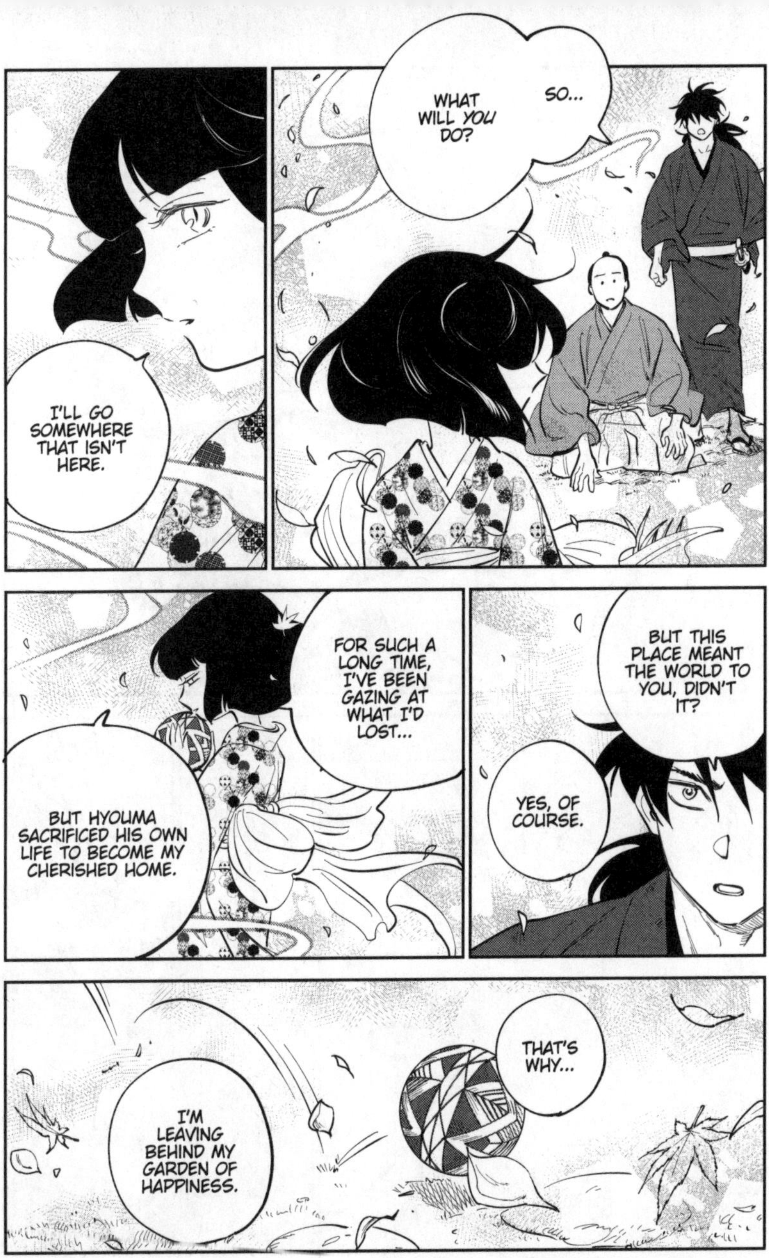
SO...
WHAT WILL YOU DO?
I'LL GO SOMEWHERE THAT ISN'T HERE.
BUT THIS PLACE MEANT THE WORLD TO YOU, DIDN'T IT?
YES, OF COURSE.
FOR SUCH A LONG TIME, I'VE BEEN GAZING AT WHAT I'D LOST...
BUT HYOUMA SACRIFICED HIS OWN LIFE TO BECOME MY CHERISHED HOME.
THAT'S WHY...
I'M LEAVING BEHIND MY GARDEN OF HAPPINESS.

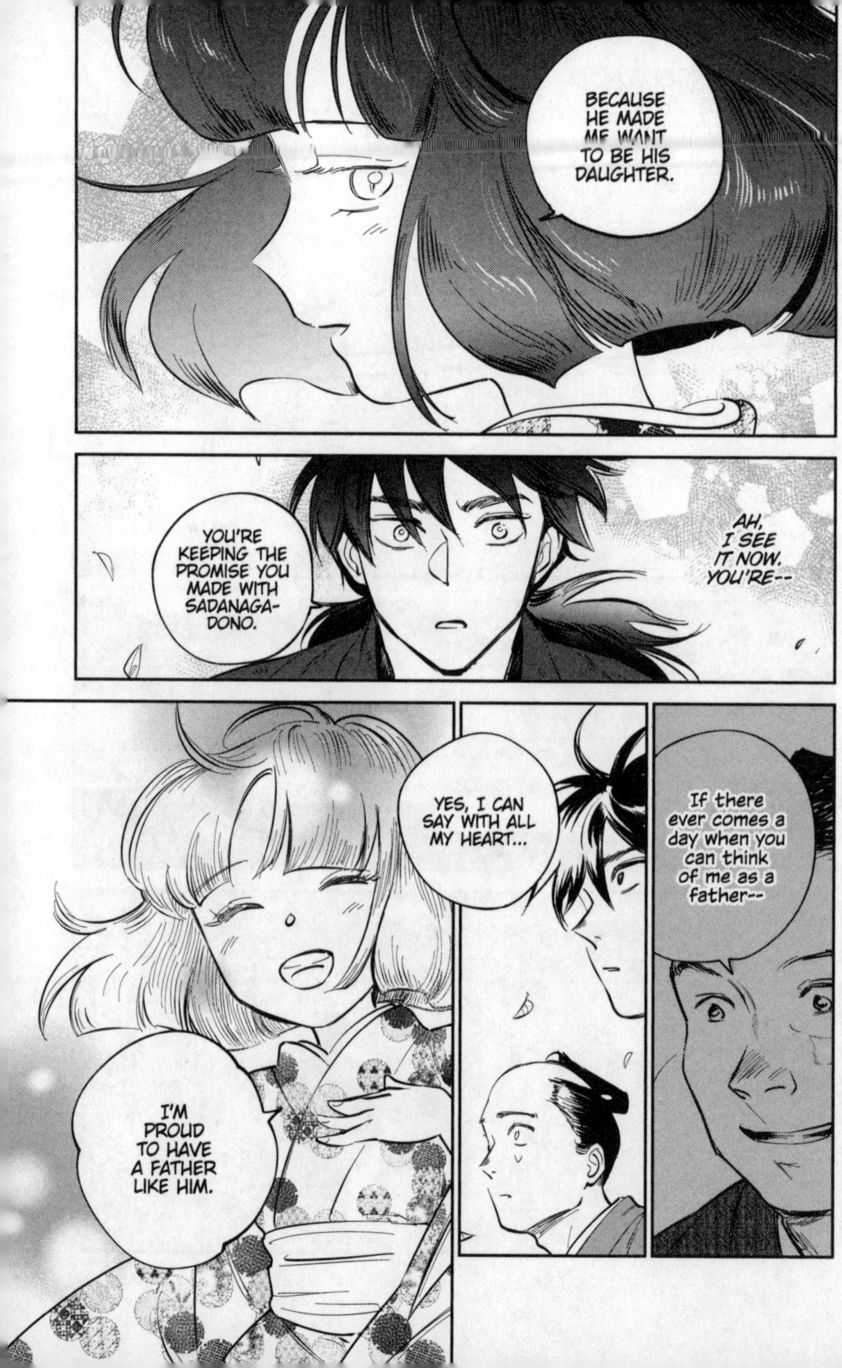
BECAUSE HE MADE ME WANT TO BE HIS DAUGHTER.
AH, I SEE IT NOW. YOU'RE--
YOU'RE KEEPING THE PROMISE YOU MADE WITH SADANAGA-DONO.
If there ever comes a day when you can think of me as a father--
YES, I CAN SAY WITH ALL MY HEART...
I'M PROUD TO HAVE A FATHER LIKE HIM.

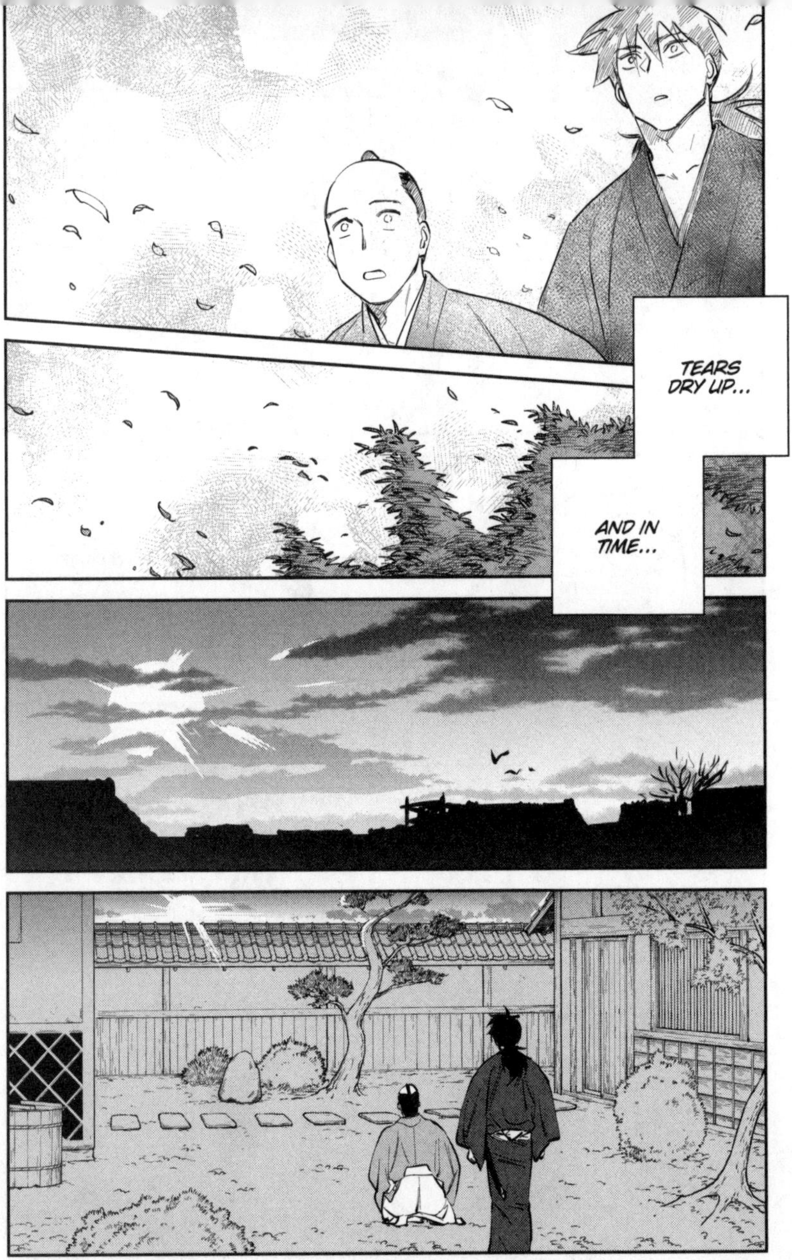
TEARS DRY UP...
AND IN TIME...

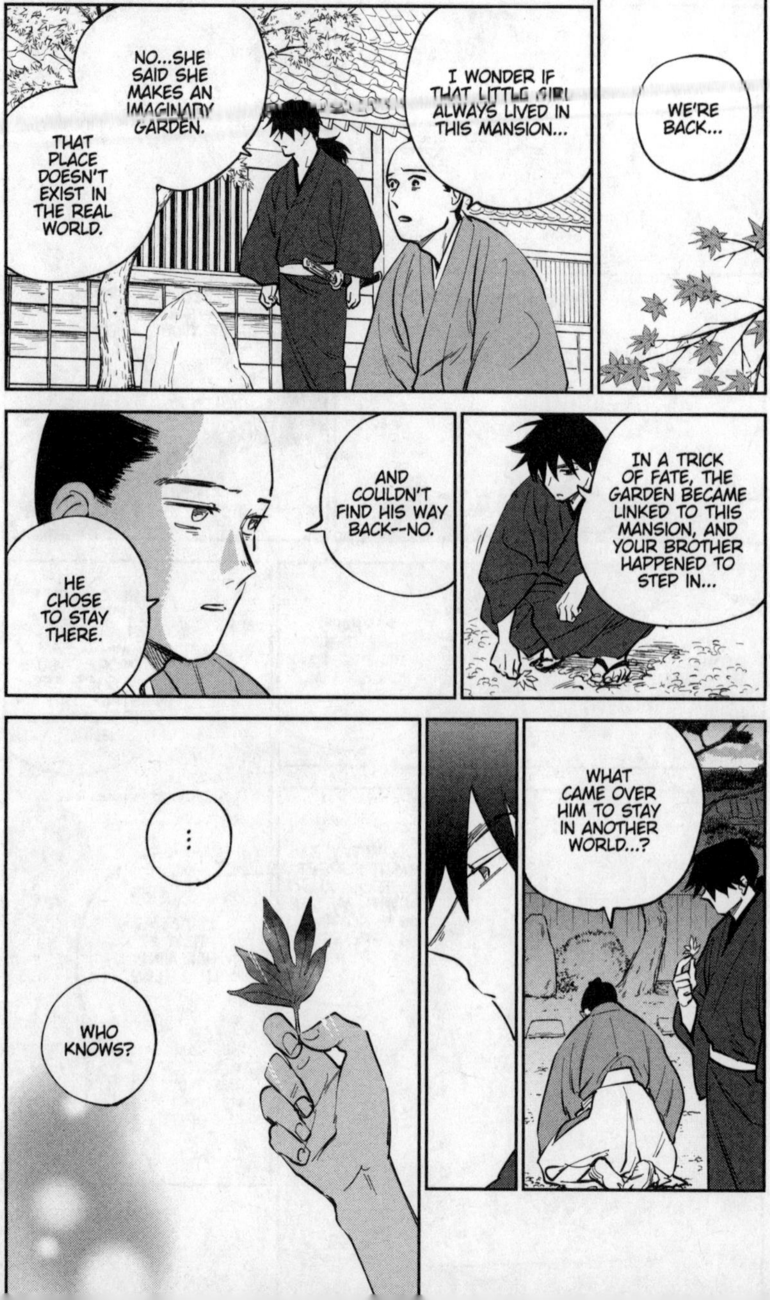
WE'RE BACK...
I WONDER IF THAT LITTLE GIRL ALWAYS LIVED IN THIS MANSION...
NO...SHE SAID SHE MAKES AN IMAGINARY GARDEN.
THAT PLACE DOESN'T EXIST IN THE REAL WORLD.
IN A TRICK OF FATE, THE GARDEN BECAME LINKED TO THIS MANSION, AND YOUR BROTHER HAPPENED TO STEP IN...
AND COULDN'T FIND HIS WAY BACK--NO.
HE CHOSE TO STAY THERE.
WHAT CAME OVER HIM TO STAY IN ANOTHER WORLD...?
...
WHO KNOWS?

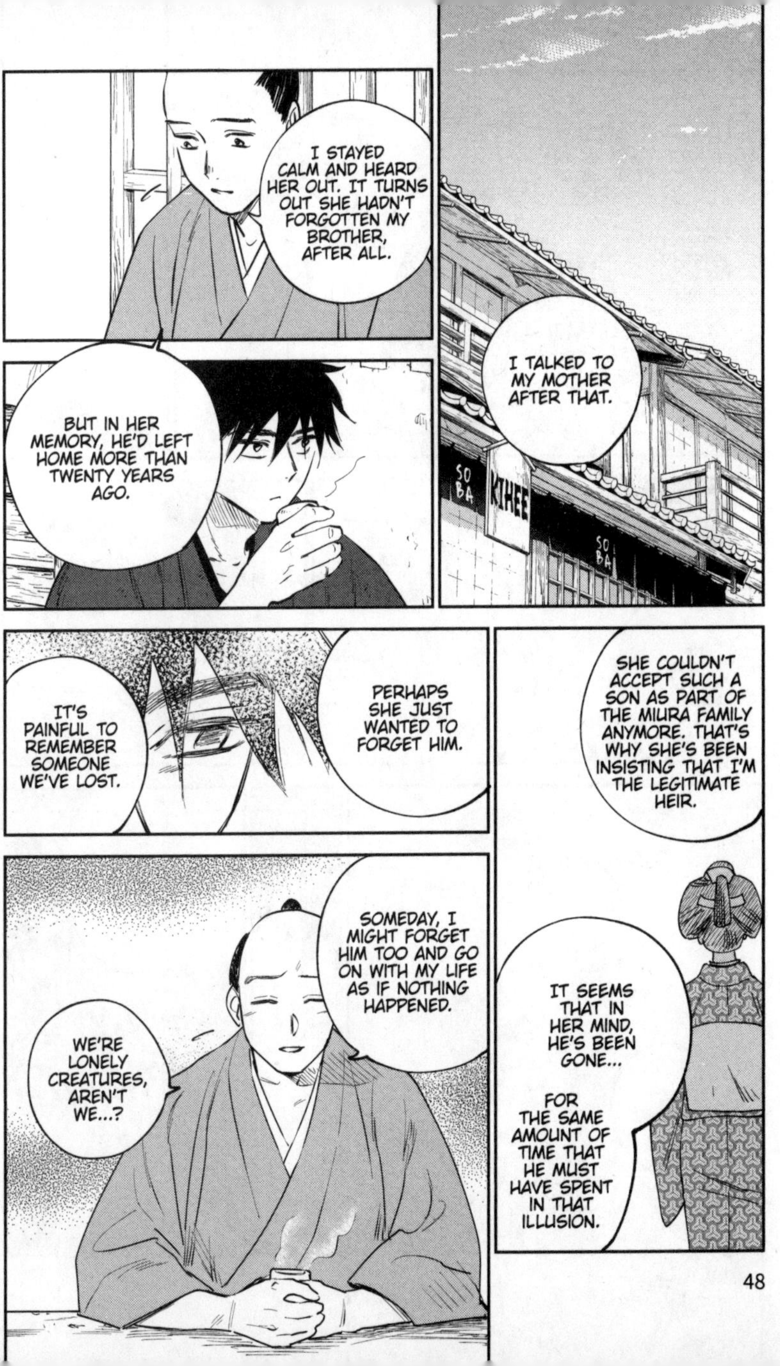
I TALKED TO MY MOTHER AFTER THAT.
SO BA
KIHEE
SO BA
I STAYED CALM AND HEARD HER OUT. IT TURNS OUT SHE HADN'T FORGOTTEN MY BROTHER, AFTER ALL.
BUT IN HER MEMORY, HE'D LEFT HOME MORE THAN TWENTY YEARS AGO.
SHE COULDN'T ACCEPT SUCH A SON AS PART OF THE MIURA FAMILY ANYMORE. THAT'S WHY SHE'S BEEN INSISTING THAT I'M THE LEGITIMATE HEIR.
PERHAPS SHE JUST WANTED TO FORGET HIM.
IT'S PAINFUL TO REMEMBER SOMEONE WE'VE LOST.
IT SEEMS THAT IN HER MIND, HE'S BEEN GONE...
FOR THE SAME AMOUNT OF TIME THAT HE MUST HAVE SPENT IN THAT ILLUSION.
SOMEDAY, I MIGHT FORGET HIM TOO AND GO ON WITH MY LIFE AS IF NOTHING HAPPENED.
WE'RE LONELY CREATURES, AREN'T WE...?

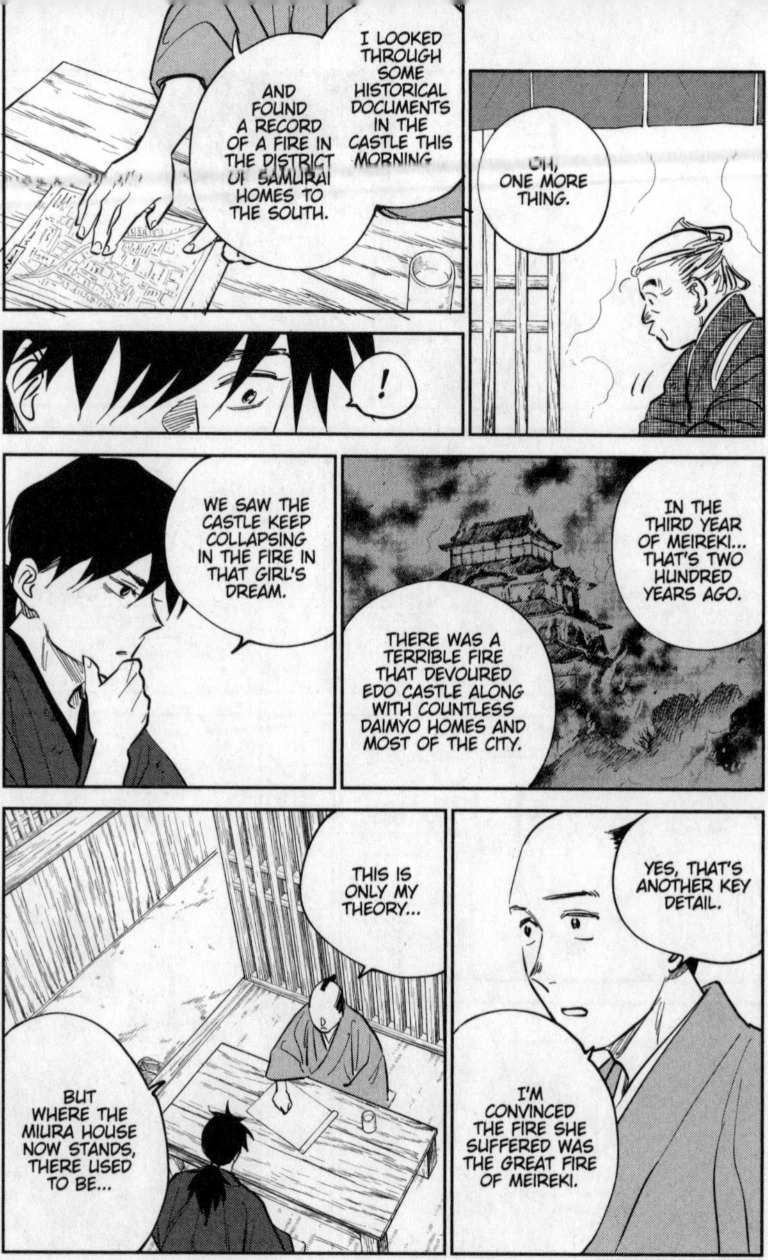

OH, ONE MORE THING.
I LOOKED THROUGH SOME HISTORICAL DOCUMENTS IN THE CASTLE THIS MORNING
AND FOUND A RECORD OF A FIRE IN THE DISTRICT OF SAMURAI HOMES TO THE SOUTH.
!
IN THE THIRD YEAR OF MEIREKI... THAT'S TWO HUNDRED YEARS AGO.
THERE WAS A TERRIBLE FIRE THAT DEVOURED EDO CASTLE ALONG WITH COUNTLESS DAIMYO HOMES AND MOST OF THE CITY.
WE SAW THE CASTLE KEEP COLLAPSING IN THE FIRE IN THAT GIRL'S DREAM.
YES, THAT'S ANOTHER KEY DETAIL.
I'M CONVINCED THE FIRE SHE SUFFERED WAS THE GREAT FIRE OF MEIREKI.
THIS IS ONLY MY THEORY...
BUT WHERE THE MIURA HOUSE NOW STANDS, THERE USED TO BE...

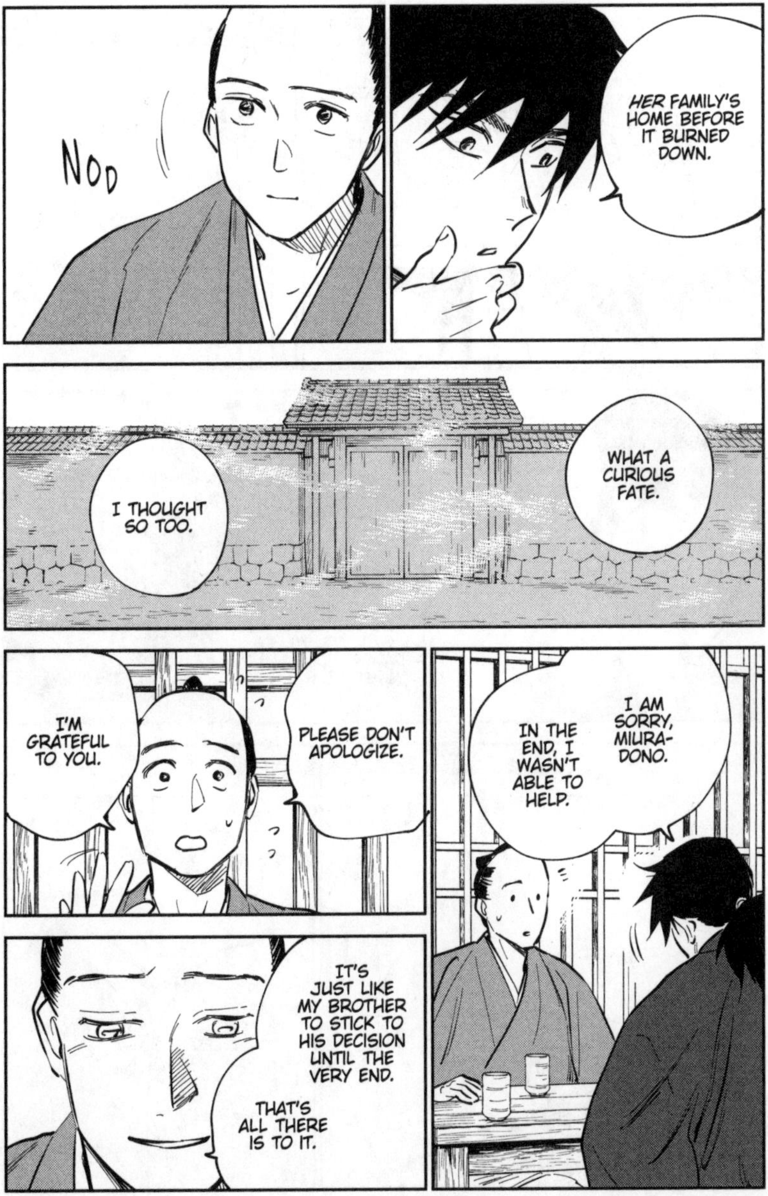
HER FAMILY'S HOME BEFORE IT BURNED DOWN.
NOD
WHAT A CURIOUS FATE.
I THOUGHT SO TOO.
I AM SORRY, MIURA-DONO.
IN THE END, I WASN'T ABLE TO HELP.
PLEASE DON'T APOLOGIZE.
I'M GRATEFUL TO YOU.
IT'S JUST LIKE MY BROTHER TO STICK TO HIS DECISION UNTIL THE VERY END.
THAT'S ALL THERE IS TO IT.

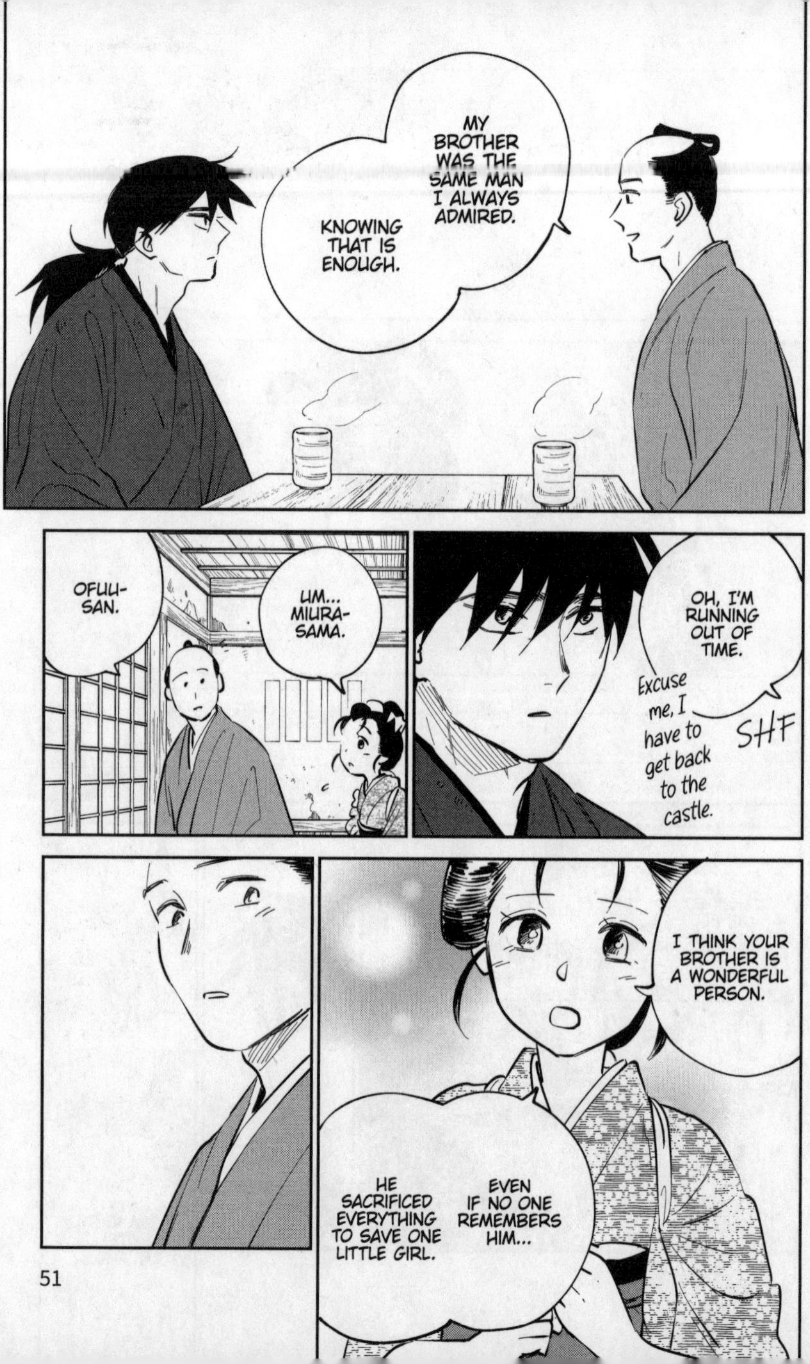
MY BROTHER WAS THE SAME MAN I ALWAYS ADMIRED.
KNOWING THAT IS ENOUGH.
OH, I'M RUNNING OUT OF TIME.
Excuse me, I have to get back to the castle.
SHF
UM... MIURA-SAMA.
OFUU-SAN.
I THINK YOUR BROTHER IS A WONDERFUL PERSON.
EVEN IF NO ONE REMEMBERS HIM...
HE SACRIFICED EVERYTHING TO SAVE ONE LITTLE GIRL.

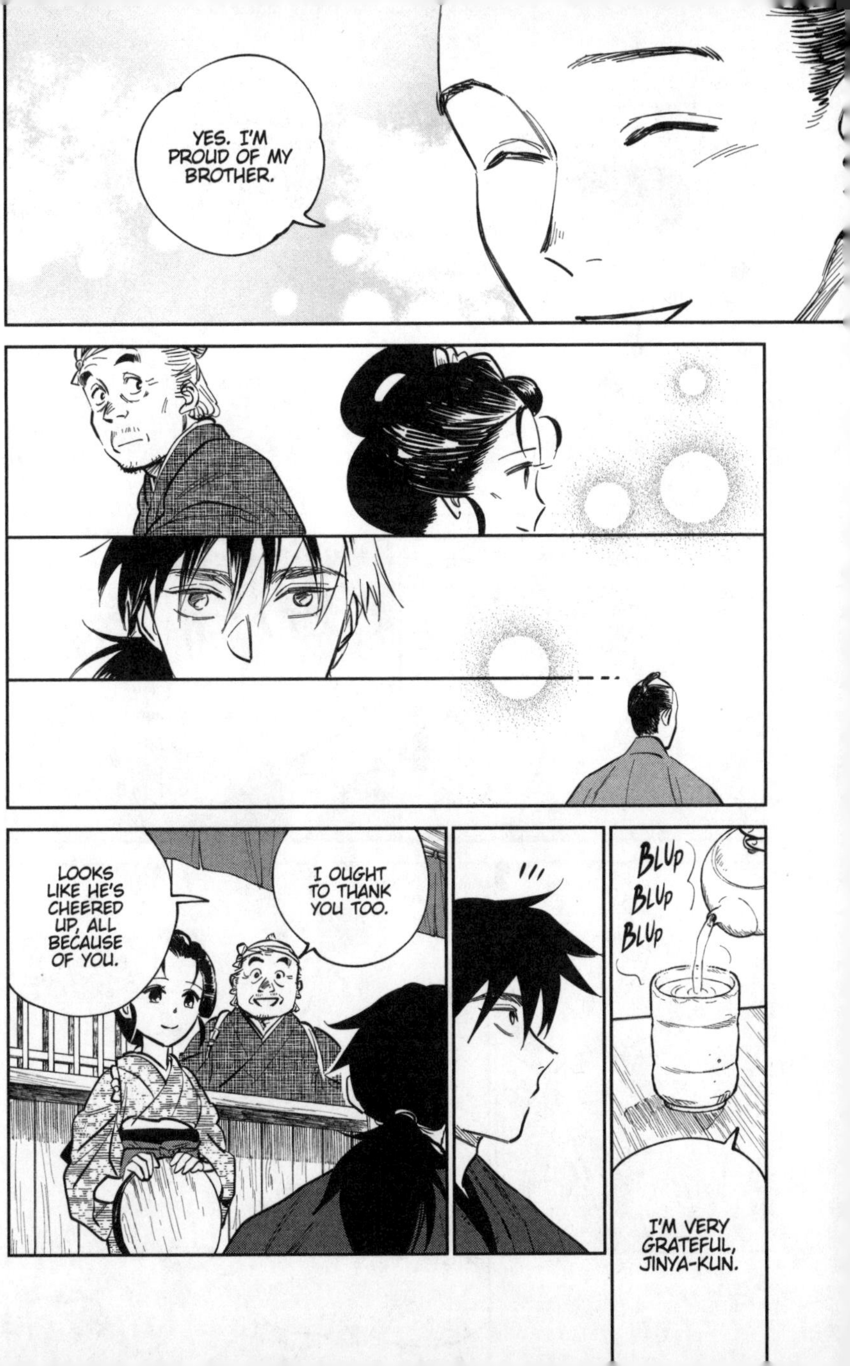
YES. I'M PROUD OF MY BROTHER.
BLUP
BLUP
BLUP
I'M VERY GRATEFUL, JINYA-KUN.
I OUGHT TO THANK YOU TOO.
LOOKS LIKE HE'S CHEERED UP, ALL BECAUSE OF YOU.

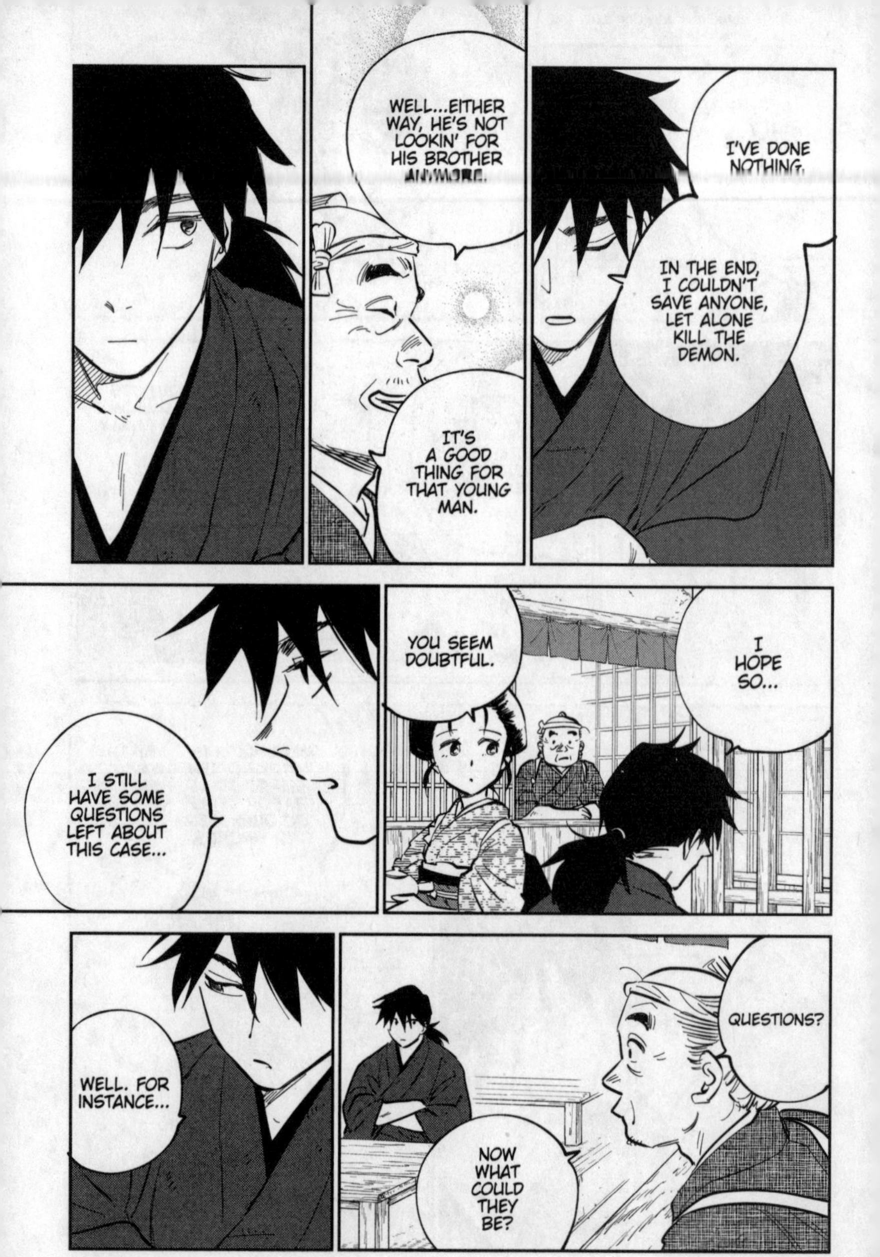
I'VE DONE NOTHING.
IN THE END, I COULDN'T SAVE ANYONE, LET ALONE KILL THE DEMON.
WELL...EITHER WAY, HE'S NOT LOOKIN' FOR HIS BROTHER ANYMORE.
IT'S A GOOD THING FOR THAT YOUNG MAN.
I HOPE SO...
YOU SEEM DOUBTFUL.
I STILL HAVE SOME QUESTIONS LEFT ABOUT THIS CASE...
QUESTIONS?
NOW WHAT COULD THEY BE?
WELL. FOR INSTANCE...

*A personal name that only one's parents or lord are allowed to use.

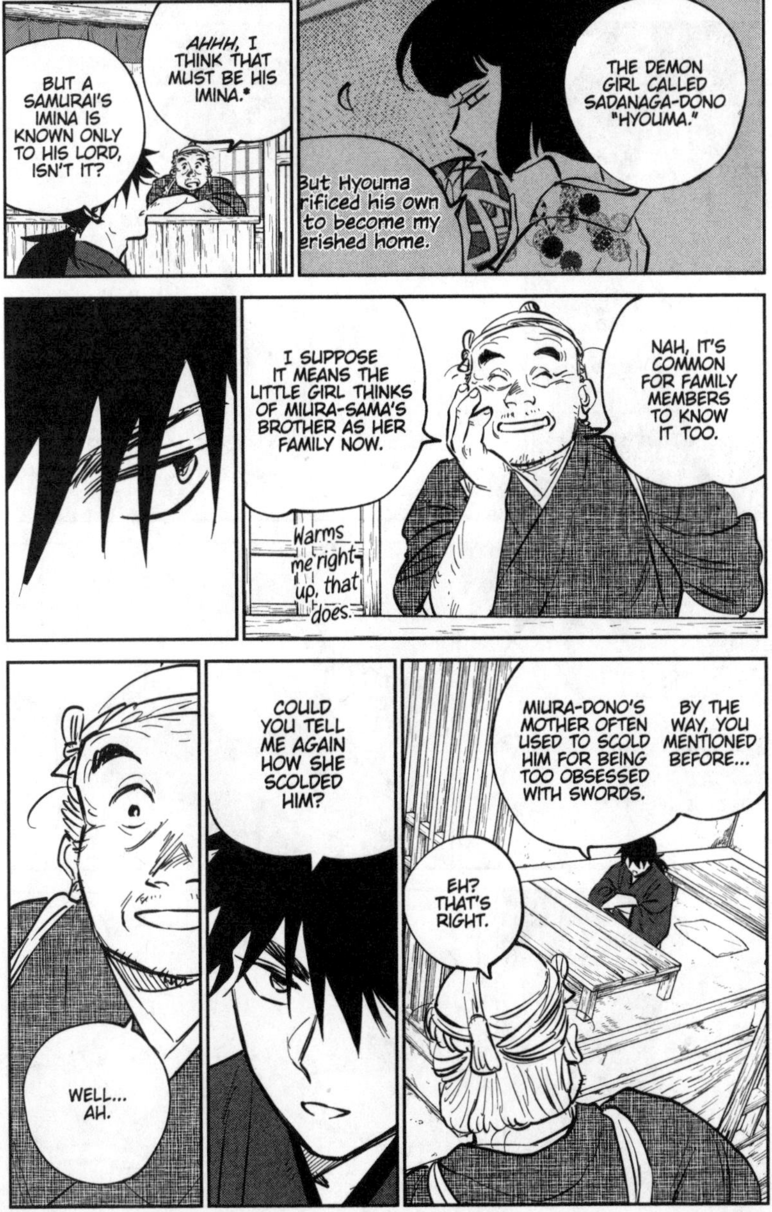
THE DEMON GIRL CALLED SADANAGA-DONO "HYOUMA."
But Hyouma rificed his own to become my erished home.
AHHH, I THINK THAT MUST BE HIS IMINA.*
BUT A SAMURAI'S IMINA IS KNOWN ONLY TO HIS LORD, ISN'T IT?
NAH, IT'S COMMON FOR FAMILY MEMBERS TO KNOW IT TOO.
I SUPPOSE IT MEANS THE LITTLE GIRL THINKS OF MIURA-SAMA'S BROTHER AS HER FAMILY NOW.
Warms me right up, that does.
BY THE WAY, YOU MENTIONED BEFORE...
MIURA-DONO'S MOTHER OFTEN USED TO SCOLD HIM FOR BEING TOO OBSESSED WITH SWORDS.
EH? THAT'S RIGHT.
COULD YOU TELL ME AGAIN HOW SHE SCOLDED HIM?
WELL... AH.

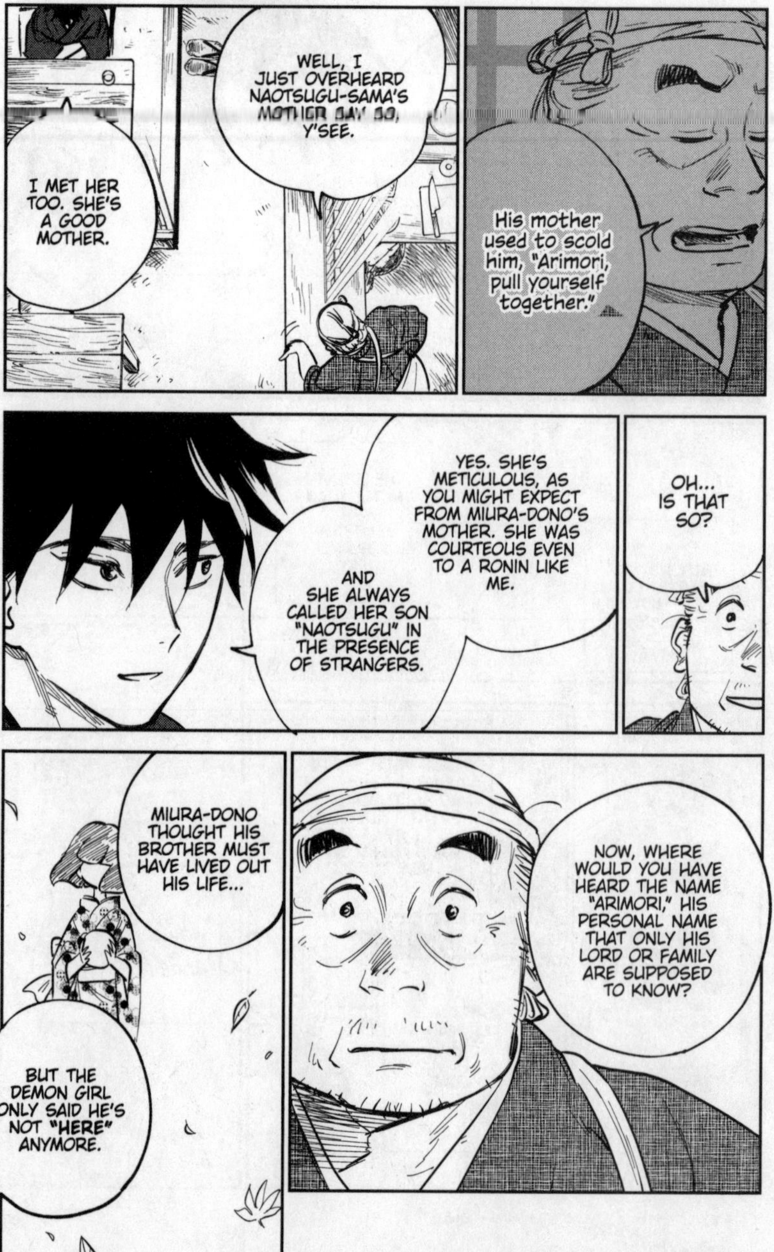
His mother used to scold him, "Arimori, pull yourself together."
WELL, I JUST OVERHEARD NAOTSUGU-SAMA'S MOTHER SAY SO, Y'SEE.
I MET HER TOO. SHE'S A GOOD MOTHER.
OH... IS THAT SO?
YES. SHE'S METICULOUS, AS YOU MIGHT EXPECT FROM MIURA-DONO'S MOTHER. SHE WAS COURTEOUS EVEN TO A RONIN LIKE ME.
AND SHE ALWAYS CALLED HER SON "NAOTSUGU" IN THE PRESENCE OF STRANGERS.
NOW, WHERE WOULD YOU HAVE HEARD THE NAME "ARIMORI," HIS PERSONAL NAME THAT ONLY HIS LORD OR FAMILY ARE SUPPOSED TO KNOW?
MIURA-DONO THOUGHT HIS BROTHER MUST HAVE LIVED OUT HIS LIFE...
BUT THE DEMON GIRL ONLY SAID HE'S NOT "HERE" ANYMORE.

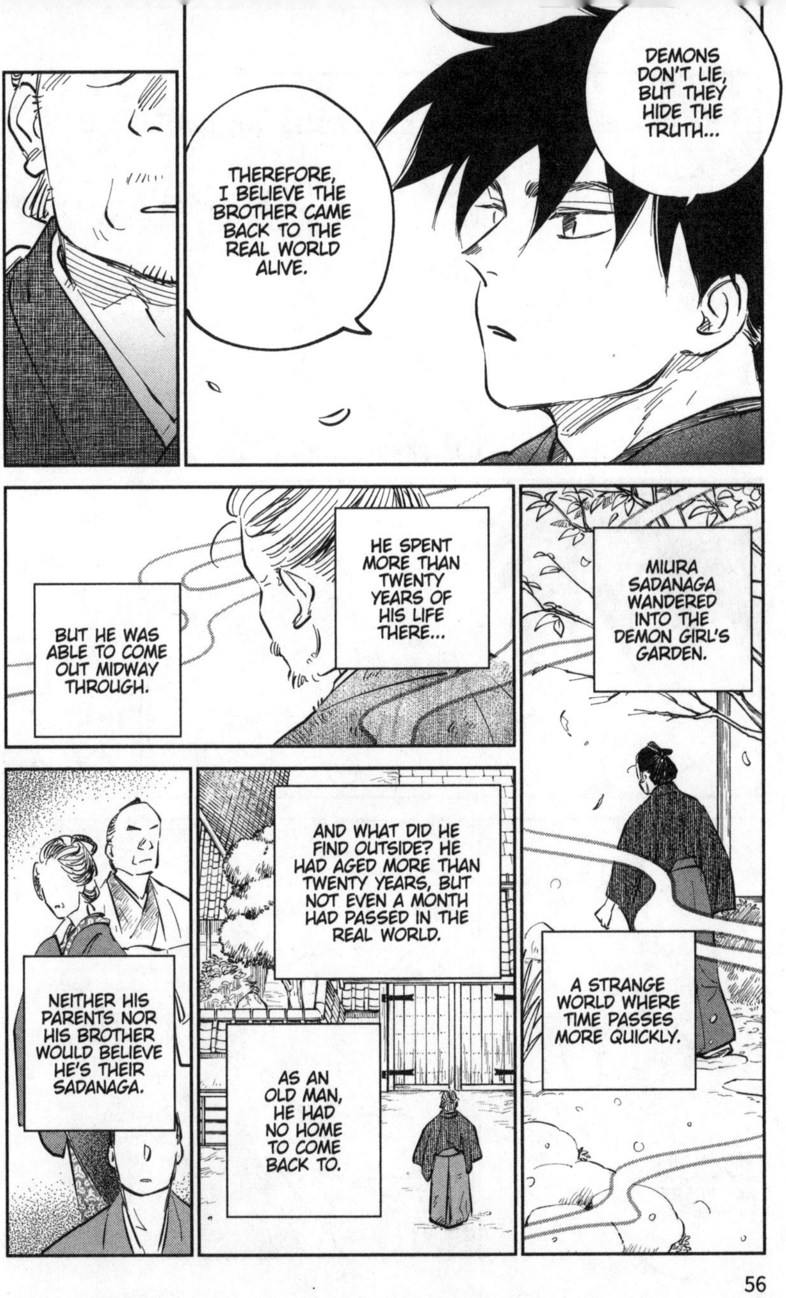
DEMONS DON'T LIE, BUT THEY HIDE THE TRUTH...
THEREFORE, I BELIEVE THE BROTHER CAME BACK TO THE REAL WORLD ALIVE.
MIURA SADANAGA WANDERED INTO THE DEMON GIRL'S GARDEN.
A STRANGE WORLD WHERE TIME PASSES MORE QUICKLY.
HE SPENT MORE THAN TWENTY YEARS OF HIS LIFE THERE...
BUT HE WAS ABLE TO COME OUT MIDWAY THROUGH.
AND WHAT DID HE FIND OUTSIDE? HE HAD AGED MORE THAN TWENTY YEARS, BUT NOT EVEN A MONTH HAD PASSED IN THE REAL WORLD.
AS AN OLD MAN, HE HAD NO HOME TO COME BACK TO.
NEITHER HIS PARENTS NOR HIS BROTHER WOULD BELIEVE HE'S THEIR SADANAGA.

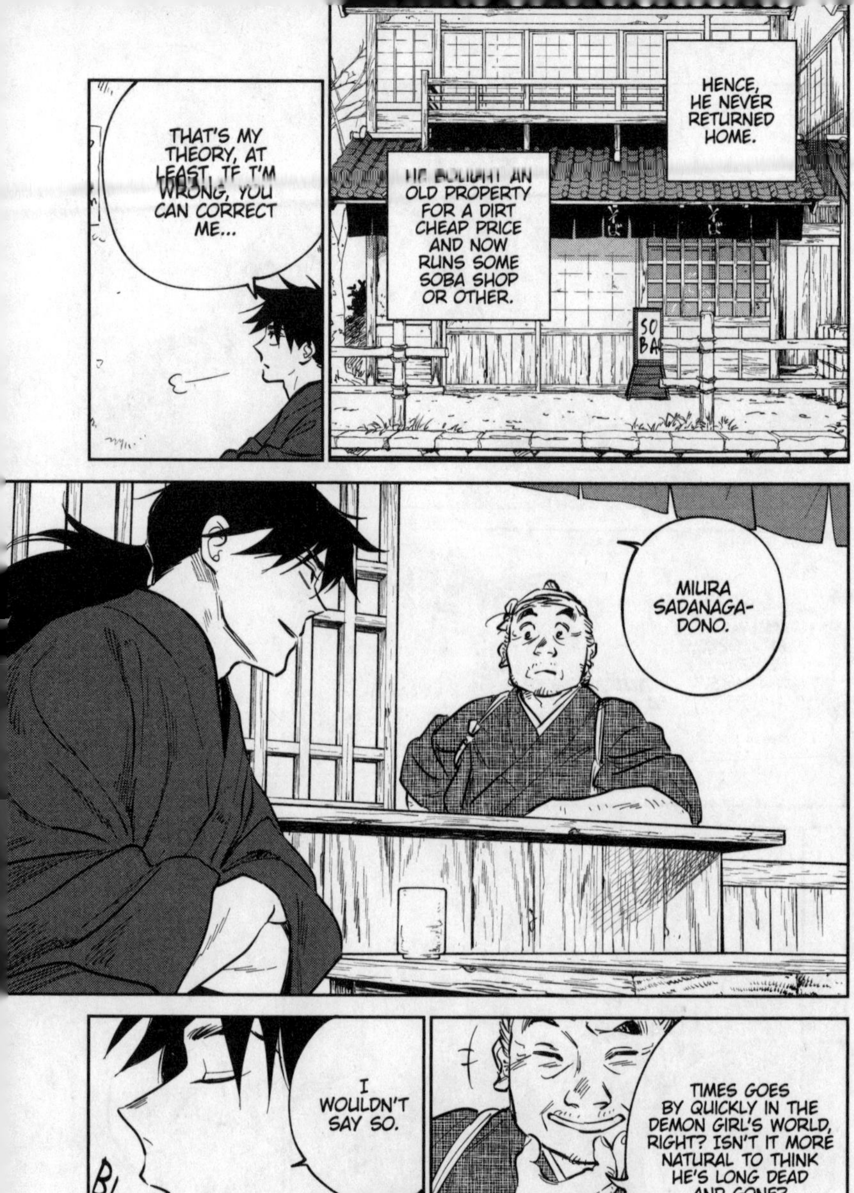
HENCE, HE NEVER RETURNED HOME.
HE BOUGHT AN OLD PROPERTY FOR A DIRT CHEAP PRICE AND NOW RUNS SOME SOBA SHOP OR OTHER.
SOBA
THAT'S MY THEORY, AT LEAST. IF I'M WRONG, YOU CAN CORRECT ME...
MIURA SADANAGA-DONO.
TIMES GOES BY QUICKLY IN THE DEMON GIRL'S WORLD, RIGHT? ISN'T IT MORE NATURAL TO THINK HE'S LONG DEAD AND GONE?
I WOULDN'T SAY SO.
BLUNT

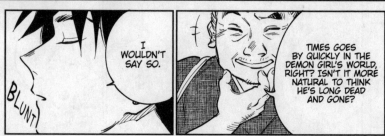

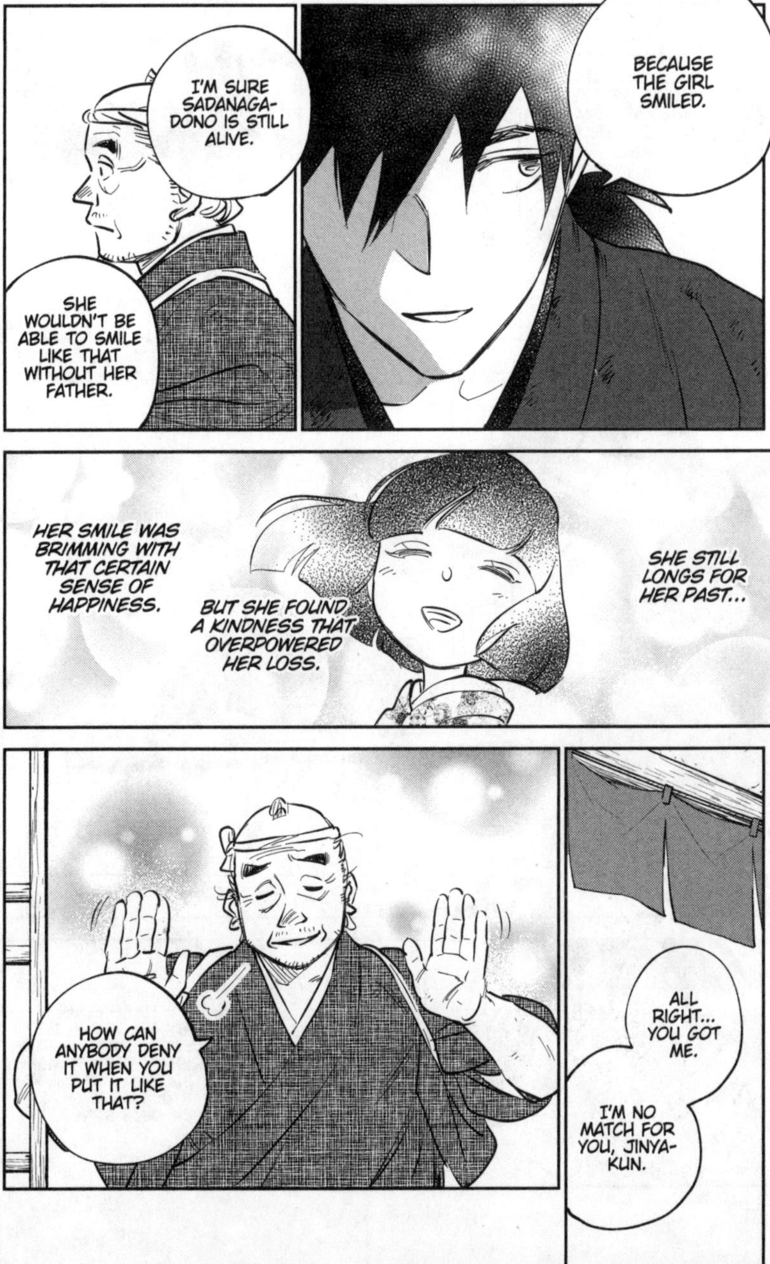
I'M SURE SADANAGA-DONO IS STILL ALIVE.
BECAUSE THE GIRL SMILED.
SHE WOULDN'T BE ABLE TO SMILE LIKE THAT WITHOUT HER FATHER.
SHE STILL LONGS FOR HER PAST...
BUT SHE FOUND A KINDNESS THAT OVERPOWERED HER LOSS.
HER SMILE WAS BRIMMING WITH THAT CERTAIN SENSE OF HAPPINESS.
ALL RIGHT... YOU GOT ME.
I'M NO MATCH FOR YOU, JINYA-KUN.
HOW CAN ANYBODY DENY IT WHEN YOU PUT IT LIKE THAT?

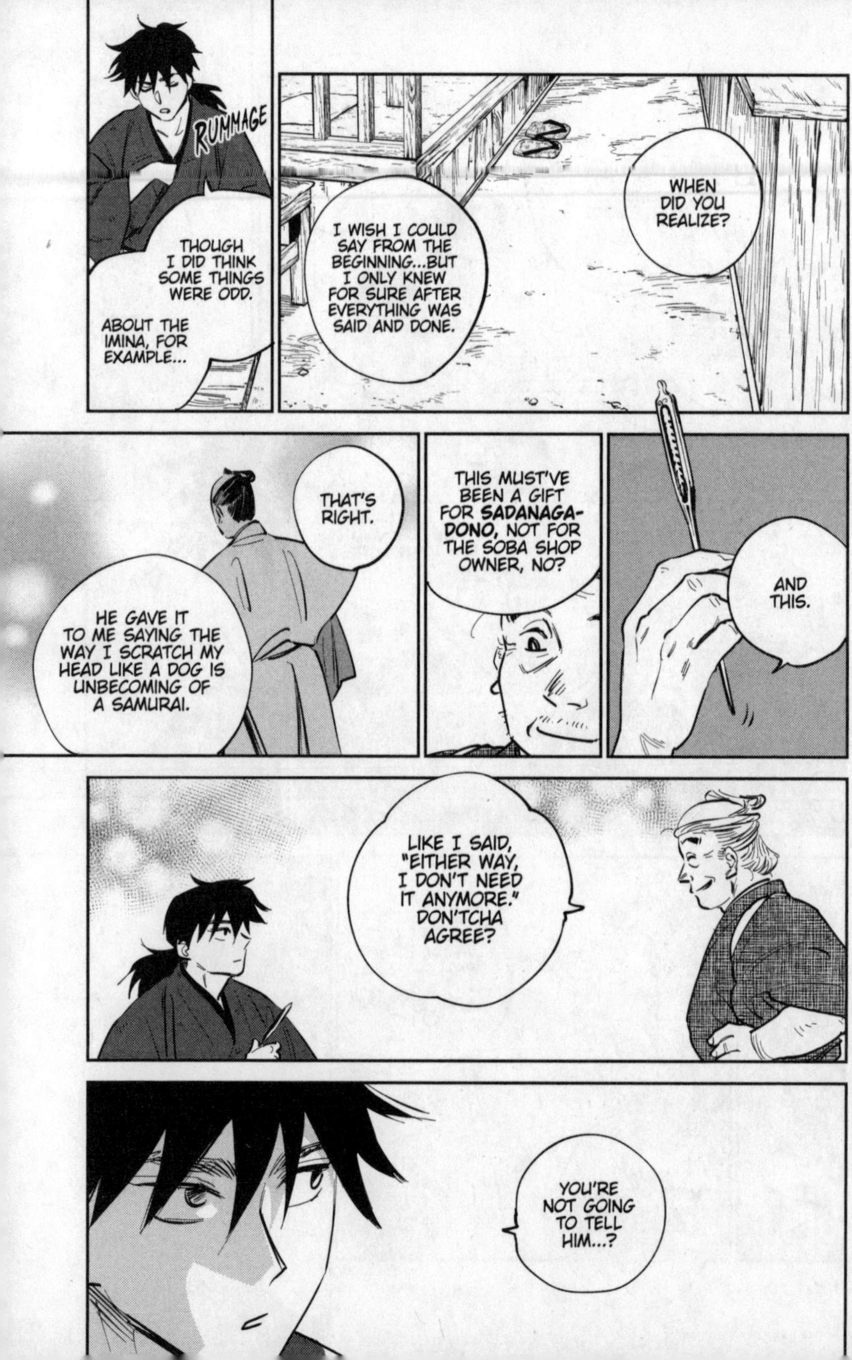
WHEN DID YOU REALIZE?
I WISH I COULD SAY FROM THE BEGINNING...BUT I ONLY KNEW FOR SURE AFTER EVERYTHING WAS SAID AND DONE.
RUMMAGE
THOUGH I DID THINK SOME THINGS WERE ODD.
ABOUT THE IMINA, FOR EXAMPLE...
AND THIS.
THIS MUST'VE BEEN A GIFT FOR **SADANAGA-DONO,** NOT FOR THE SOBA SHOP OWNER, NO?
THAT'S RIGHT.
HE GAVE IT TO ME SAYING THE WAY I SCRATCH MY HEAD LIKE A DOG IS UNBECOMING OF A SAMURAI.
LIKE I SAID, "EITHER WAY, I DON'T NEED IT ANYMORE." DON'TCHA AGREE?
YOU'RE NOT GOING TO TELL HIM...?

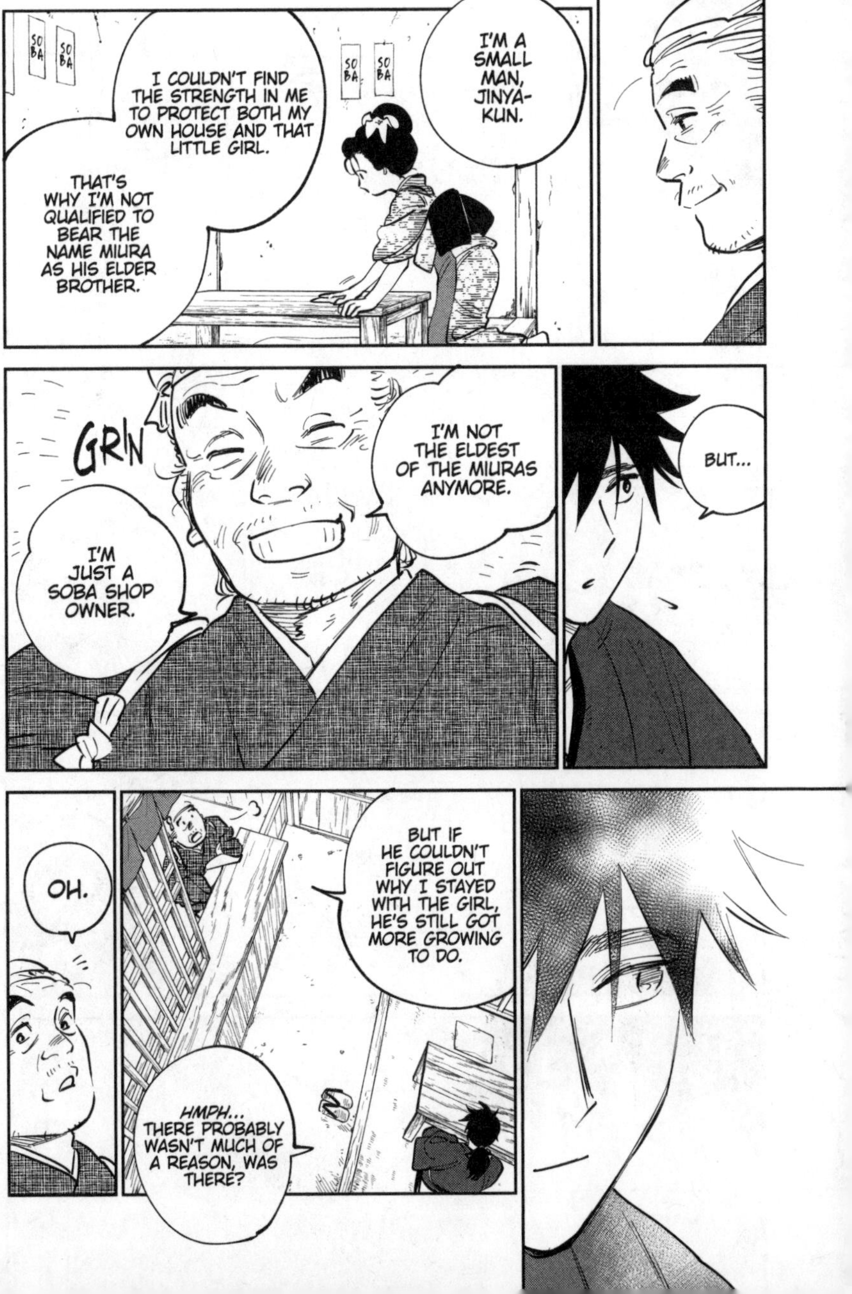

I'M A SMALL MAN, JINYA-KUN.
SO BA
SO BA
I COULDN'T FIND THE STRENGTH IN ME TO PROTECT BOTH MY OWN HOUSE AND THAT LITTLE GIRL.
SO BA
SO BA
THAT'S WHY I'M NOT QUALIFIED TO BEAR THE NAME MIURA AS HIS ELDER BROTHER.
BUT...
I'M NOT THE ELDEST OF THE MIURAS ANYMORE.
GRIN
I'M JUST A SOBA SHOP OWNER.
BUT IF HE COULDN'T FIGURE OUT WHY I STAYED WITH THE GIRL, HE'S STILL GOT MORE GROWING TO DO.
*HMPH...* THERE PROBABLY WASN'T MUCH OF A REASON, WAS THERE?
OH.

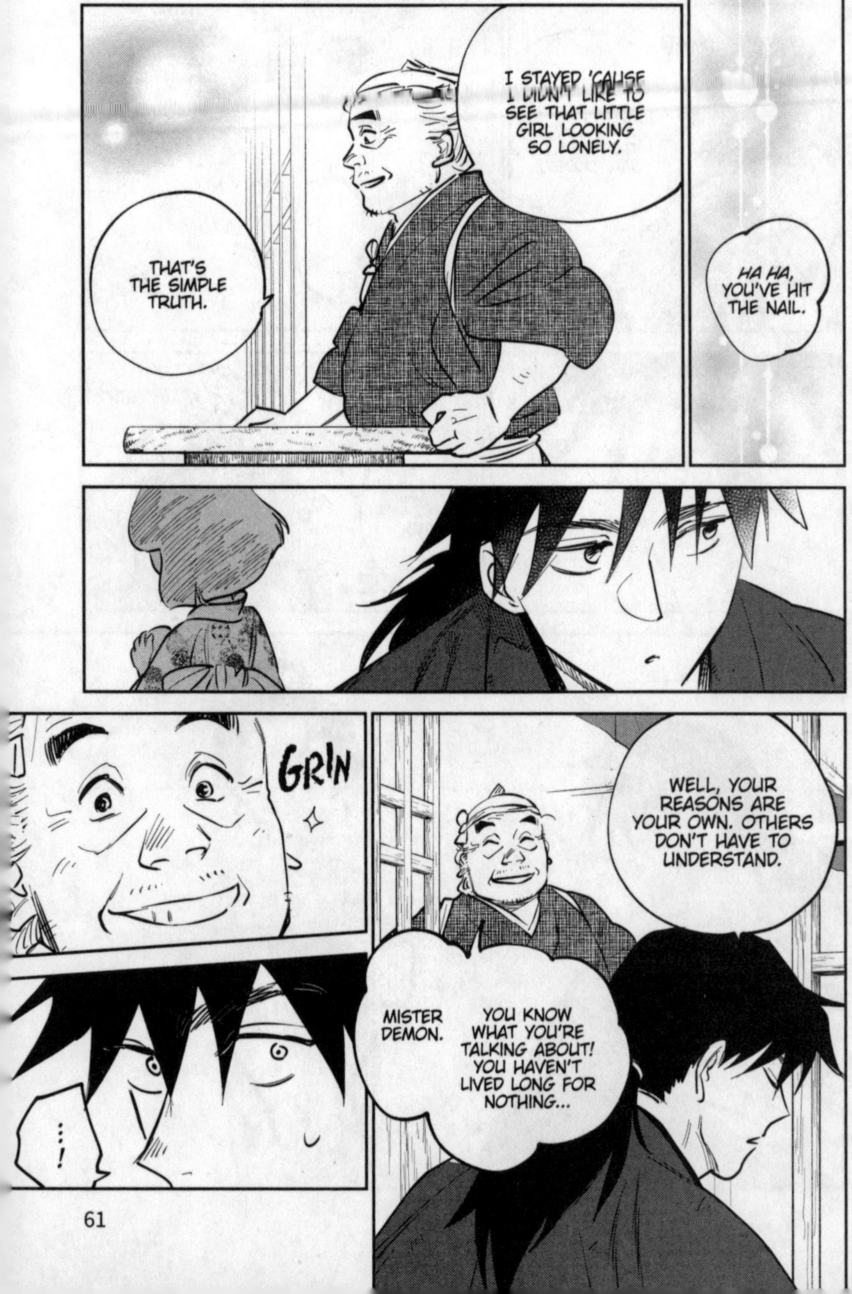
HA HA, YOU'VE HIT THE NAIL.
I STAYED 'CAUSE I DIDN'T LIKE TO SEE THAT LITTLE GIRL LOOKING SO LONELY.
THAT'S THE SIMPLE TRUTH.
WELL, YOUR REASONS ARE YOUR OWN. OTHERS DON'T HAVE TO UNDERSTAND.
MISTER DEMON.
YOU KNOW WHAT YOU'RE TALKING ABOUT! YOU HAVEN'T LIVED LONG FOR NOTHING...
GRIN
...!

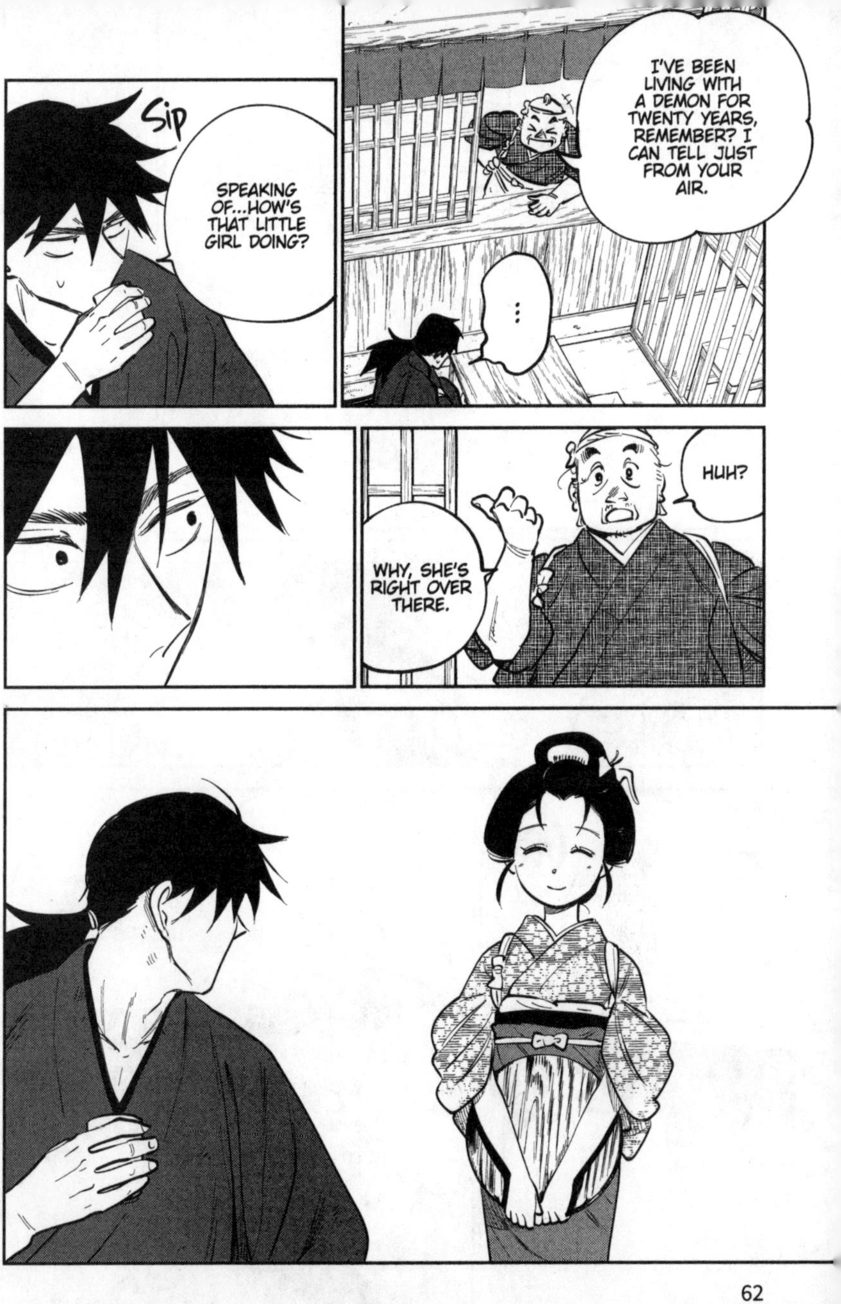
I'VE BEEN LIVING WITH A DEMON FOR TWENTY YEARS, REMEMBER? I CAN TELL JUST FROM YOUR AIR.
...
Sip
SPEAKING OF...HOW'S THAT LITTLE GIRL DOING?
HUH?
WHY, SHE'S RIGHT OVER THERE.

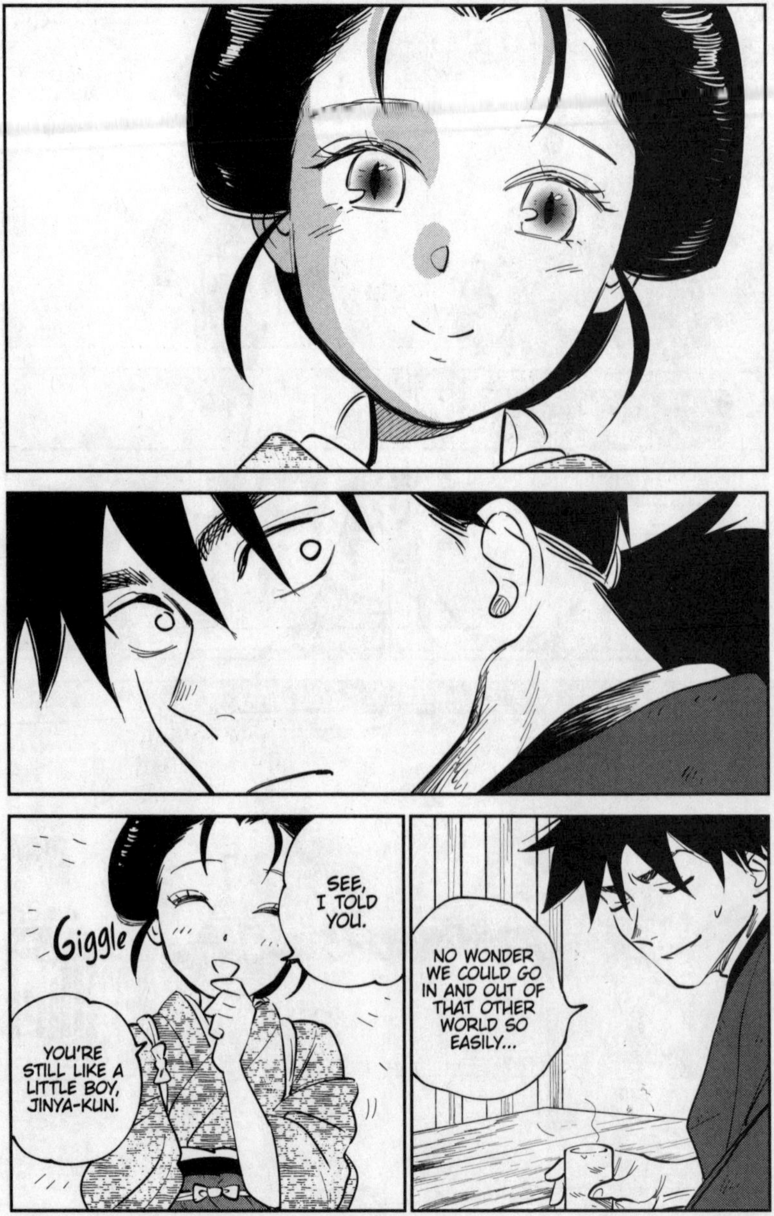
NO WONDER WE COULD GO IN AND OUT OF THAT OTHER WORLD SO EASILY...
SEE, I TOLD YOU.
Giggle
YOU'RE STILL LIKE A LITTLE BOY, JINYA-KUN.

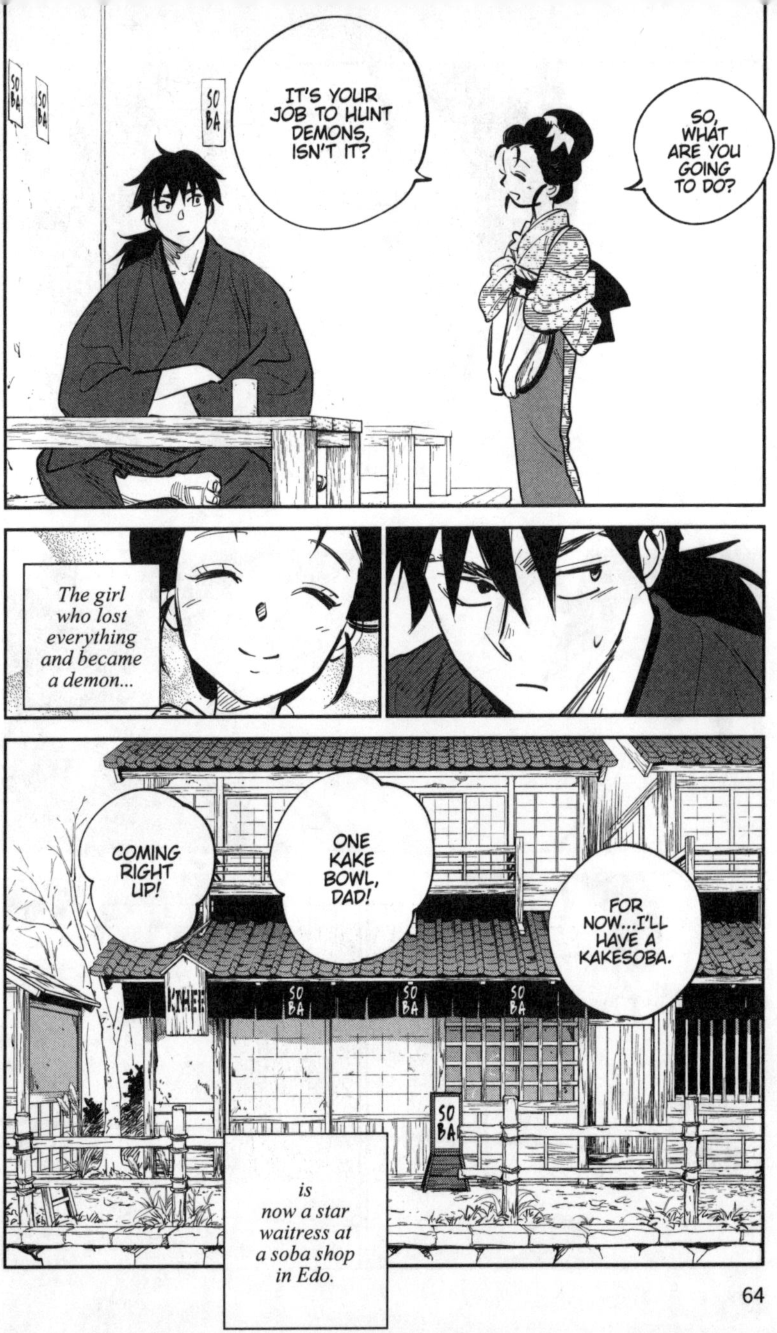
SO, WHAT ARE YOU GOING TO DO?
IT'S YOUR JOB TO HUNT DEMONS, ISN'T IT?
The girl who lost everything and became a demon...
FOR NOW...I'LL HAVE A KAKESOBA.
ONE KAKE BOWL, DAD!
COMING RIGHT UP!
is now a star waitress at a soba shop in Edo.

Sword
of the Demon
Hunter KIJIN
GENTŌSHŌ

Sword
of the Demon
Hunter KIJIN
GENTŌSHŌ

## CHAPTER 22: THE HAUNTING OF KUDANZAKA ①

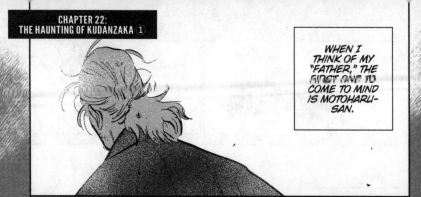

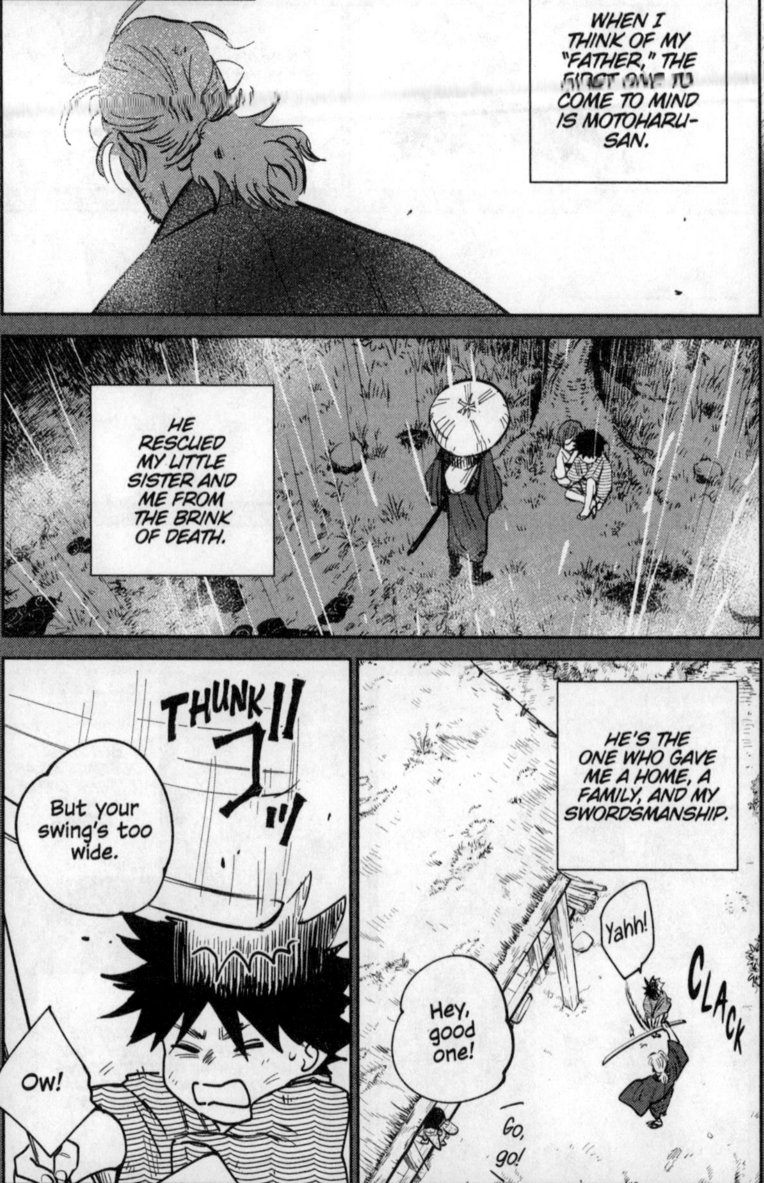
WHEN I THINK OF MY "FATHER," THE FIRST ONE TO COME TO MIND IS MOTOHARU-SAN.
HE RESCUED MY LITTLE SISTER AND ME FROM THE BRINK OF DEATH.
HE'S THE ONE WHO GAVE ME A HOME, A FAMILY, AND MY SWORDSMANSHIP.
Yahh!
CLACK
Hey, good one!
Go, go!
THUNK!!
But your swing's too wide.
Ow!

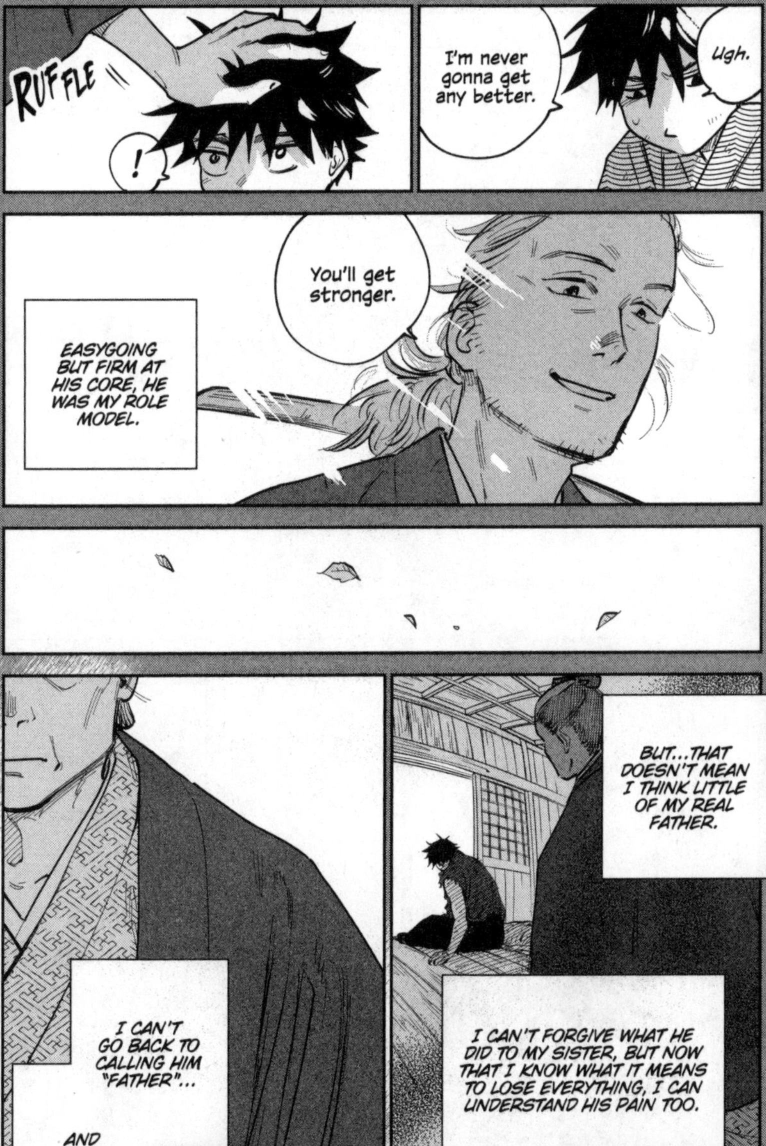
Ugh.
I'm never gonna get any better.
RUFFLE
!
You'll get stronger.
EASYGOING BUT FIRM AT HIS CORE, HE WAS MY ROLE MODEL.
BUT...THAT DOESN'T MEAN I THINK LITTLE OF MY REAL FATHER.
I CAN'T FORGIVE WHAT HE DID TO MY SISTER, BUT NOW THAT I KNOW WHAT IT MEANS TO LOSE EVERYTHING, I CAN UNDERSTAND HIS PAIN TOO.
I CAN'T GO BACK TO CALLING HIM "FATHER"...
AND YET...

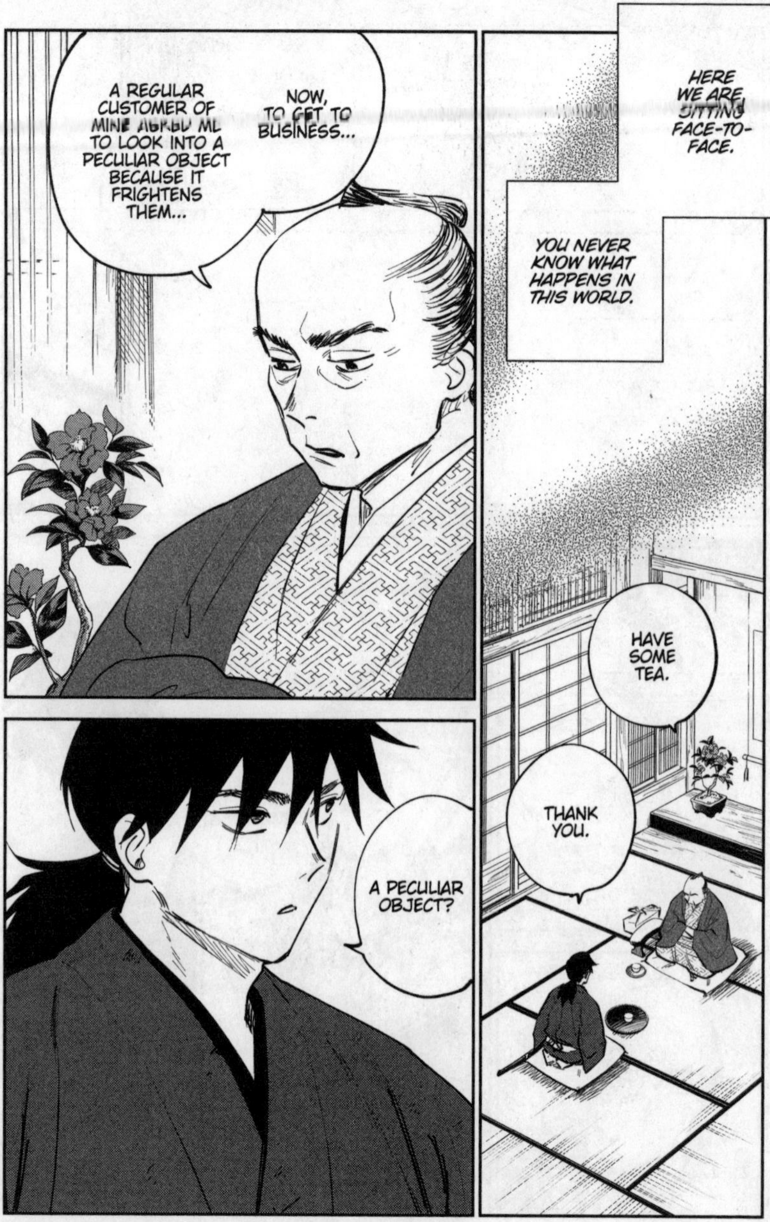

HERE WE ARE SITTING FACE-TO-FACE.
YOU NEVER KNOW WHAT HAPPENS IN THIS WORLD.
HAVE SOME TEA.
THANK YOU.
NOW, TO GET TO BUSINESS...
A REGULAR CUSTOMER OF MINE ASKED ME TO LOOK INTO A PECULIAR OBJECT BECAUSE IT FRIGHTENS THEM...
A PECULIAR OBJECT?

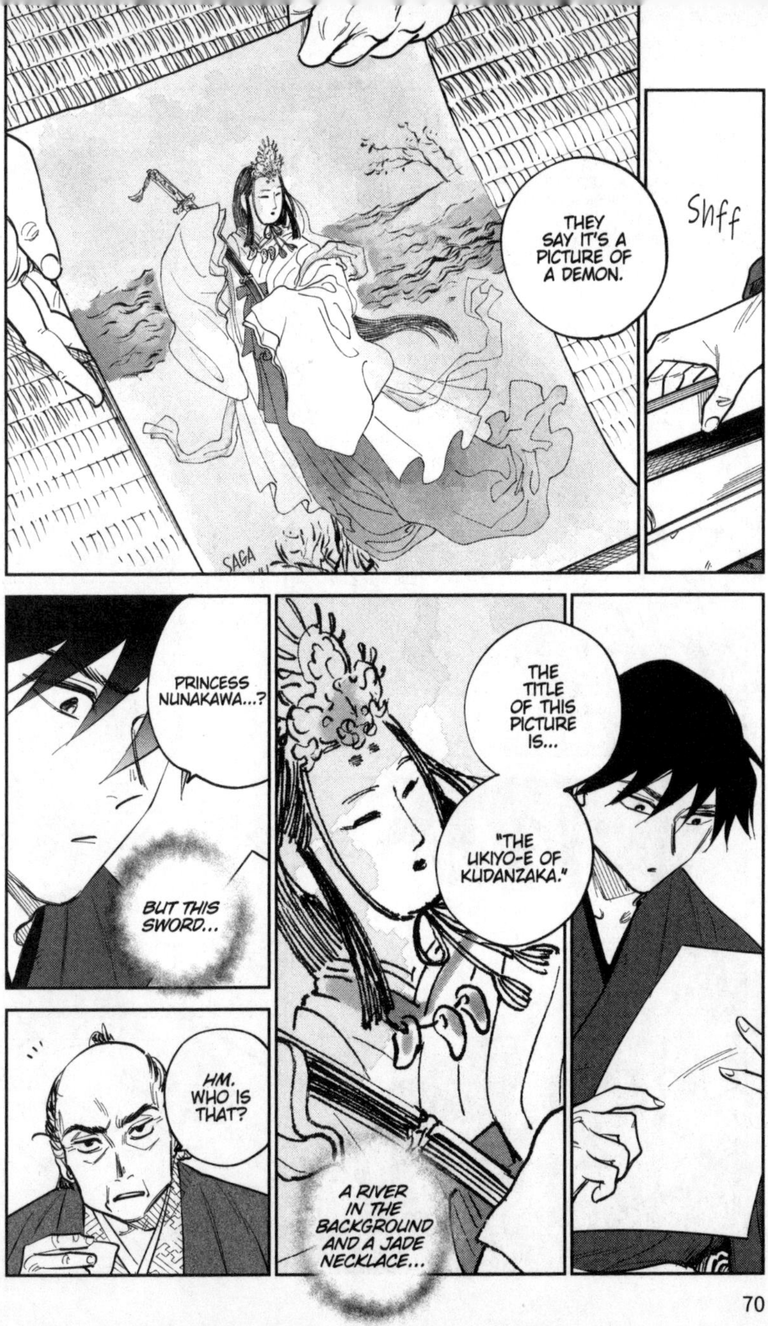
Shff
THEY SAY IT'S A PICTURE OF A DEMON.
SAGA
THE TITLE OF THIS PICTURE IS...
"THE UKIYO-E OF KUDANZAKA."
A RIVER IN THE BACKGROUND AND A JADE NECKLACE...
PRINCESS NUNAKAWA...?
BUT THIS SWORD...
HM. WHO IS THAT?

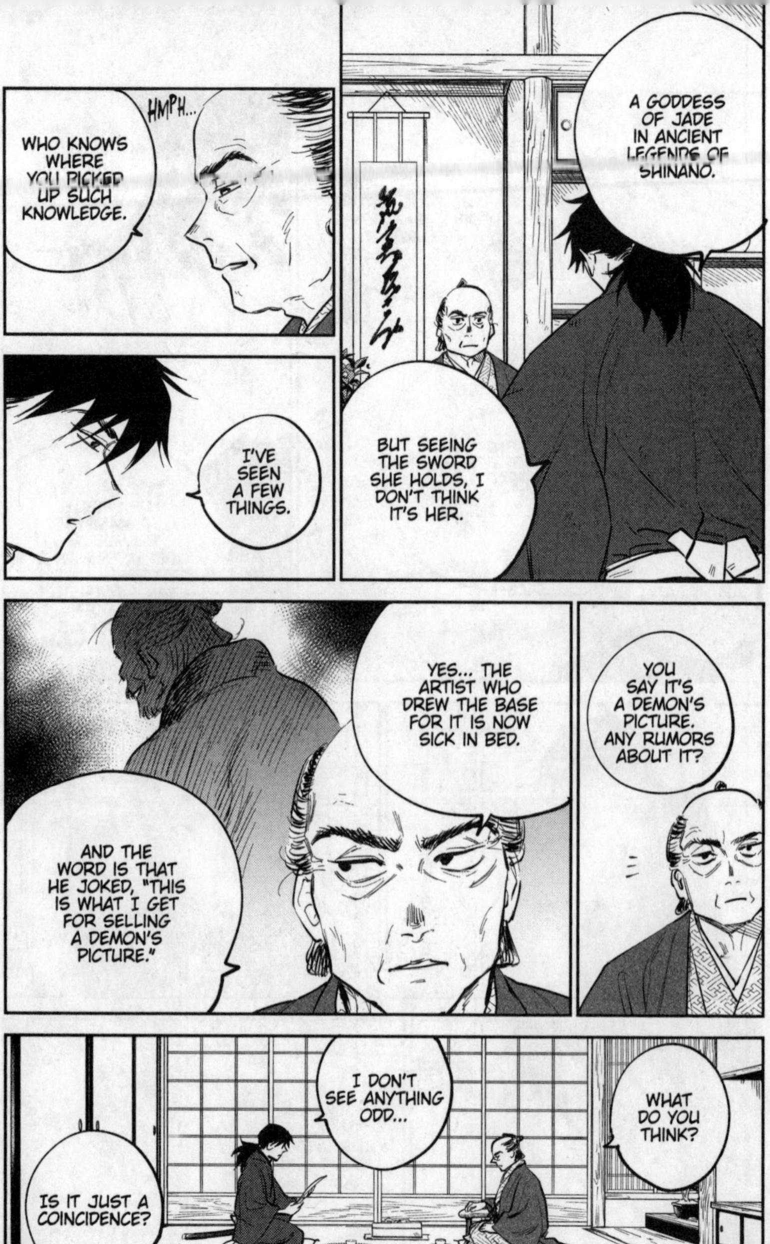
A GODDESS OF JADE IN ANCIENT LEGENDS OF SHINANO.
BUT SEEING THE SWORD SHE HOLDS, I DON'T THINK IT'S HER.
HMPH...
WHO KNOWS WHERE YOU PICKED UP SUCH KNOWLEDGE.
I'VE SEEN A FEW THINGS.
YOU SAY IT'S A DEMON'S PICTURE. ANY RUMORS ABOUT IT?
YES... THE ARTIST WHO DREW THE BASE FOR IT IS NOW SICK IN BED.
AND THE WORD IS THAT HE JOKED, "THIS IS WHAT I GET FOR SELLING A DEMON'S PICTURE."
WHAT DO YOU THINK?
I DON'T SEE ANYTHING ODD...
IS IT JUST A COINCIDENCE?

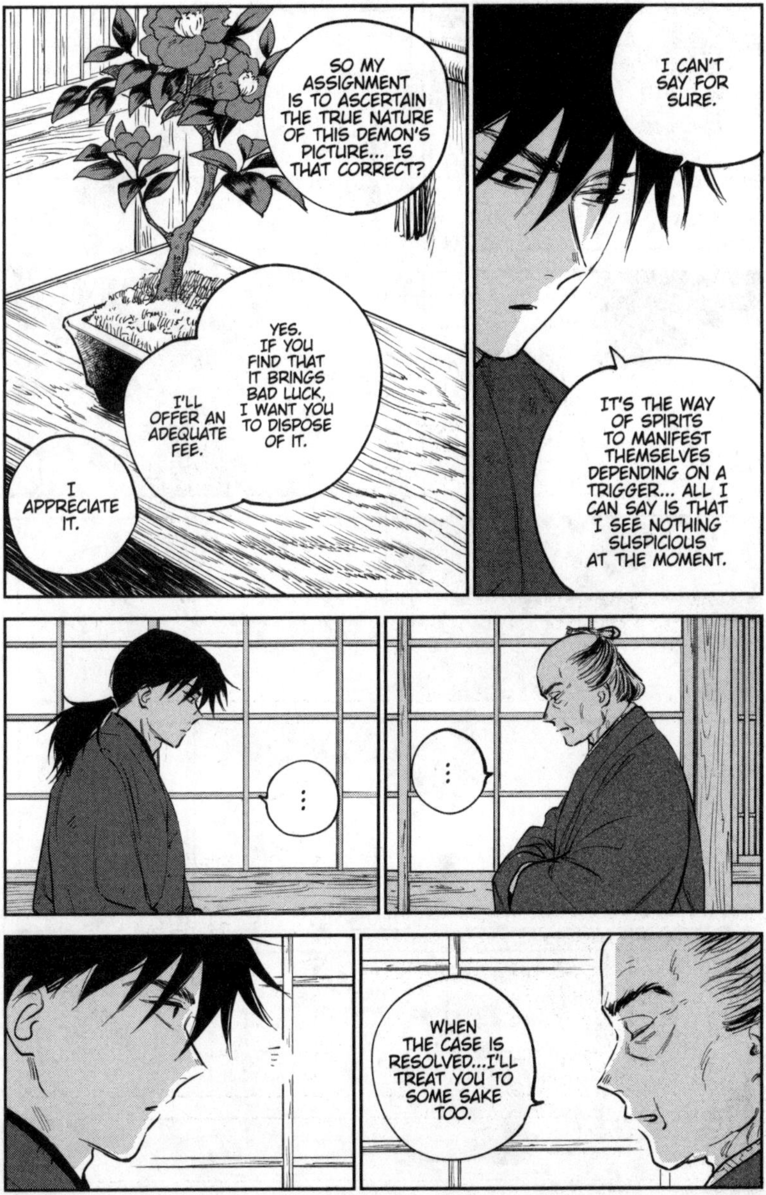
I CAN'T SAY FOR SURE.
IT'S THE WAY OF SPIRITS TO MANIFEST THEMSELVES DEPENDING ON A TRIGGER... ALL I CAN SAY IS THAT I SEE NOTHING SUSPICIOUS AT THE MOMENT.
SO MY ASSIGNMENT IS TO ASCERTAIN THE TRUE NATURE OF THIS DEMON'S PICTURE... IS THAT CORRECT?
YES. IF YOU FIND THAT IT BRINGS BAD LUCK, I WANT YOU TO DISPOSE OF IT.
I'LL OFFER AN ADEQUATE FEE.
I APPRECIATE IT.
...
...
WHEN THE CASE IS RESOLVED...I'LL TREAT YOU TO SOME SAKE TOO.

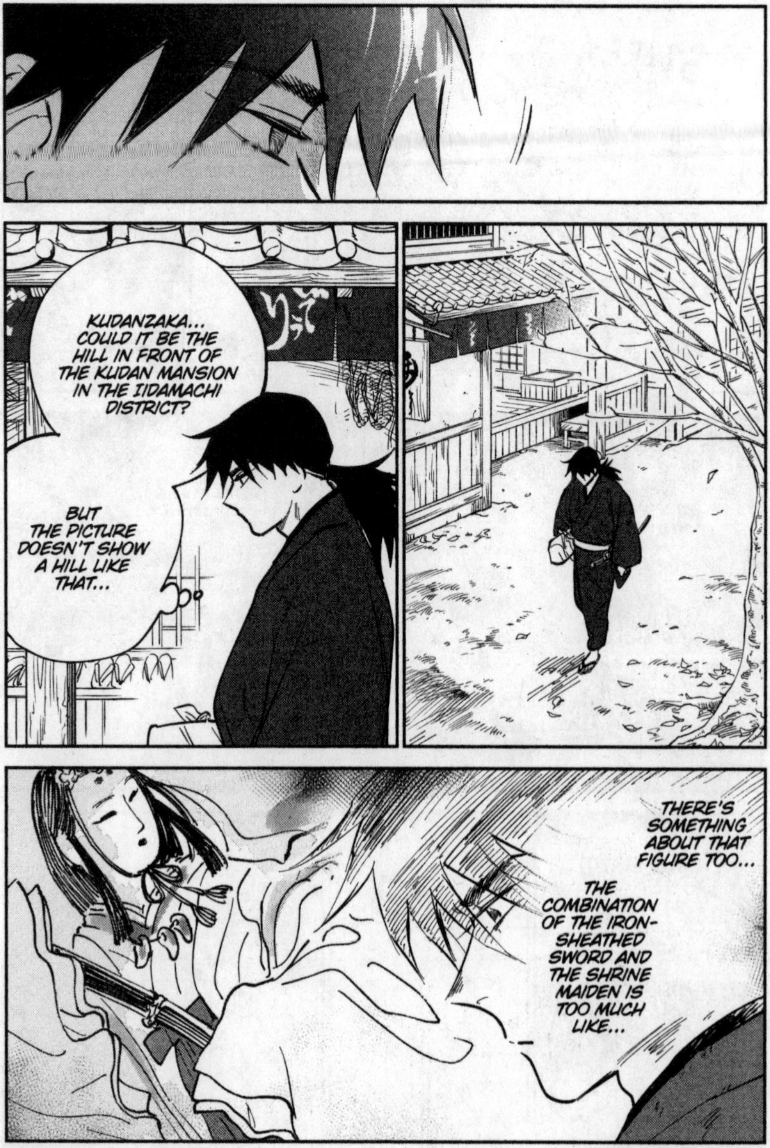
KUDANZAKA... COULD IT BE THE HILL IN FRONT OF THE KUDAN MANSION IN THE IIDAMACHI DISTRICT?
BUT THE PICTURE DOESN'T SHOW A HILL LIKE THAT...
THERE'S SOMETHING ABOUT THAT FIGURE TOO...
THE COMBINATION OF THE IRON-SHEATHED SWORD AND THE SHRINE MAIDEN IS TOO MUCH LIKE...

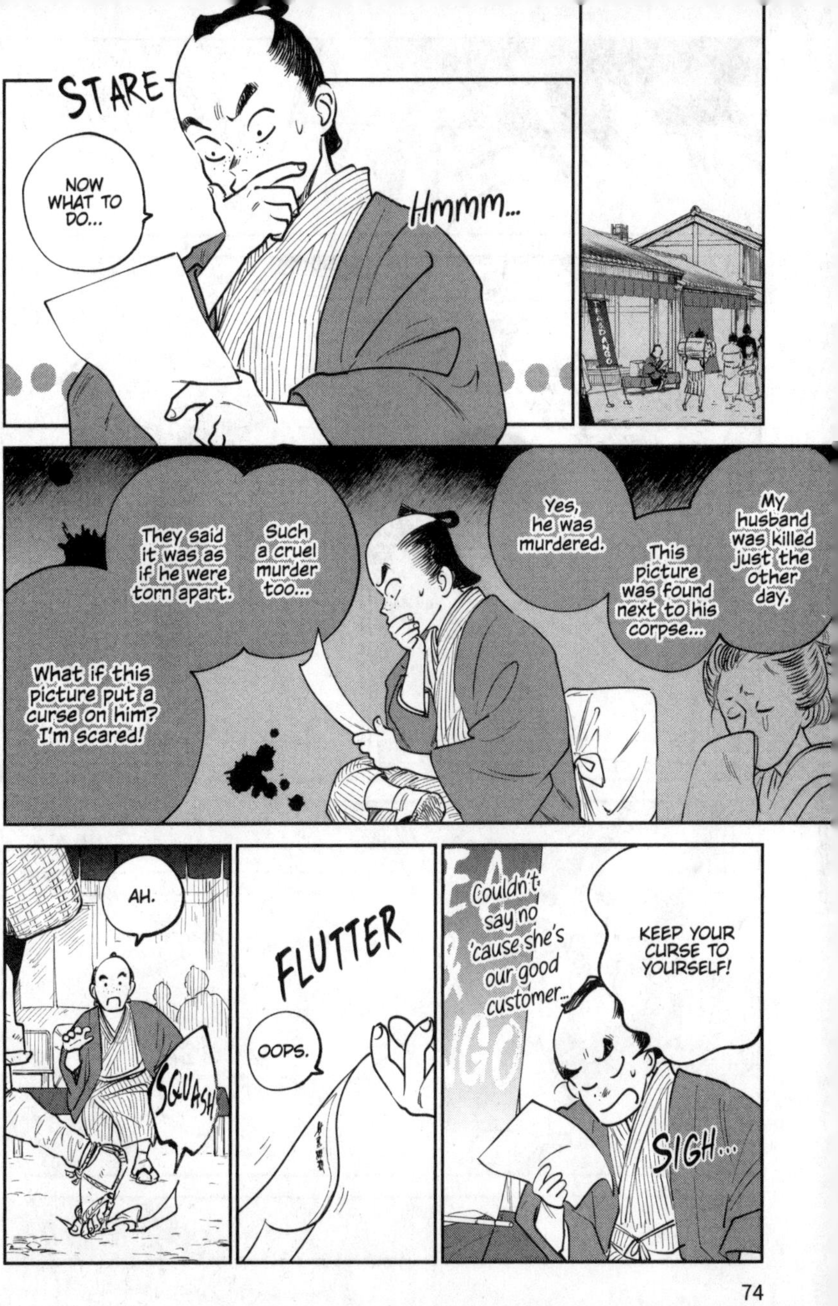
STARE
NOW WHAT TO DO...
Hmmm...
My husband was killed just the other day.
Yes, he was murdered.
This picture was found next to his corpse...
Such a cruel murder too...
They said it was as if he were torn apart.
What if this picture put a curse on him? I'm scared!
KEEP YOUR CURSE TO YOURSELF!
Couldn't say no 'cause she's our good customer...
SIGH...
FLUTTER
OOPS.
AH.
SQUASH

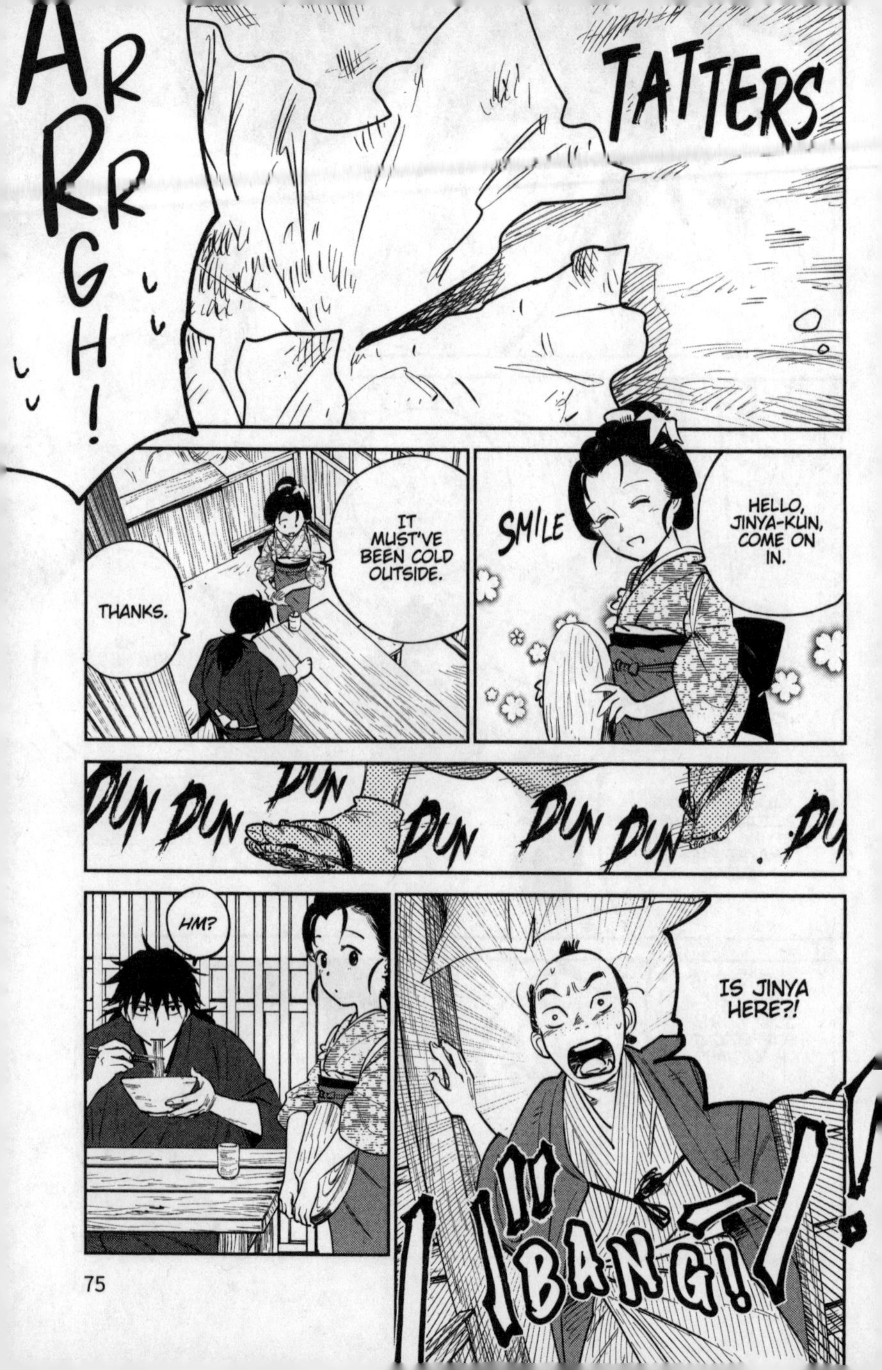
TATTERS
ARRRGH!
SMILE
HELLO, JINYA-KUN, COME ON IN.
IT MUST'VE BEEN COLD OUTSIDE.
THANKS.
DUN DUN DUN DUN DUN DUN DUN DUN
IS JINYA HERE?!
BANG!
HM?

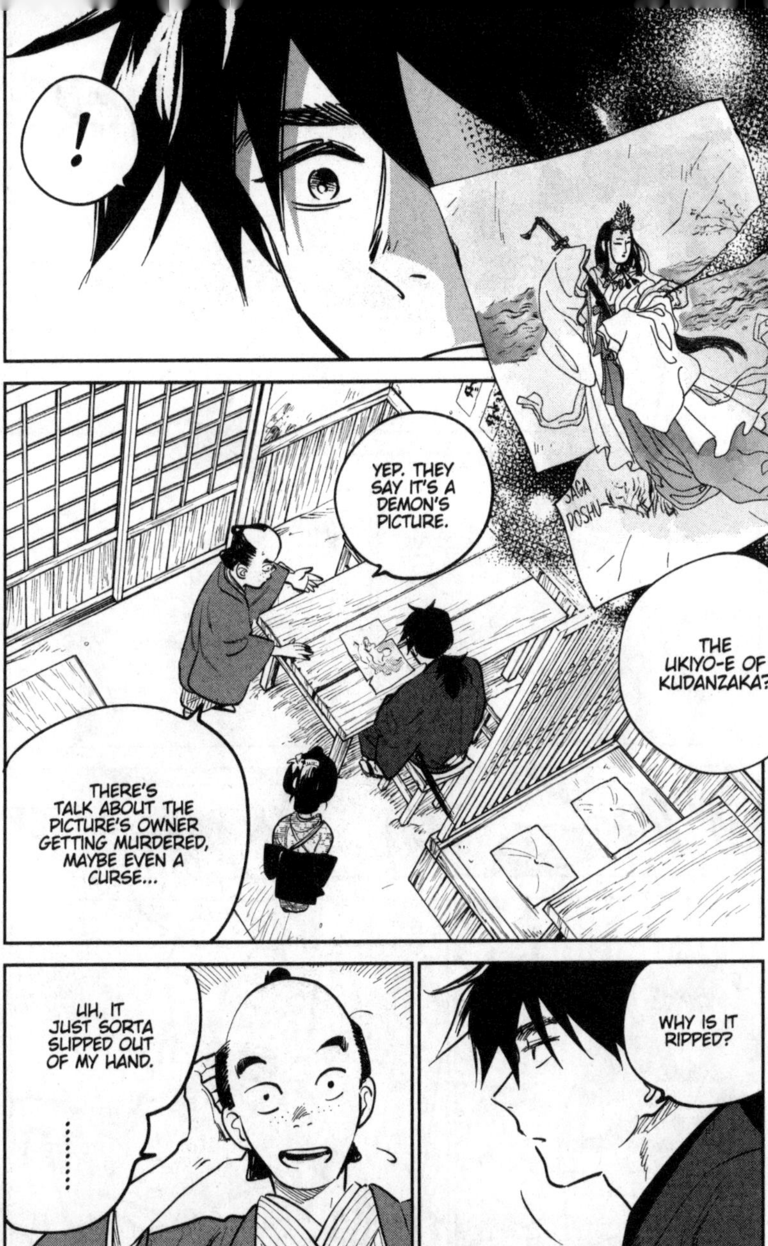
!
SAGA DOSHU
THE UKIYO-E OF KUDANZAKA?
YEP. THEY SAY IT'S A DEMON'S PICTURE.
THERE'S TALK ABOUT THE PICTURE'S OWNER GETTING MURDERED, MAYBE EVEN A CURSE...
WHY IS IT RIPPED?
UH, IT JUST SORTA SLIPPED OUT OF MY HAND.
......

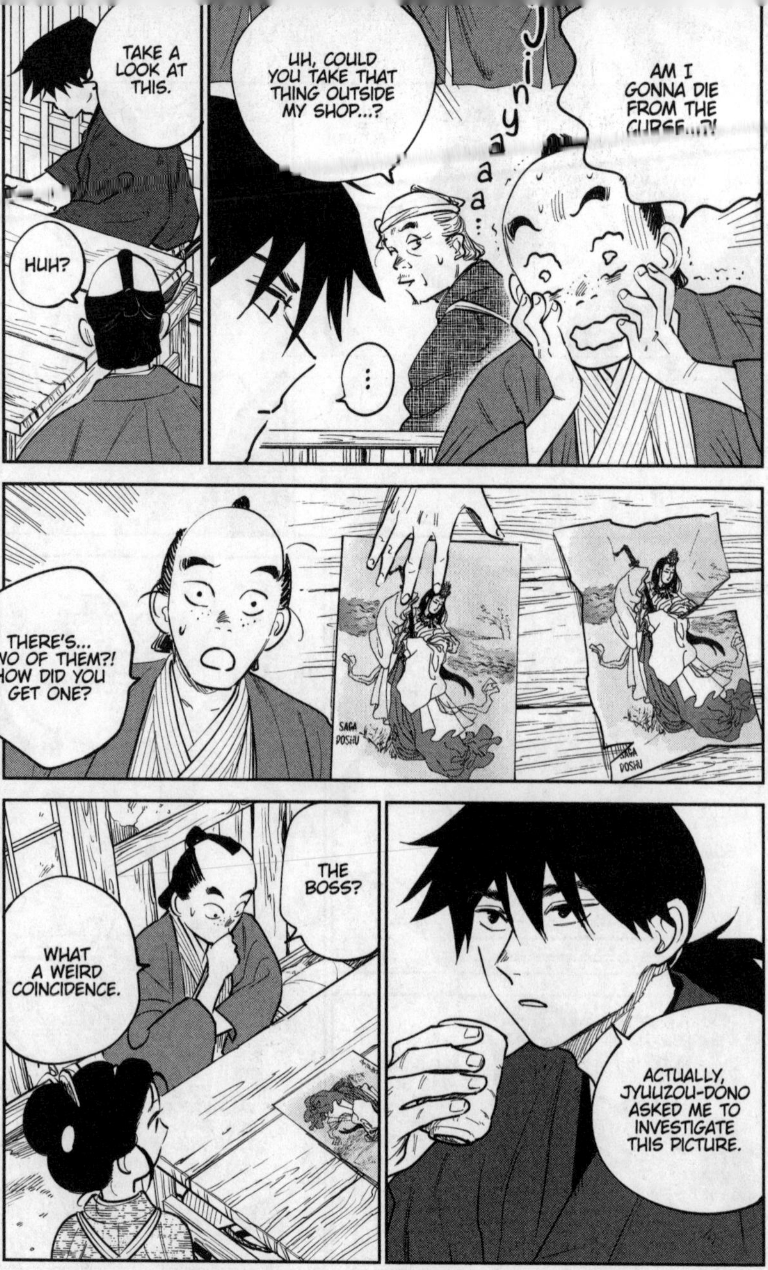
AM I GONNA DIE FROM THE CURSE...?!
Jinyaaaa...
UH, COULD YOU TAKE THAT THING OUTSIDE MY SHOP...?
...
TAKE A LOOK AT THIS.
HUH?
THERE'S... TWO OF THEM?! HOW DID YOU GET ONE?
SAGA DOSHU
SAGA DOSHU
ACTUALLY, JYUUZOU-DONO ASKED ME TO INVESTIGATE THIS PICTURE.
THE BOSS?
WHAT A WEIRD COINCIDENCE.

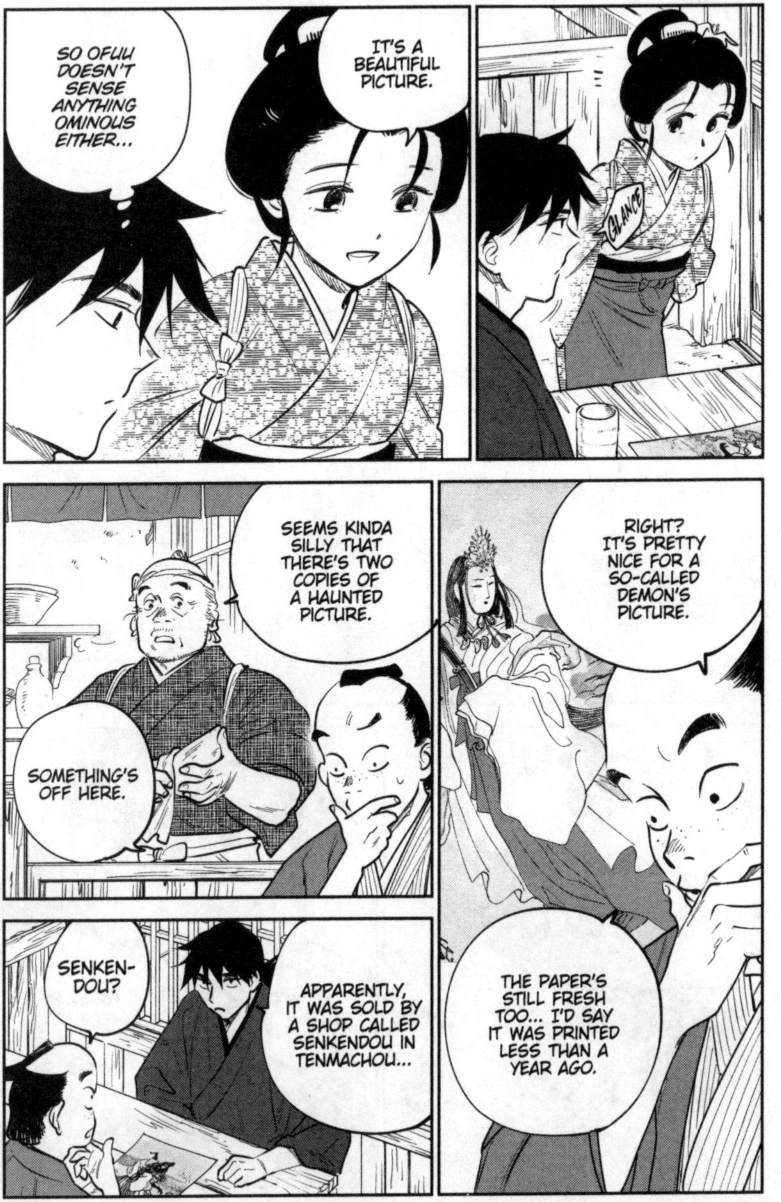
GLANCE
IT'S A BEAUTIFUL PICTURE.
SO OFUU DOESN'T SENSE ANYTHING OMINOUS EITHER...
RIGHT? IT'S PRETTY NICE FOR A SO-CALLED DEMON'S PICTURE.
THE PAPER'S STILL FRESH TOO... I'D SAY IT WAS PRINTED LESS THAN A YEAR AGO.
SEEMS KINDA SILLY THAT THERE'S TWO COPIES OF A HAUNTED PICTURE.
SOMETHING'S OFF HERE.
APPARENTLY, IT WAS SOLD BY A SHOP CALLED SENKENDOU IN TENMACHOU...
SENKEN-DOU?

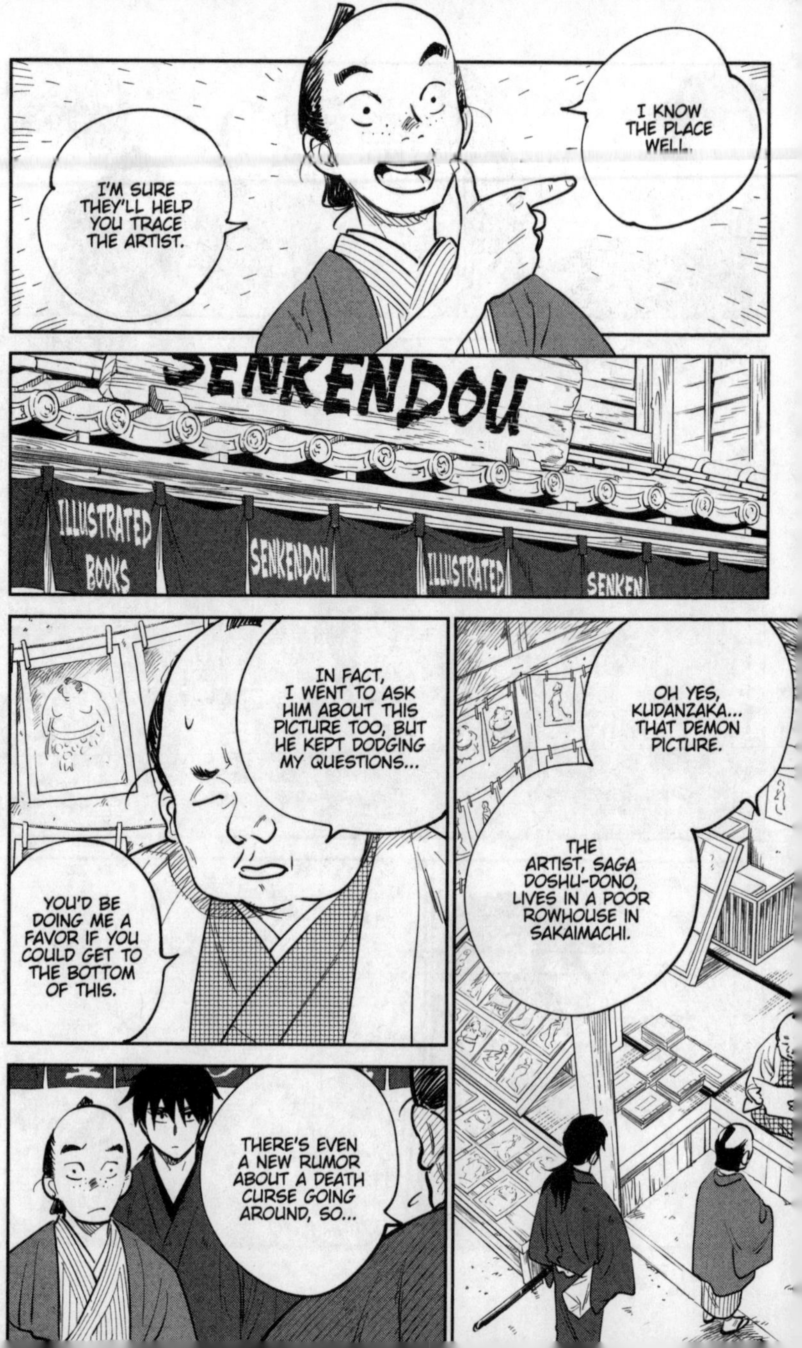
I KNOW THE PLACE WELL.
I'M SURE THEY'LL HELP YOU TRACE THE ARTIST.
SENKENDOU
ILLUSTRATED BOOKS
SENKENDOU
ILLUSTRATED
OH YES, KUDANZAKA... THAT DEMON PICTURE.
THE ARTIST, SAGA DOSHU-DONO, LIVES IN A POOR ROWHOUSE IN SAKAIMACHI.
IN FACT, I WENT TO ASK HIM ABOUT THIS PICTURE TOO, BUT HE KEPT DODGING MY QUESTIONS...
YOU'D BE DOING ME A FAVOR IF YOU COULD GET TO THE BOTTOM OF THIS.
THERE'S EVEN A NEW RUMOR ABOUT A DEATH CURSE GOING AROUND, SO...

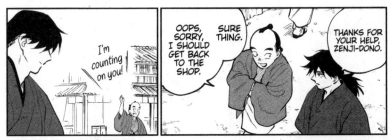

THANKS FOR YOUR HELP, ZENJI-DONO.
SURE THING.
OOPS, SORRY, I SHOULD GET BACK TO THE SHOP.
I'm counting on you!
EXCUSE ME. IS SAGA DOSHU-DONO THERE?
YEAH. JUST COME IN.

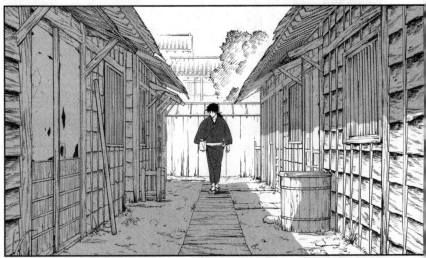

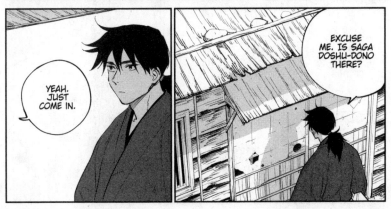

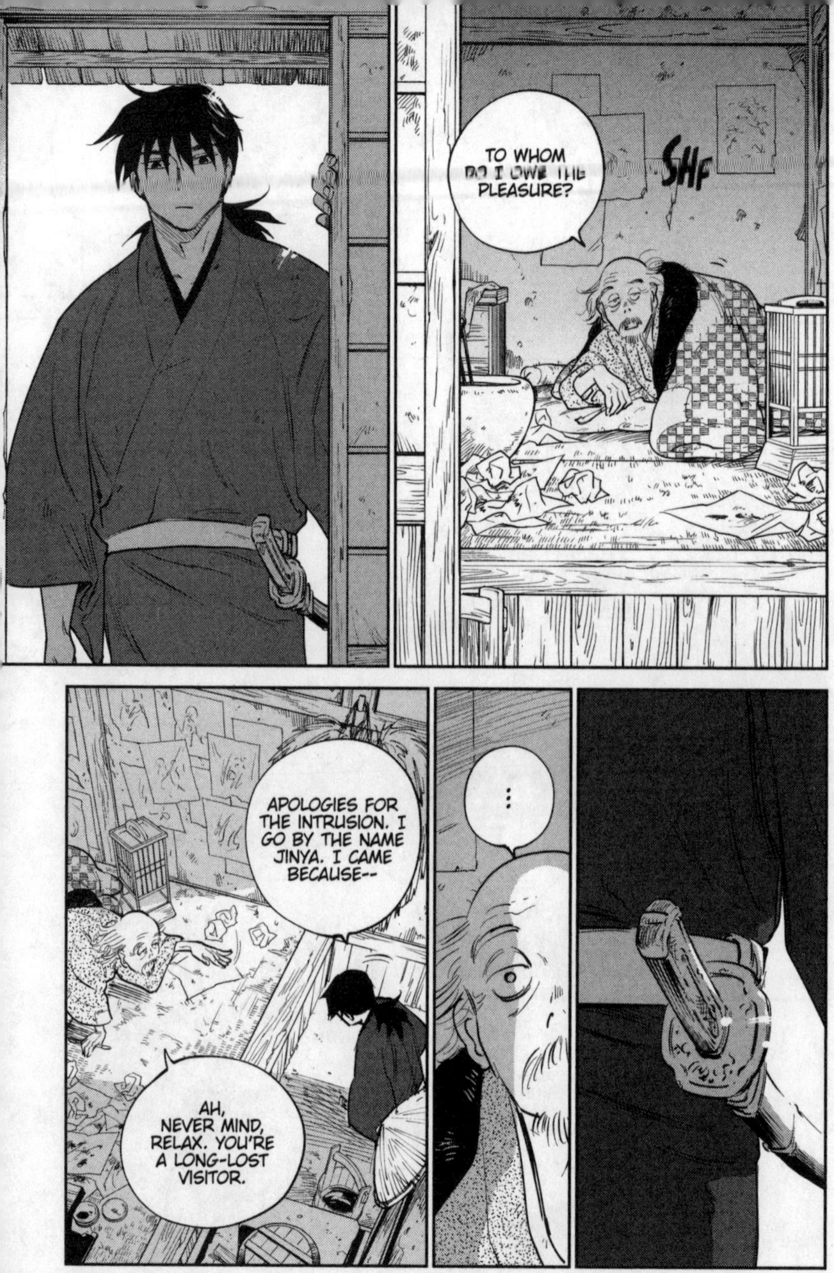
TO WHOM DO I OWE THE PLEASURE?
SHF
...
APOLOGIES FOR THE INTRUSION. I GO BY THE NAME JINYA. I CAME BECAUSE--
AH, NEVER MIND, RELAX. YOU'RE A LONG-LOST VISITOR.

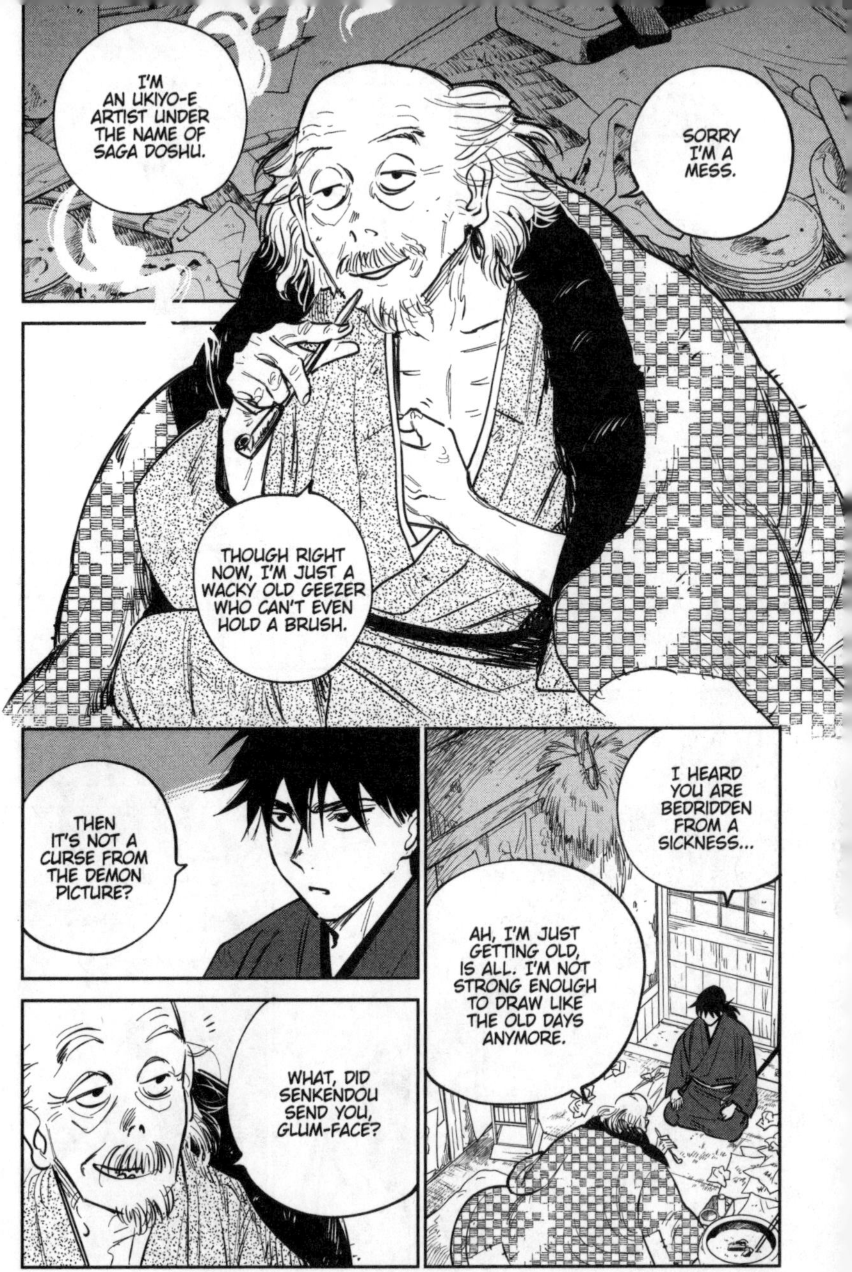
SORRY I'M A MESS.
I'M AN UKIYO-E ARTIST UNDER THE NAME OF SAGA DOSHU.
THOUGH RIGHT NOW, I'M JUST A WACKY OLD GEEZER WHO CAN'T EVEN HOLD A BRUSH.
I HEARD YOU ARE BEDRIDDEN FROM A SICKNESS...
AH, I'M JUST GETTING OLD, IS ALL. I'M NOT STRONG ENOUGH TO DRAW LIKE THE OLD DAYS ANYMORE.
THEN IT'S NOT A CURSE FROM THE DEMON PICTURE?
WHAT, DID SENKENDOU SEND YOU, GLUM-FACE?

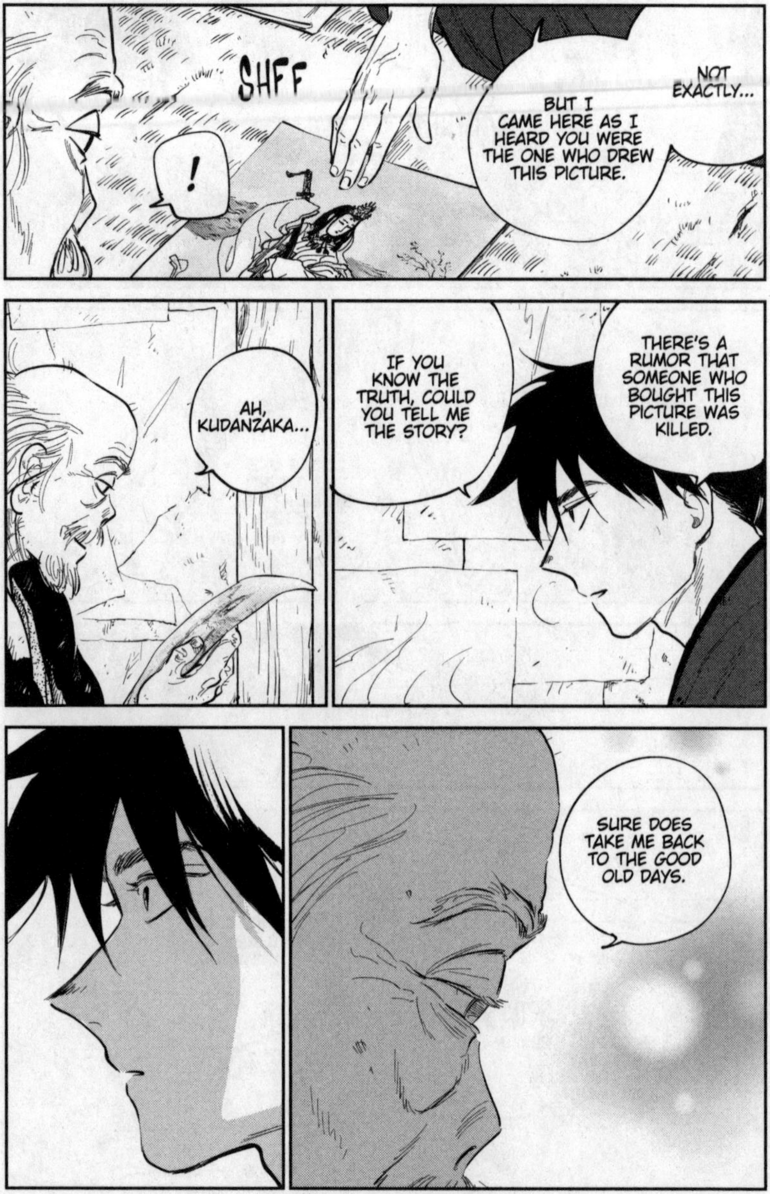
NOT EXACTLY...
BUT I CAME HERE AS I HEARD YOU WERE THE ONE WHO DREW THIS PICTURE.
SHFF
!
THERE'S A RUMOR THAT SOMEONE WHO BOUGHT THIS PICTURE WAS KILLED.
IF YOU KNOW THE TRUTH, COULD YOU TELL ME THE STORY?
AH, KUDANZAKA...
SURE DOES TAKE ME BACK TO THE GOOD OLD DAYS.

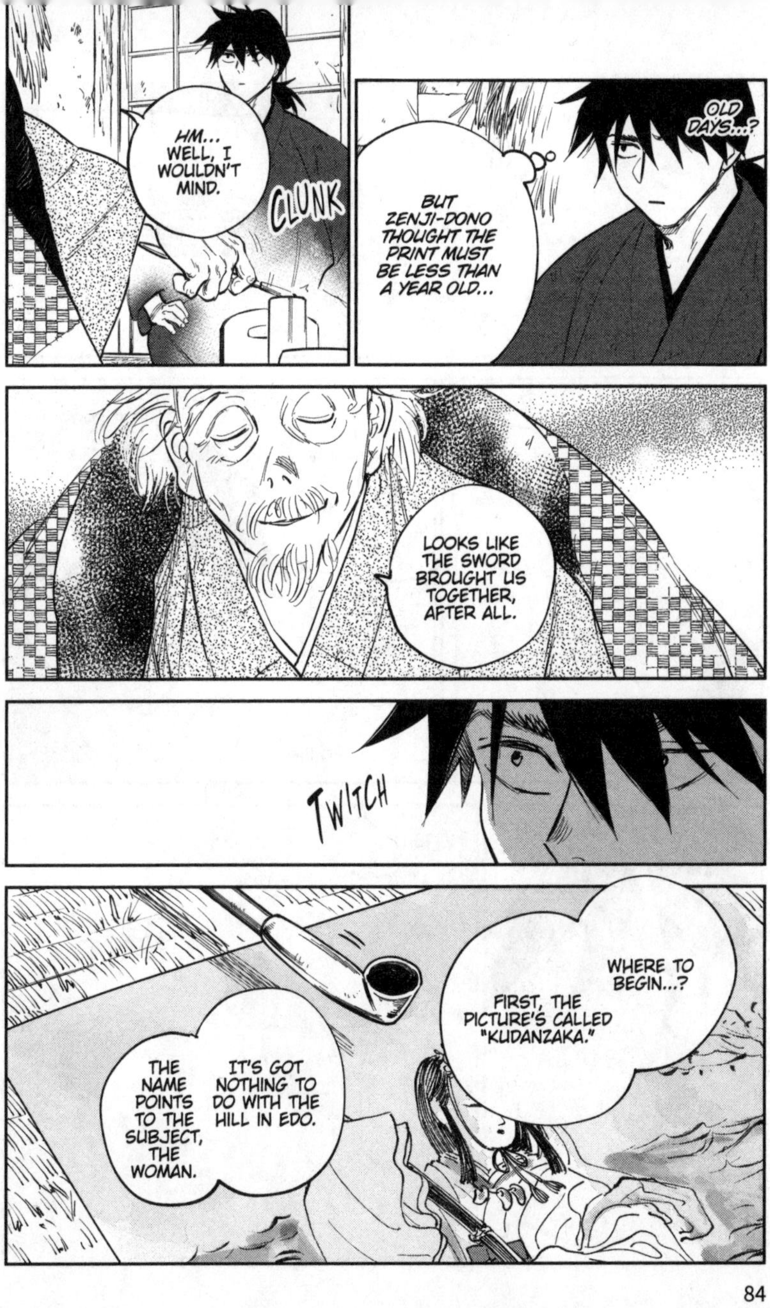
OLD DAYS...?
BUT ZENJI-DONO THOUGHT THE PRINT MUST BE LESS THAN A YEAR OLD...
HM... WELL, I WOULDN'T MIND.
CLUNK
LOOKS LIKE THE SWORD BROUGHT US TOGETHER, AFTER ALL.
TWITCH
WHERE TO BEGIN...?
FIRST, THE PICTURE'S CALLED "KUDANZAKA."
IT'S GOT NOTHING TO DO WITH THE HILL IN EDO.
THE NAME POINTS TO THE SUBJECT, THE WOMAN.

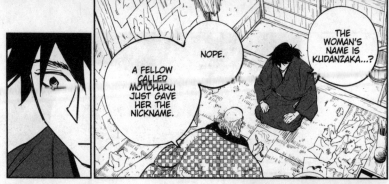

NOPE.

THE WOMAN'S NAME IS KUDANZAKA...?

A FELLOW CALLED MOTOHARU JUST GAVE HER THE NICKNAME.

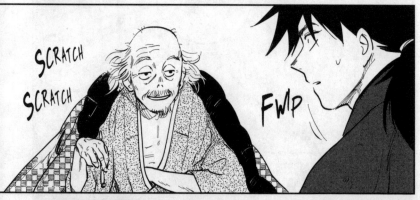

SCRATCH

SCRATCH

FWP

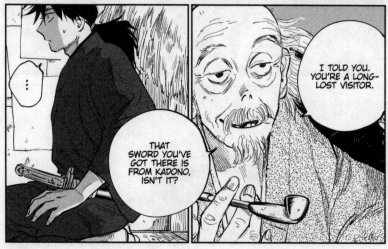

...

I TOLD YOU. YOU'RE A LONG-LOST VISITOR.

THAT SWORD YOU'VE GOT THERE IS FROM KADONO, ISN'T IT?

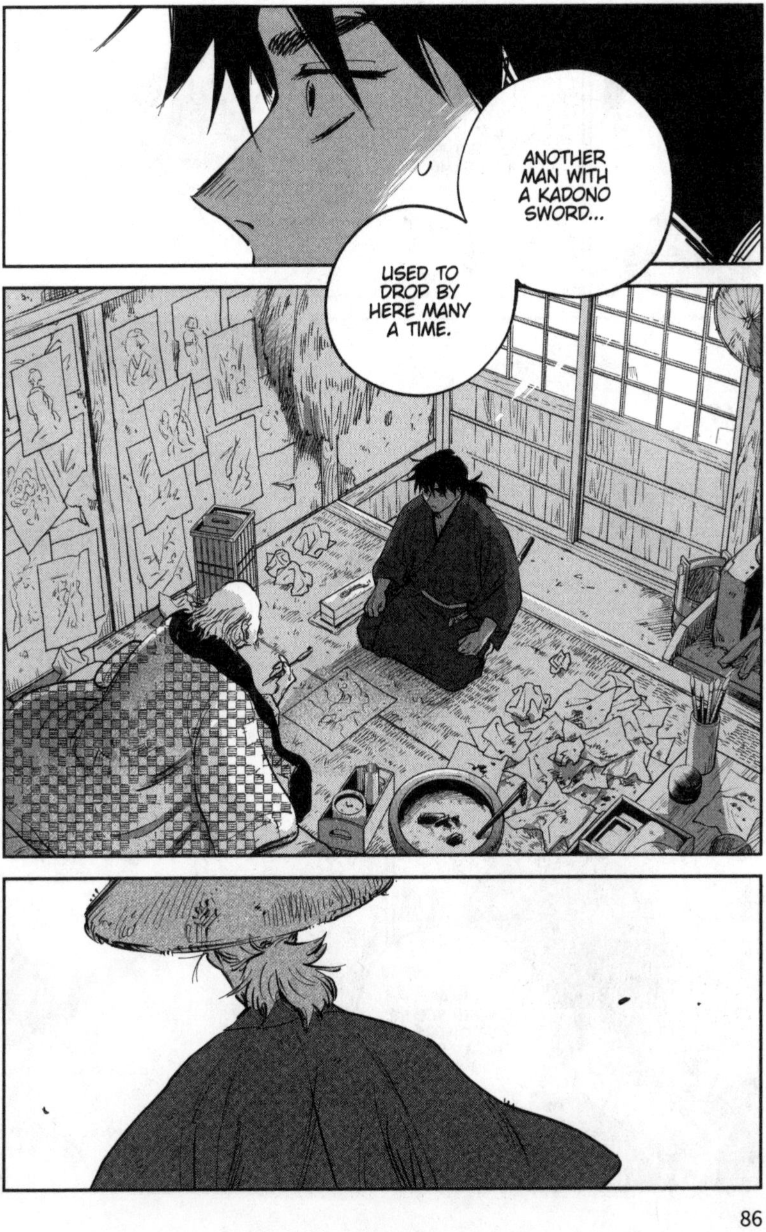
ANOTHER MAN WITH A KADONO SWORD...
USED TO DROP BY HERE MANY A TIME.

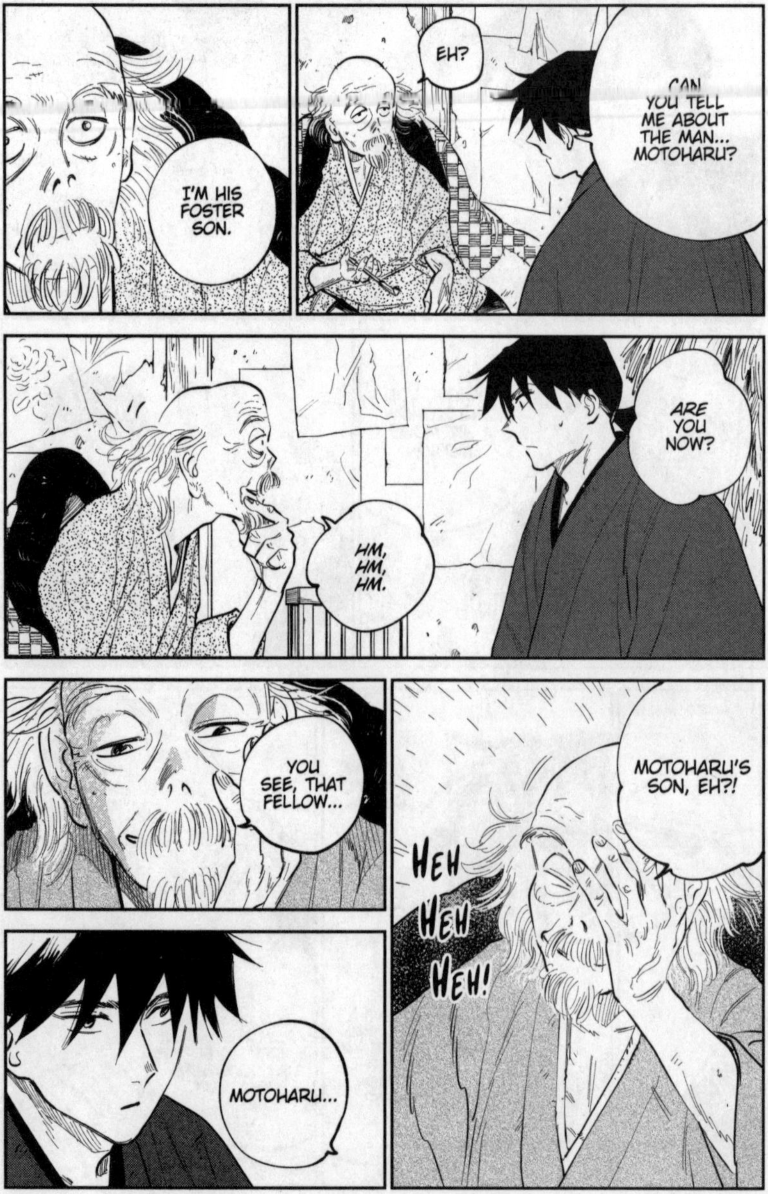
CAN YOU TELL ME ABOUT THE MAN... MOTOHARU?
EH?
I'M HIS FOSTER SON.
ARE YOU NOW?
HM, HM, HM.
MOTOHARU'S SON, EH?!
HEH HEH HEH!
YOU SEE, THAT FELLOW...
MOTOHARU...

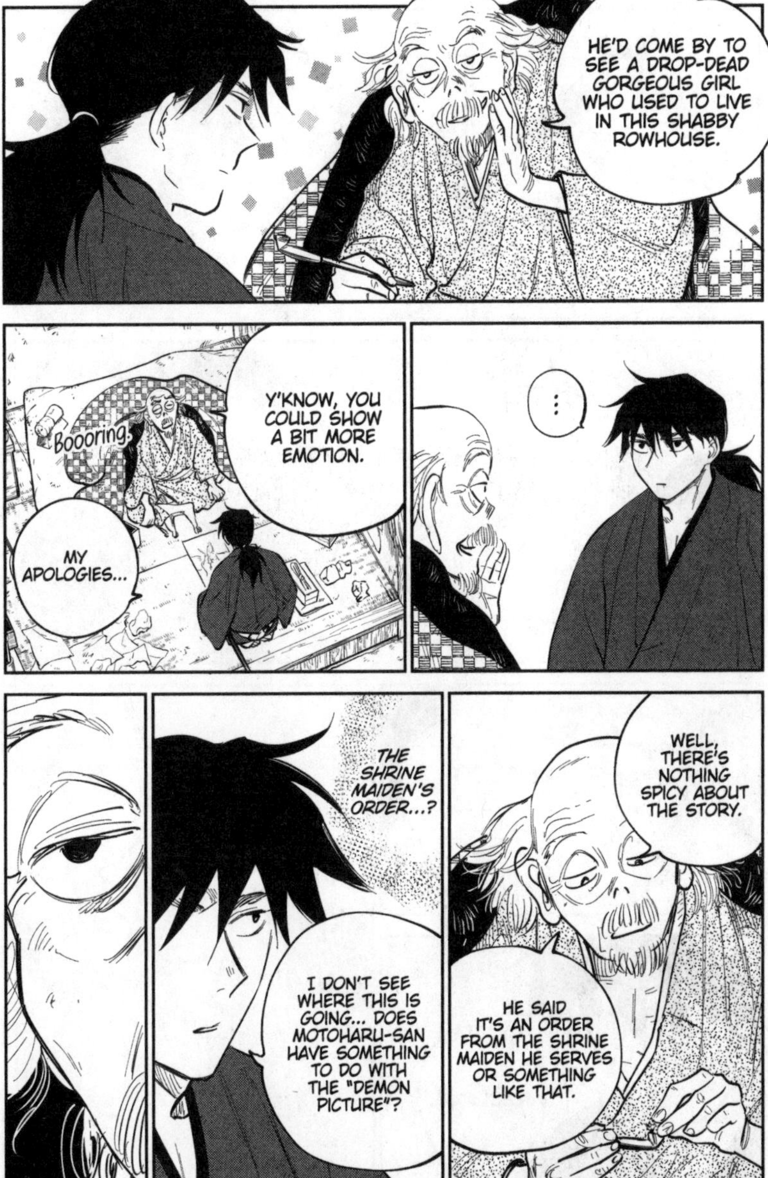
HE'D COME BY TO SEE A DROP-DEAD GORGEOUS GIRL WHO USED TO LIVE IN THIS SHABBY ROWHOUSE.
...
Y'KNOW, YOU COULD SHOW A BIT MORE EMOTION.
Boooring.
MY APOLOGIES...
WELL, THERE'S NOTHING SPICY ABOUT THE STORY.
HE SAID IT'S AN ORDER FROM THE SHRINE MAIDEN HE SERVES OR SOMETHING LIKE THAT.
THE SHRINE MAIDEN'S ORDER...?
I DON'T SEE WHERE THIS IS GOING... DOES MOTOHARU-SAN HAVE SOMETHING TO DO WITH THE "DEMON PICTURE"?

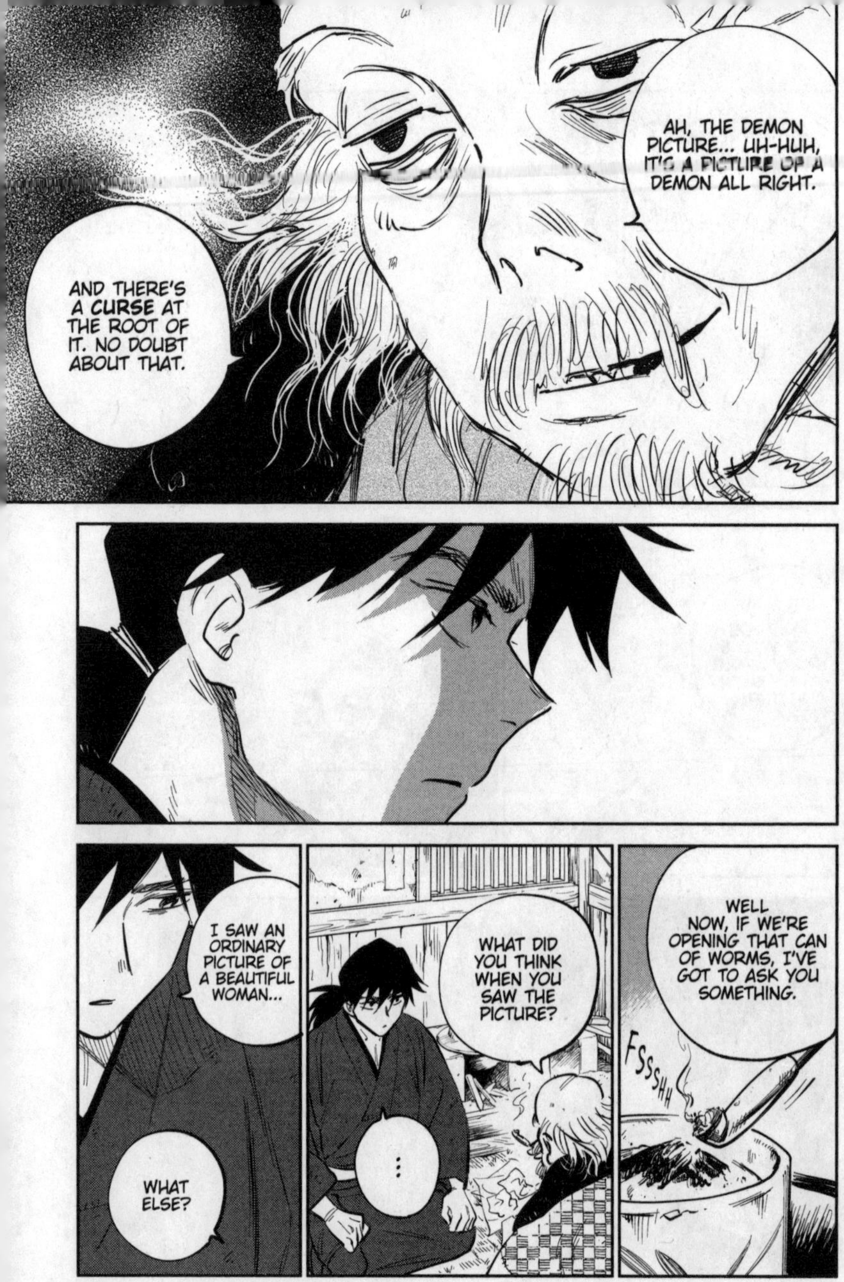
AH, THE DEMON PICTURE... UH-HUH, IT'S A PICTURE OF A DEMON ALL RIGHT.
AND THERE'S A **CURSE** AT THE ROOT OF IT. NO DOUBT ABOUT THAT.
WELL NOW, IF WE'RE OPENING THAT CAN OF WORMS, I'VE GOT TO ASK YOU SOMETHING.
FSSSHH
WHAT DID YOU THINK WHEN YOU SAW THE PICTURE?
...
I SAW AN ORDINARY PICTURE OF A BEAUTIFUL WOMAN...
WHAT ELSE?

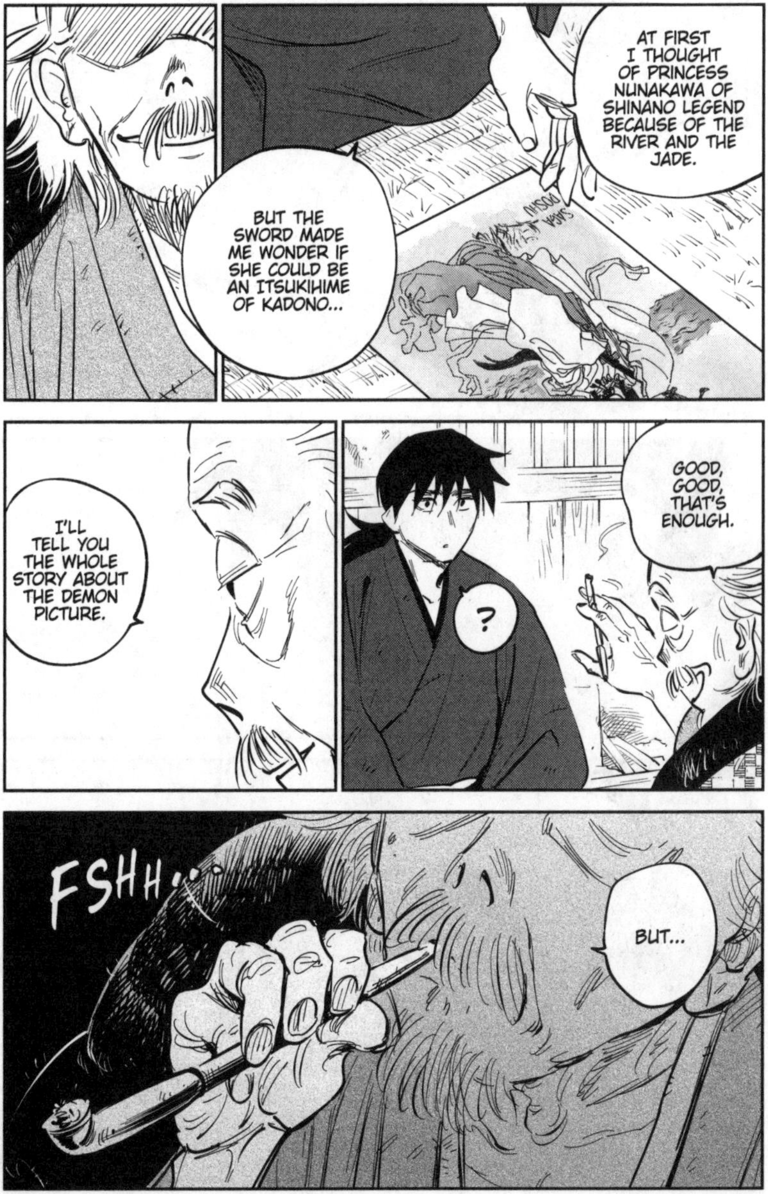
AT FIRST I THOUGHT OF PRINCESS NUNAKAWA OF SHINANO LEGEND BECAUSE OF THE RIVER AND THE JADE.
BUT THE SWORD MADE ME WONDER IF SHE COULD BE AN ITSUKIHIME OF KADONO...
GOOD, GOOD, THAT'S ENOUGH.
?
I'LL TELL YOU THE WHOLE STORY ABOUT THE DEMON PICTURE.
BUT...
FSHH...

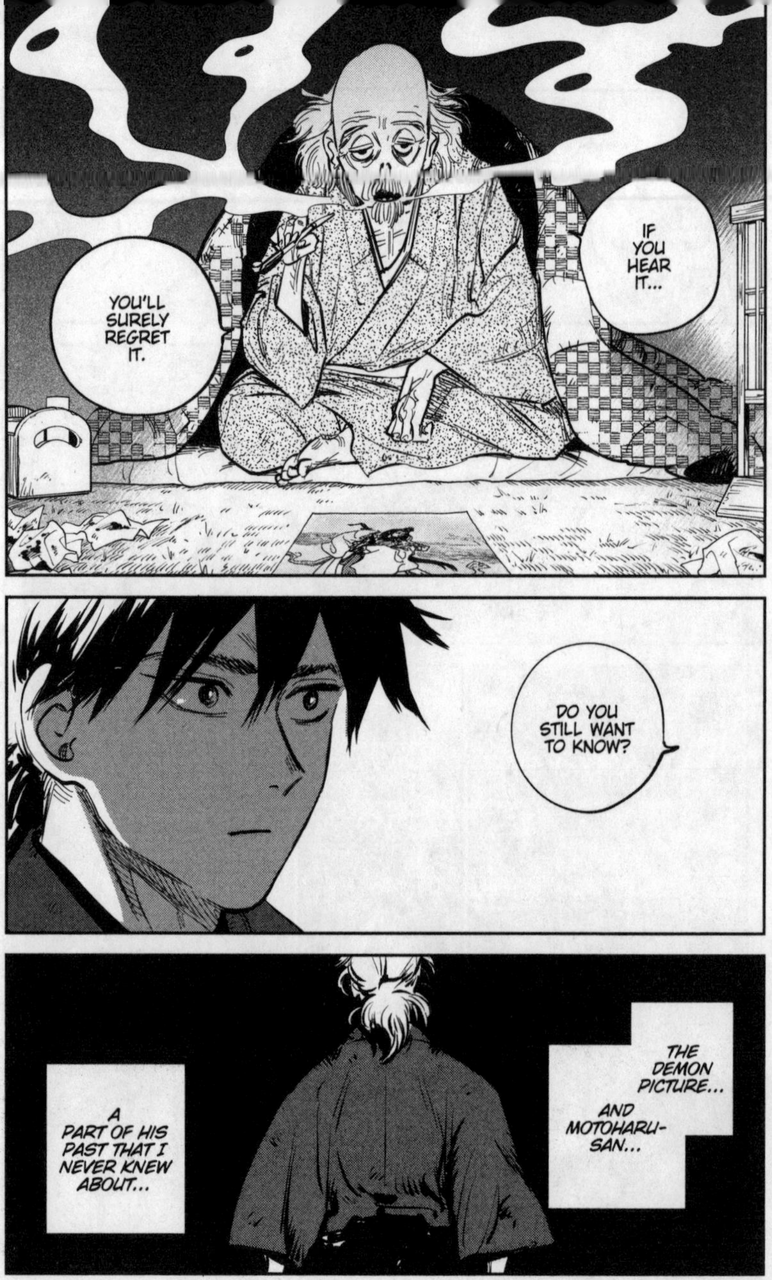
IF YOU HEAR IT...
YOU'LL SURELY REGRET IT.
DO YOU STILL WANT TO KNOW?
THE DEMON PICTURE...
AND MOTOHARU-SAN...
A PART OF HIS PAST THAT I NEVER KNEW ABOUT...

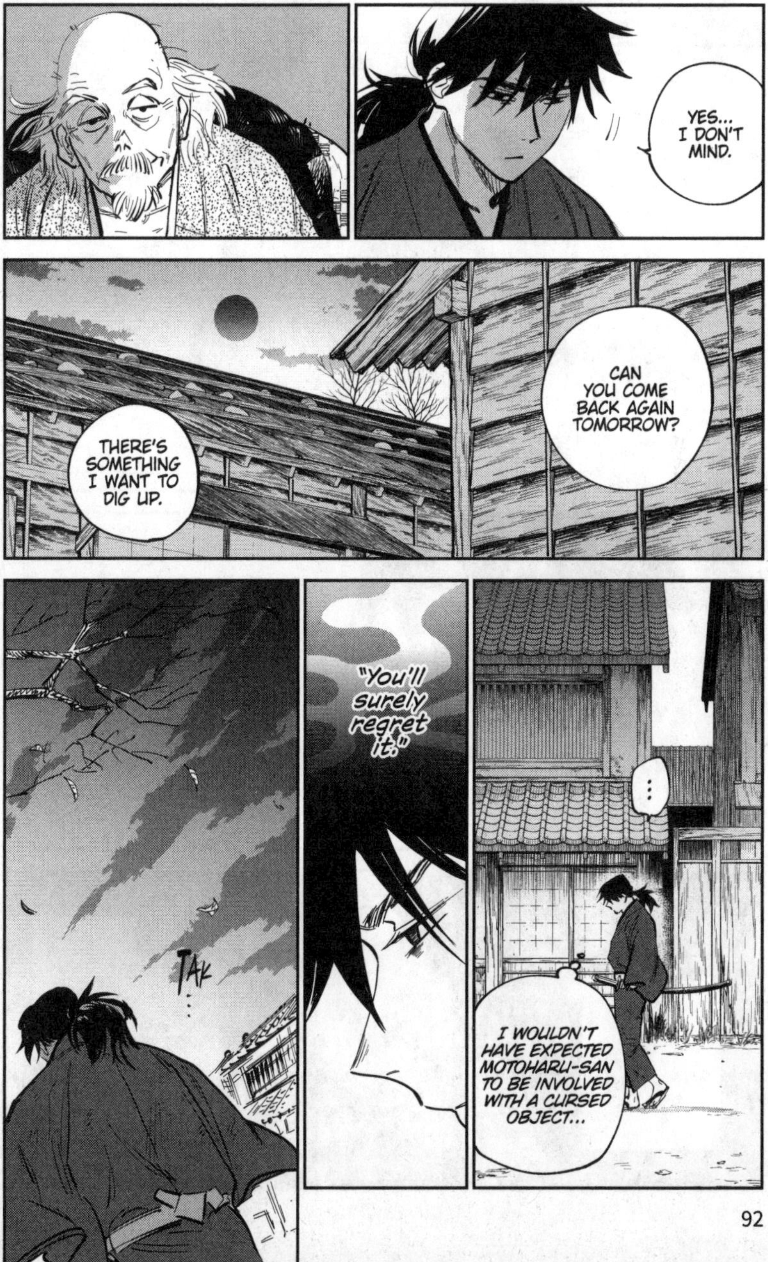
YES... I DON'T MIND.
CAN YOU COME BACK AGAIN TOMORROW?
THERE'S SOMETHING I WANT TO DIG UP.
...
I WOULDN'T HAVE EXPECTED MOTOHARU-SAN TO BE INVOLVED WITH A CURSED OBJECT...
"You'll surely regret it."
TAK

## CHAPTER 23: THE HAUNTING OF KUDANZAKA ②

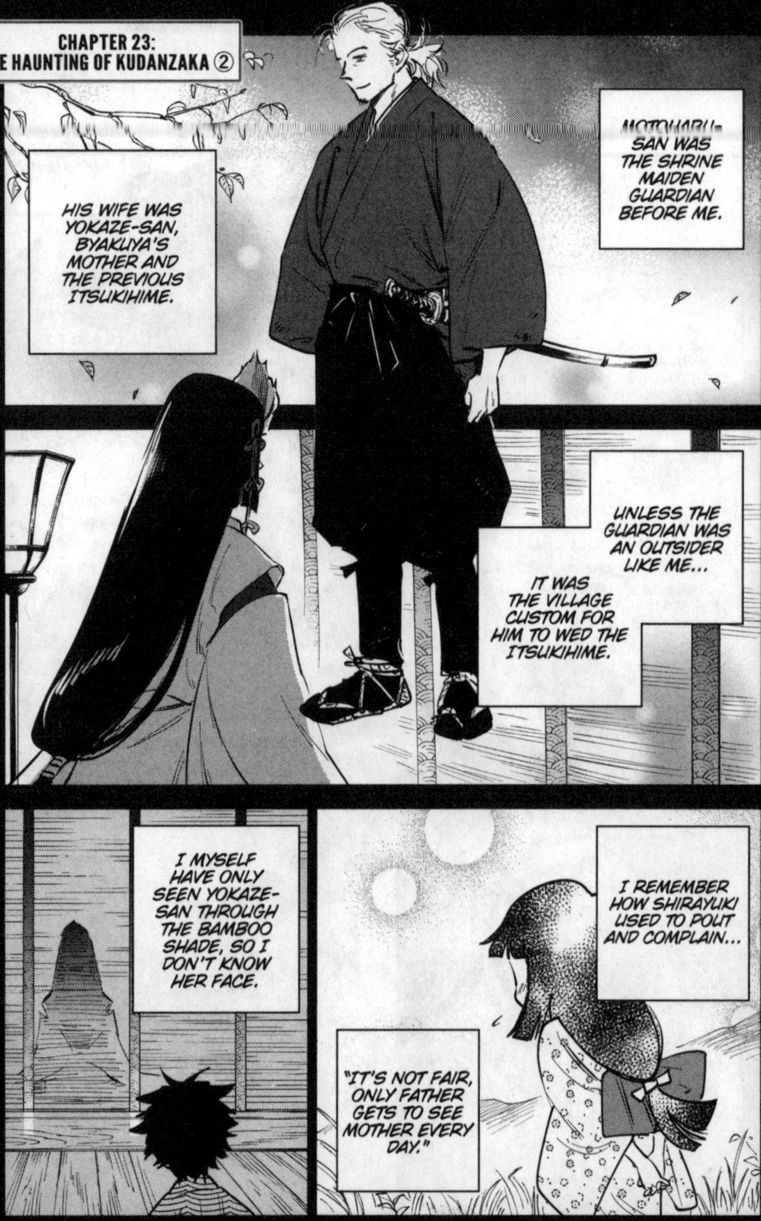
MOTOHARU-SAN WAS THE SHRINE MAIDEN GUARDIAN BEFORE ME.
HIS WIFE WAS YOKAZE-SAN, BYAKUYA'S MOTHER AND THE PREVIOUS ITSUKIHIME.
UNLESS THE GUARDIAN WAS AN OUTSIDER LIKE ME...
IT WAS THE VILLAGE CUSTOM FOR HIM TO WED THE ITSUKIHIME.
I REMEMBER HOW SHIRAYUKI USED TO POUT AND COMPLAIN...
"IT'S NOT FAIR, ONLY FATHER GETS TO SEE MOTHER EVERY DAY."
I MYSELF HAVE ONLY SEEN YOKAZE-SAN THROUGH THE BAMBOO SHADE, SO I DON'T KNOW HER FACE.

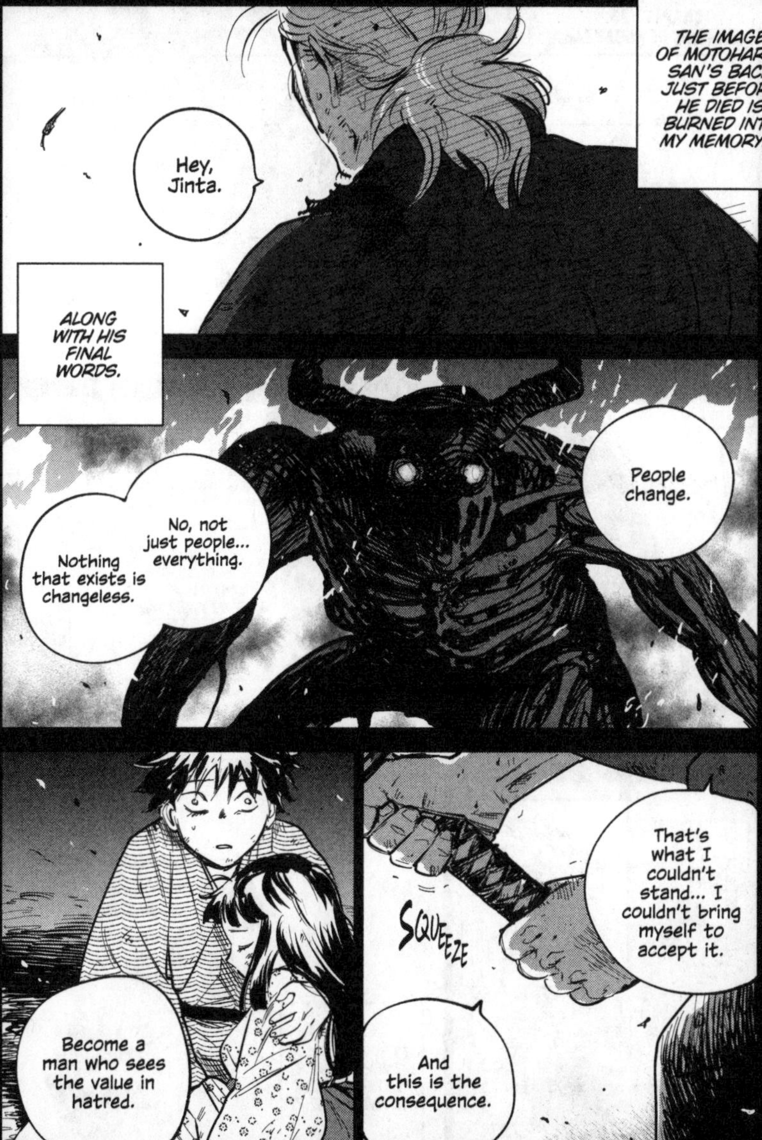
THE IMAGE OF MOTOHARU-SAN'S BACK JUST BEFORE HE DIED IS BURNED INTO MY MEMORY...
Hey, Jinta.
ALONG WITH HIS FINAL WORDS.
People change.
No, not just people... everything.
Nothing that exists is changeless.
That's what I couldn't stand... I couldn't bring myself to accept it.
SQUEEZE
And this is the consequence.
Become a man who sees the value in hatred.

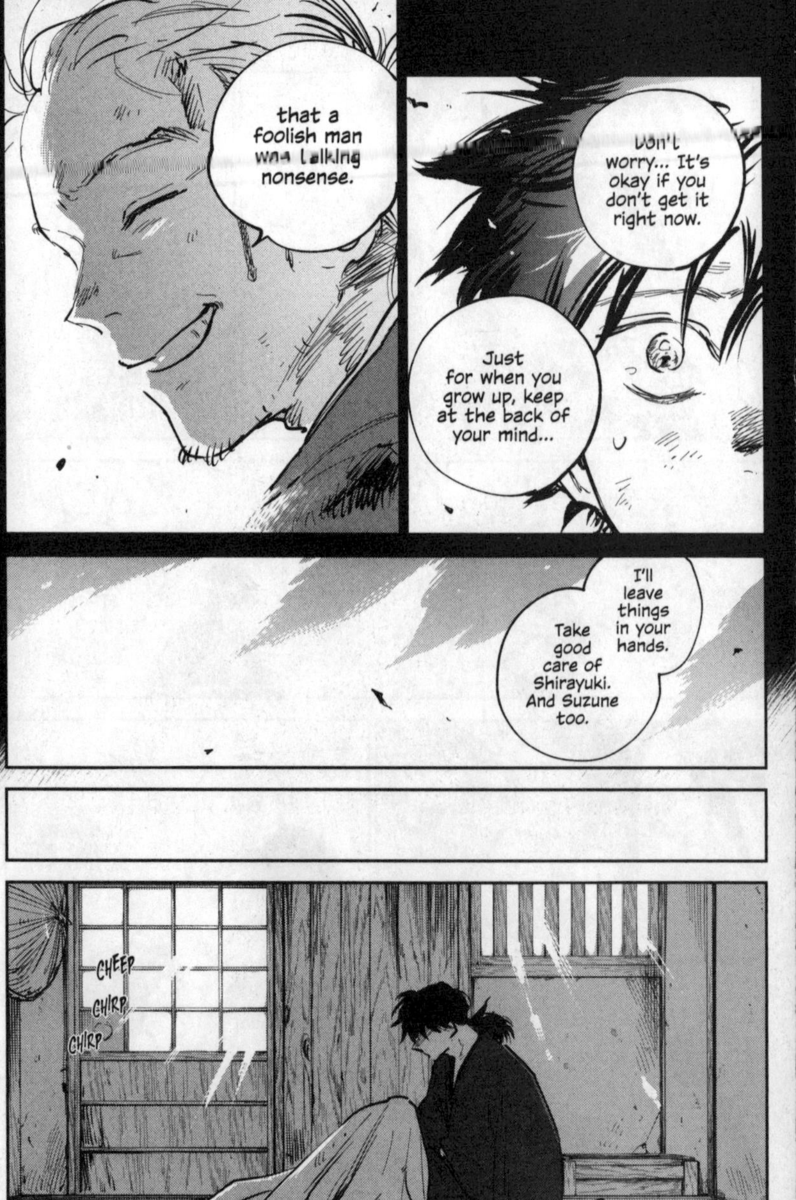

Don't worry... It's okay if you don't get it right now.
Just for when you grow up, keep at the back of your mind...
that a foolish man was talking nonsense.
I'll leave things in your hands.
Take good care of Shirayuki. And Suzune too.
CHEEP
CHIRP
CHIRP

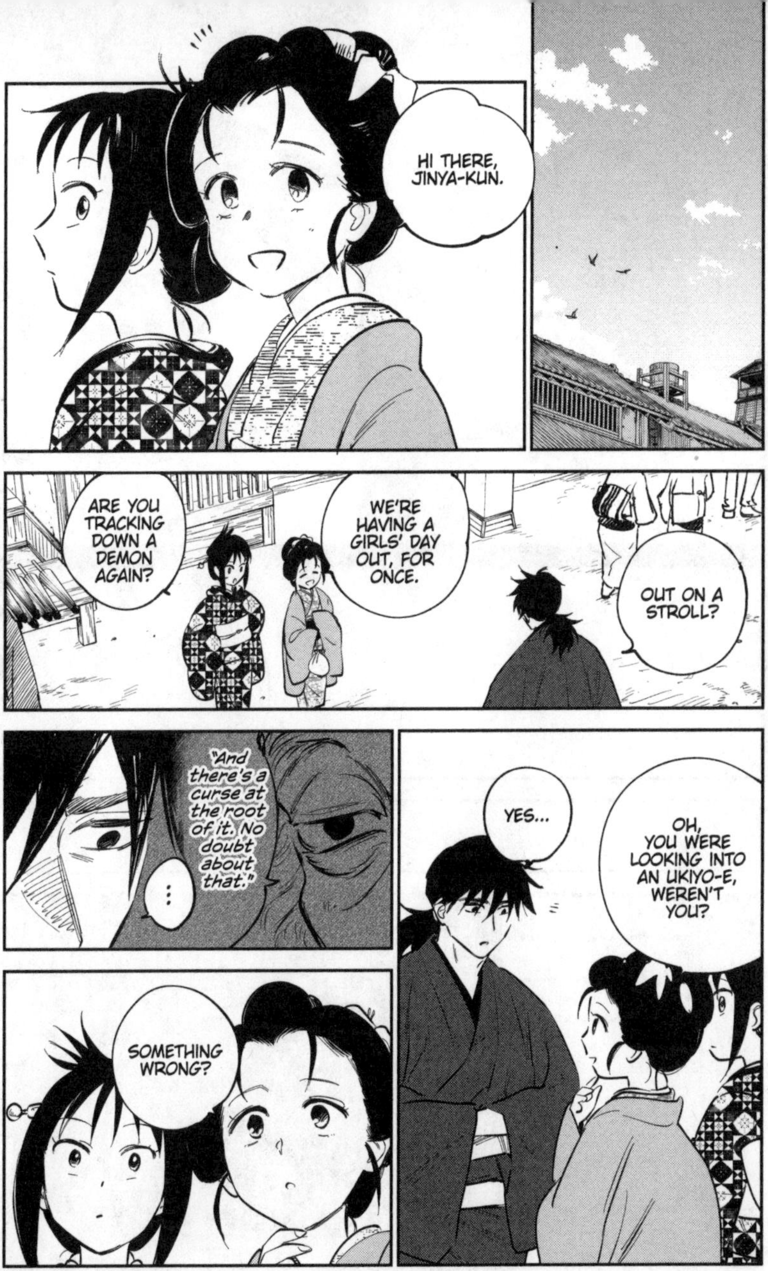
HI THERE, JINYA-KUN.
OUT ON A STROLL?
WE'RE HAVING A GIRLS' DAY OUT, FOR ONCE.
ARE YOU TRACKING DOWN A DEMON AGAIN?
OH, YOU WERE LOOKING INTO AN UKIYO-E, WEREN'T YOU?
YES...
"And there's a curse at the root of it. No doubt about that."
...
SOMETHING WRONG?

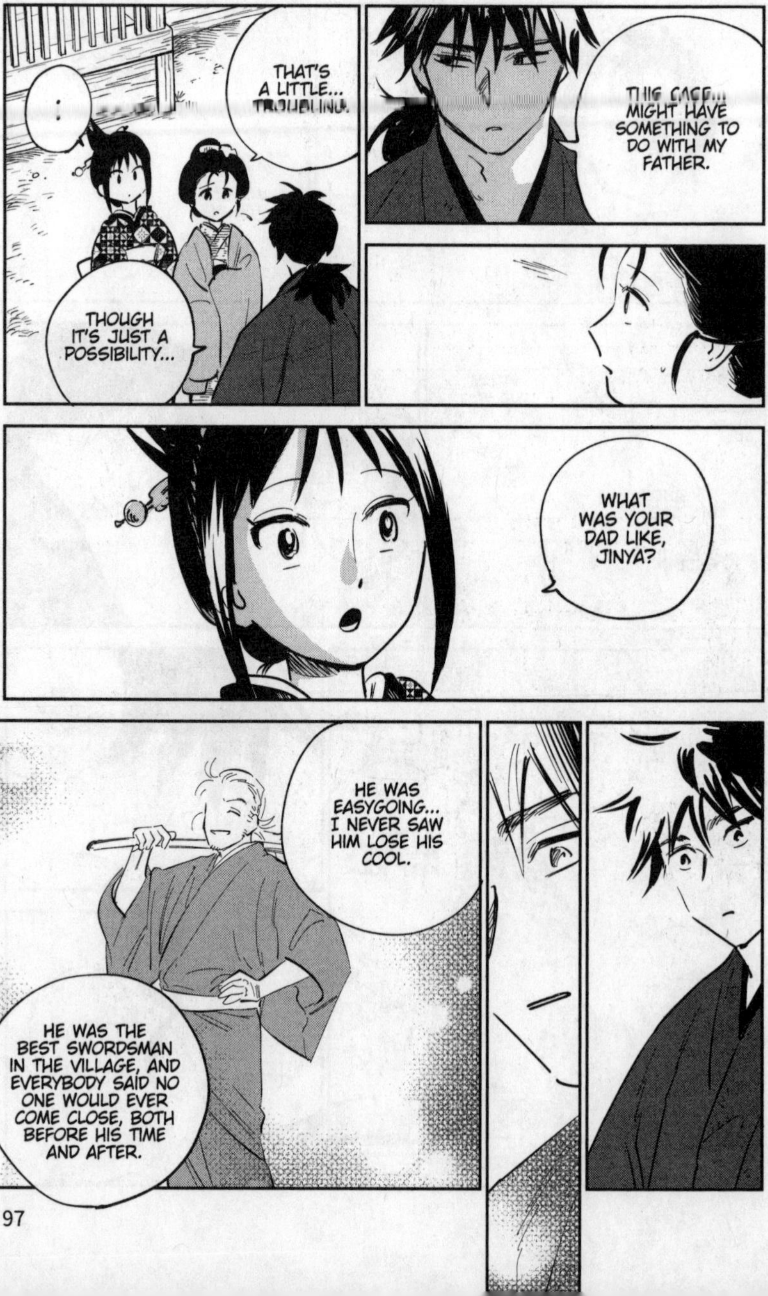
THIS CASE... MIGHT HAVE SOMETHING TO DO WITH MY FATHER.
THAT'S A LITTLE... TROUBLING.
...
THOUGH IT'S JUST A POSSIBILITY...
WHAT WAS YOUR DAD LIKE, JINYA?
HE WAS EASYGOING... I NEVER SAW HIM LOSE HIS COOL.
HE WAS THE BEST SWORDSMAN IN THE VILLAGE, AND EVERYBODY SAID NO ONE WOULD EVER COME CLOSE, BOTH BEFORE HIS TIME AND AFTER.

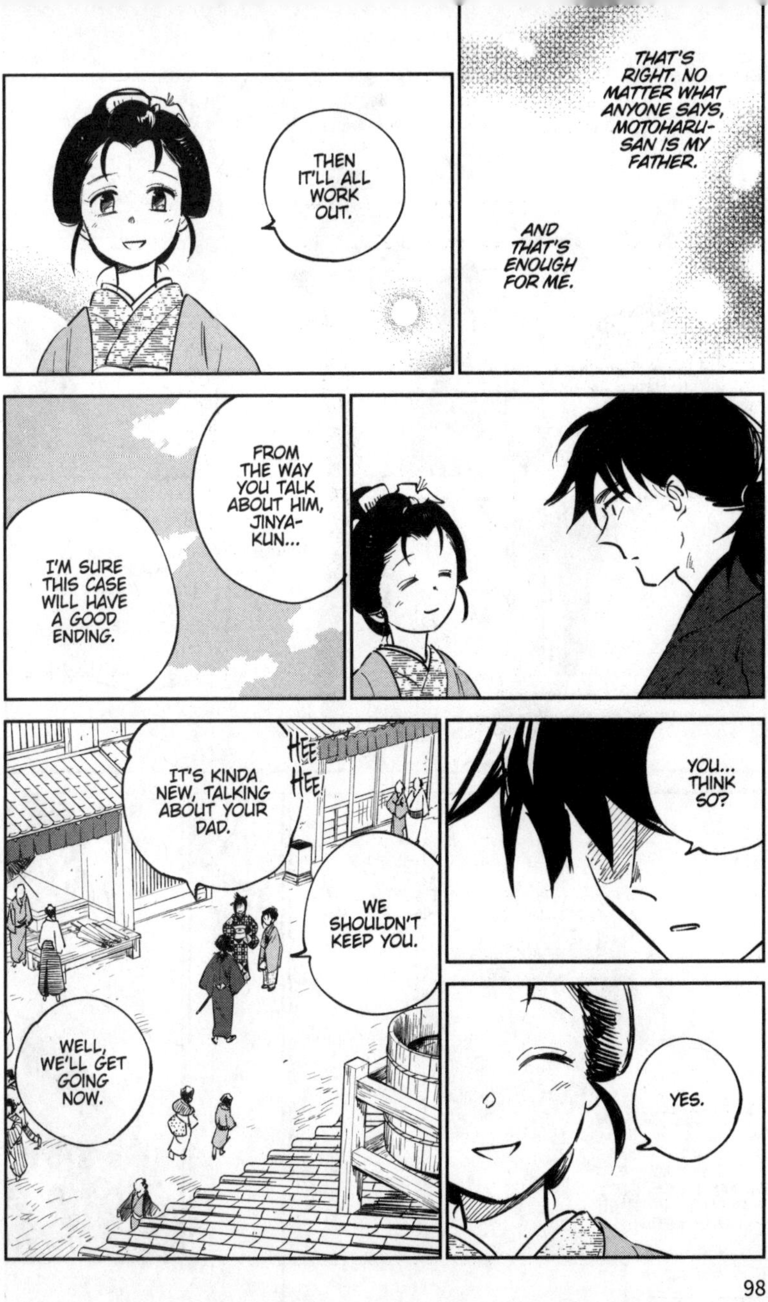
THAT'S RIGHT. NO MATTER WHAT ANYONE SAYS, MOTOHARU-SAN IS MY FATHER.
AND THAT'S ENOUGH FOR ME.
THEN IT'LL ALL WORK OUT.
FROM THE WAY YOU TALK ABOUT HIM, JINYA-KUN...
I'M SURE THIS CASE WILL HAVE A GOOD ENDING.
YOU... THINK SO?
YES.
HEE HEE!
IT'S KINDA NEW, TALKING ABOUT YOUR DAD.
WE SHOULDN'T KEEP YOU.
WELL, WE'LL GET GOING NOW.

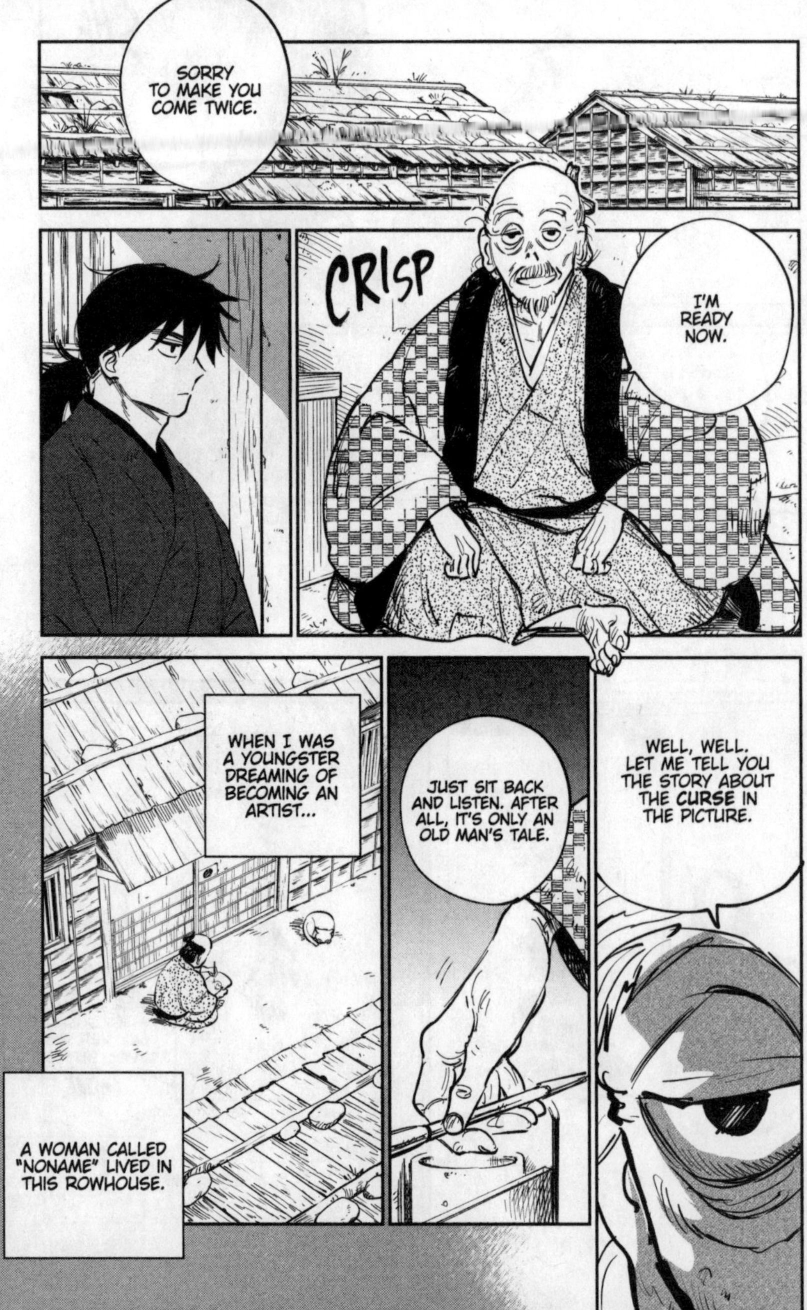
SORRY TO MAKE YOU COME TWICE.
CRISP
I'M READY NOW.
WELL, WELL. LET ME TELL YOU THE STORY ABOUT THE **CURSE** IN THE PICTURE.
JUST SIT BACK AND LISTEN. AFTER ALL, IT'S ONLY AN OLD MAN'S TALE.
WHEN I WAS A YOUNGSTER DREAMING OF BECOMING AN ARTIST...
A WOMAN CALLED "NONAME" LIVED IN THIS ROWHOUSE.

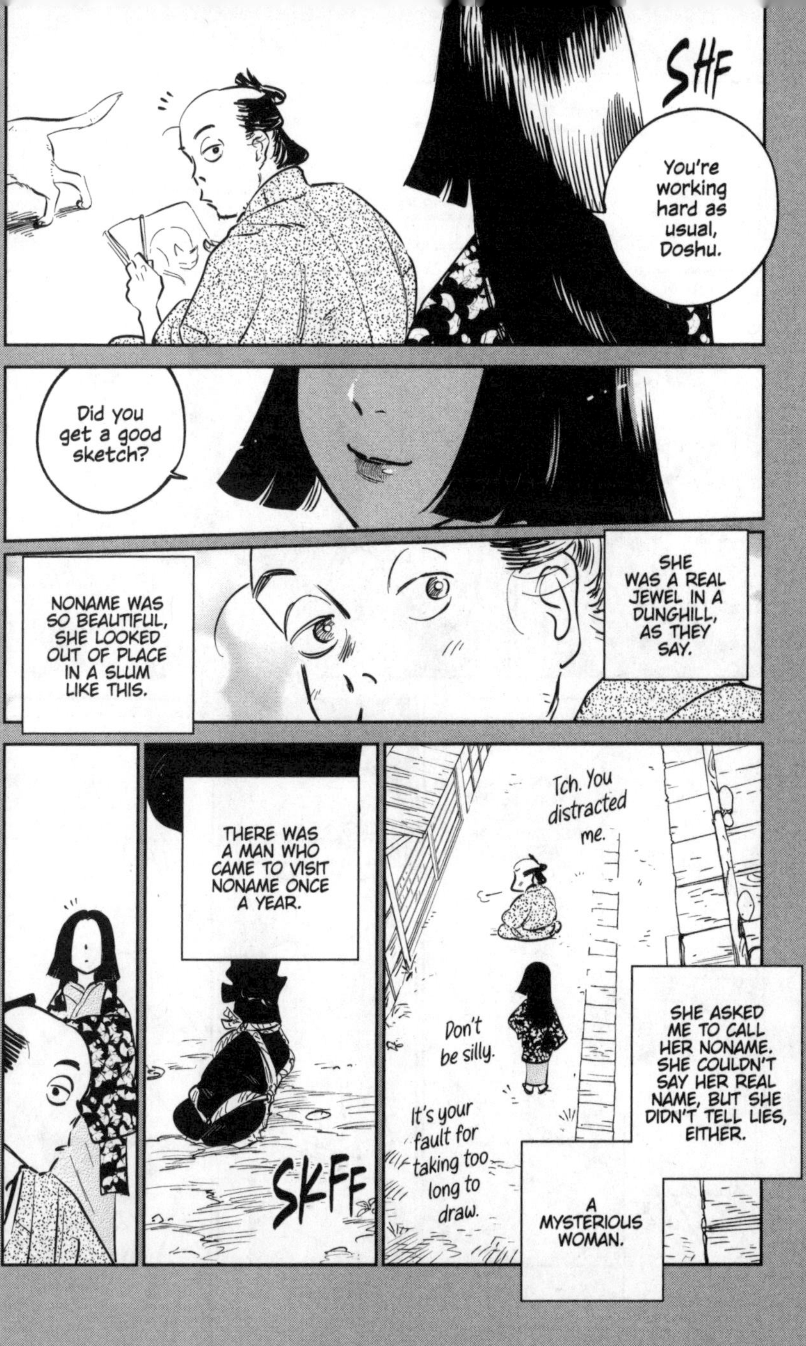
SHF
You're working hard as usual, Doshu.
Did you get a good sketch?
SHE WAS A REAL JEWEL IN A DUNGHILL, AS THEY SAY.
NONAME WAS SO BEAUTIFUL, SHE LOOKED OUT OF PLACE IN A SLUM LIKE THIS.
Tch. You distracted me.
Don't be silly.
It's your fault for taking too long to draw.
SHE ASKED ME TO CALL HER NONAME. SHE COULDN'T SAY HER REAL NAME, BUT SHE DIDN'T TELL LIES, EITHER.
A MYSTERIOUS WOMAN.
THERE WAS A MAN WHO CAME TO VISIT NONAME ONCE A YEAR.
SKFF

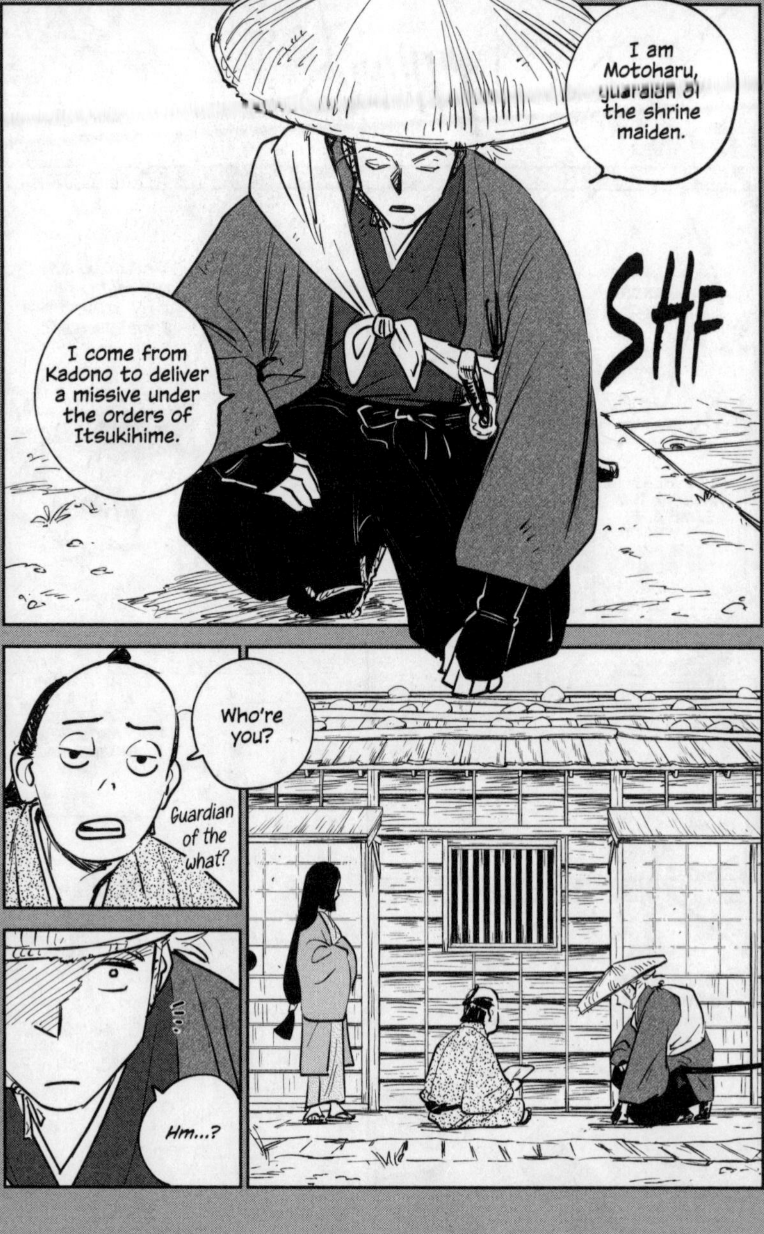
I am Motoharu, guardian of the shrine maiden.
SHF
I come from Kadono to deliver a missive under the orders of Itsukihime.
Who're you?
Guardian of the what?
Hm...?

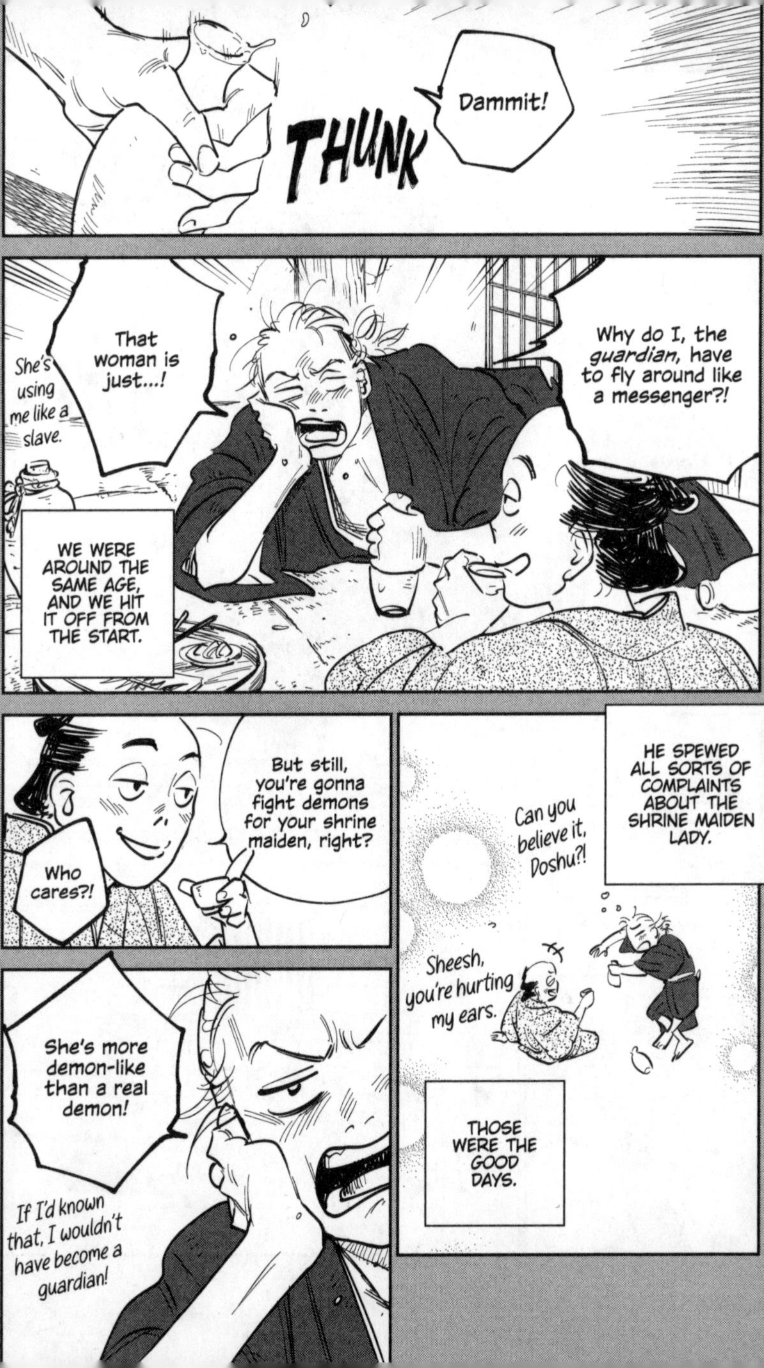

Dammit!
THUNK
Why do I, the *guardian*, have to fly around like a messenger?!
That woman is just...!
She's using me like a slave.
WE WERE AROUND THE SAME AGE, AND WE HIT IT OFF FROM THE START.
HE SPEWED ALL SORTS OF COMPLAINTS ABOUT THE SHRINE MAIDEN LADY.
Can you believe it, Doshu?!
Sheesh, you're hurting my ears.
THOSE WERE THE GOOD DAYS.
But still, you're gonna fight demons for your shrine maiden, right?
Who cares?!
She's more demon-like than a real demon!
If I'd known that, I wouldn't have become a guardian!

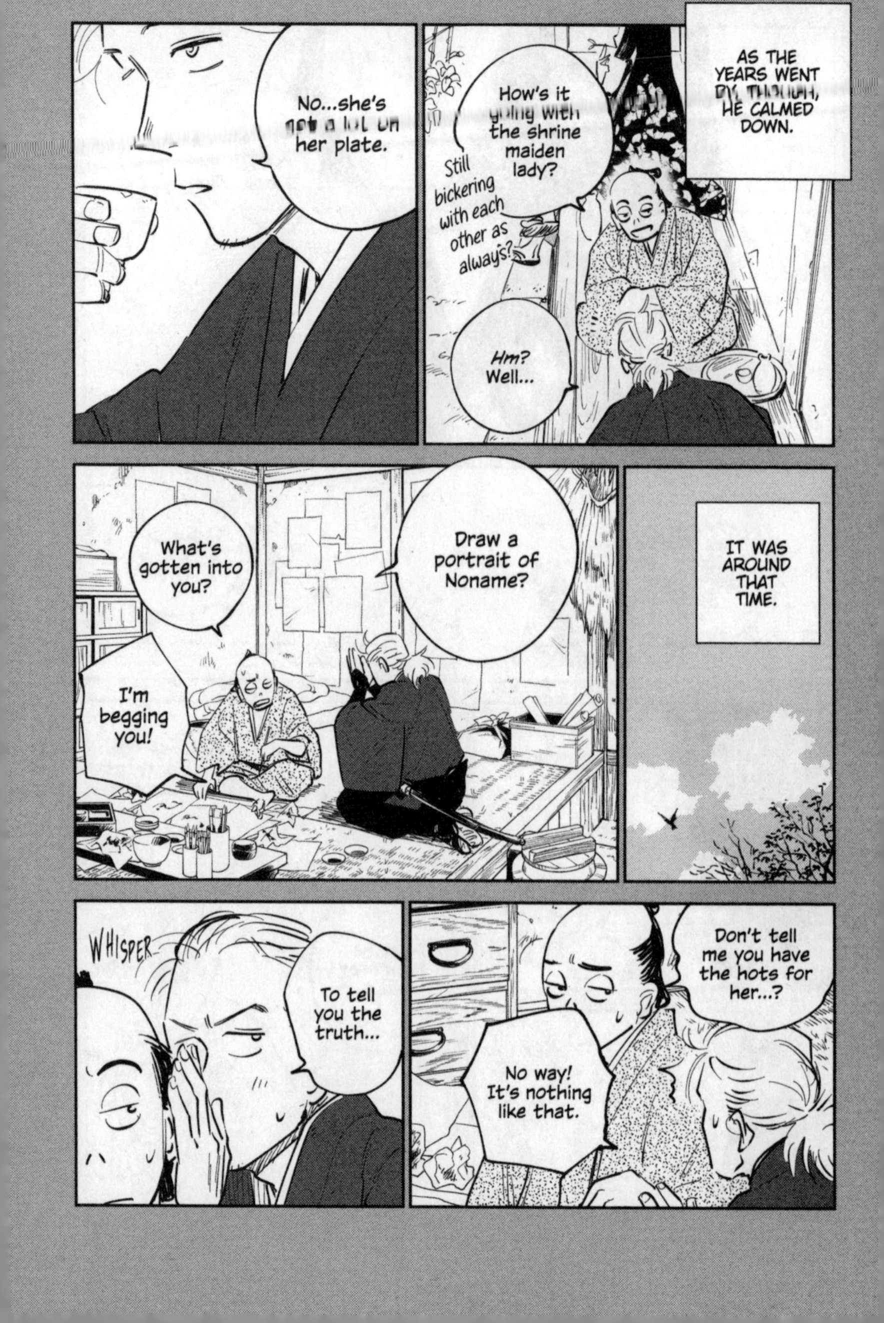
AS THE YEARS WENT BY, THOUGH, HE CALMED DOWN.
How's it going with the shrine maiden lady?
Still bickering with each other as always?
Hm? Well...
No...she's got a lot on her plate.
IT WAS AROUND THAT TIME.
Draw a portrait of Noname?
What's gotten into you?
I'm begging you!
Don't tell me you have the hots for her...?
No way! It's nothing like that.
To tell you the truth...
WHISPER

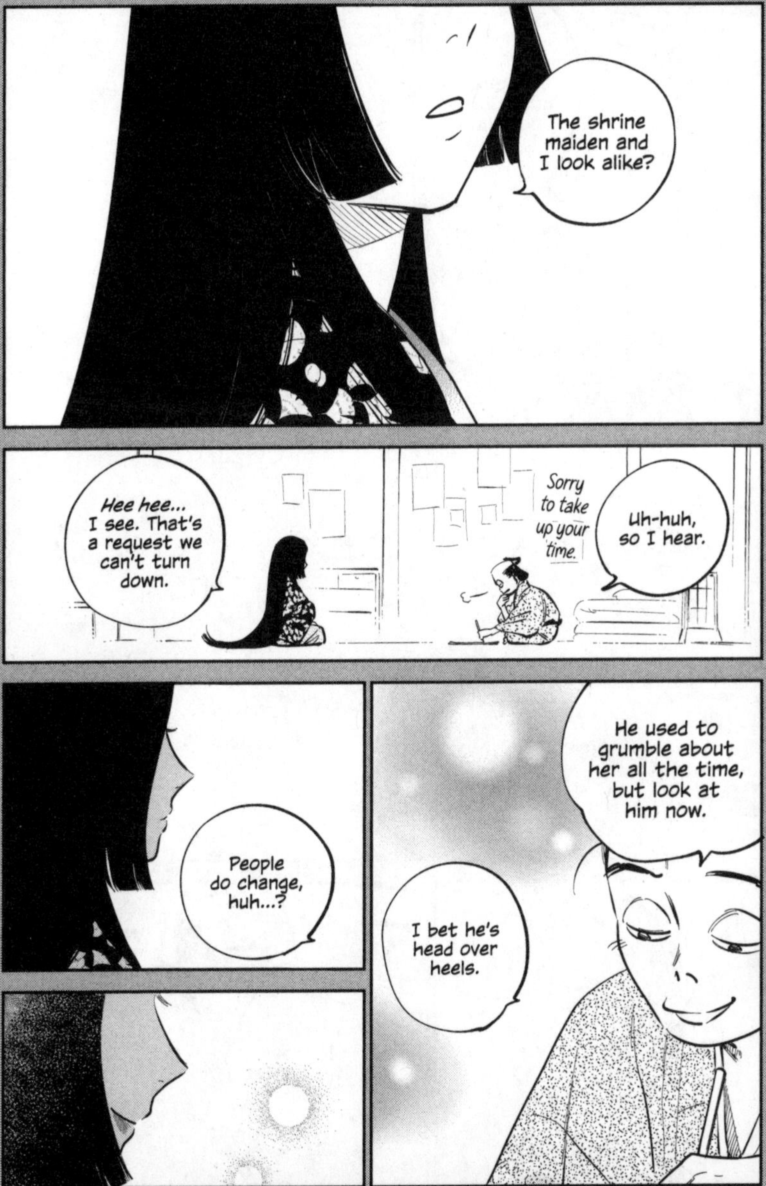
The shrine maiden and I look alike?
Uh-huh, so I hear.
Sorry to take up your time.
Hee hee... I see. That's a request we can't turn down.
He used to grumble about her all the time, but look at him now.
I bet he's head over heels.
People do change, huh...?

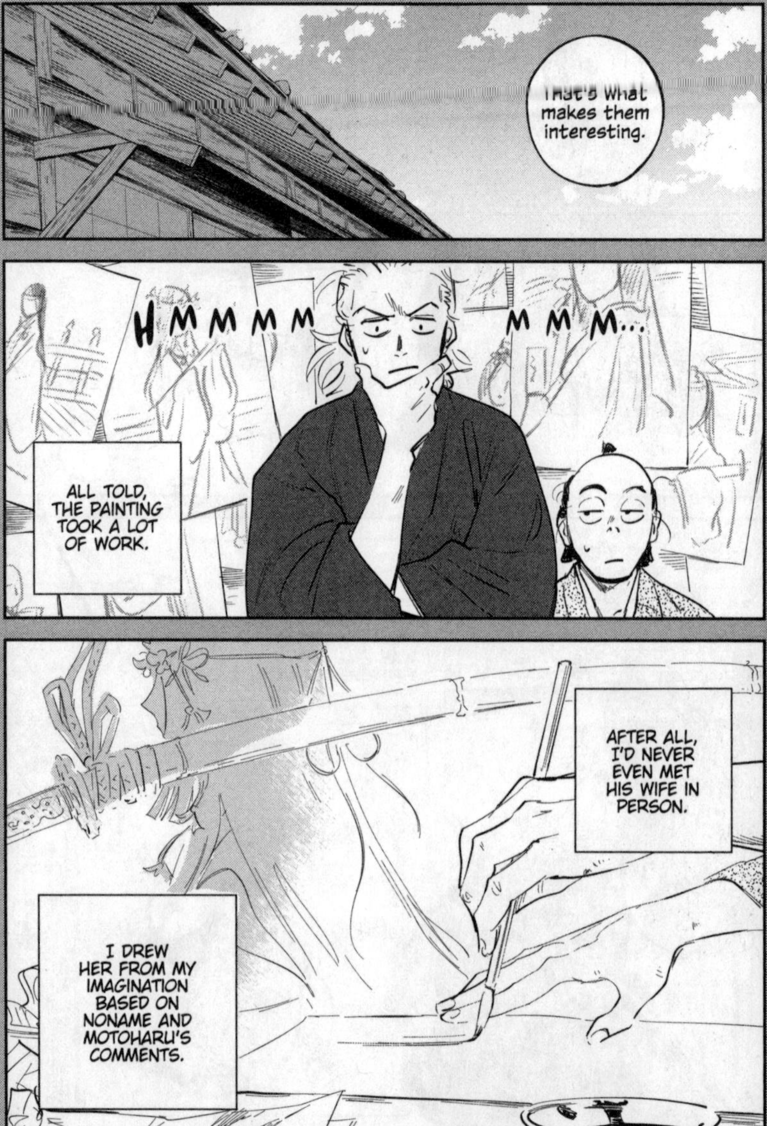
That's what makes them interesting.
HMMMM MMM...
ALL TOLD, THE PAINTING TOOK A LOT OF WORK.
AFTER ALL, I'D NEVER EVEN MET HIS WIFE IN PERSON.
I DREW HER FROM MY IMAGINATION BASED ON NONAME AND MOTOHARU'S COMMENTS.

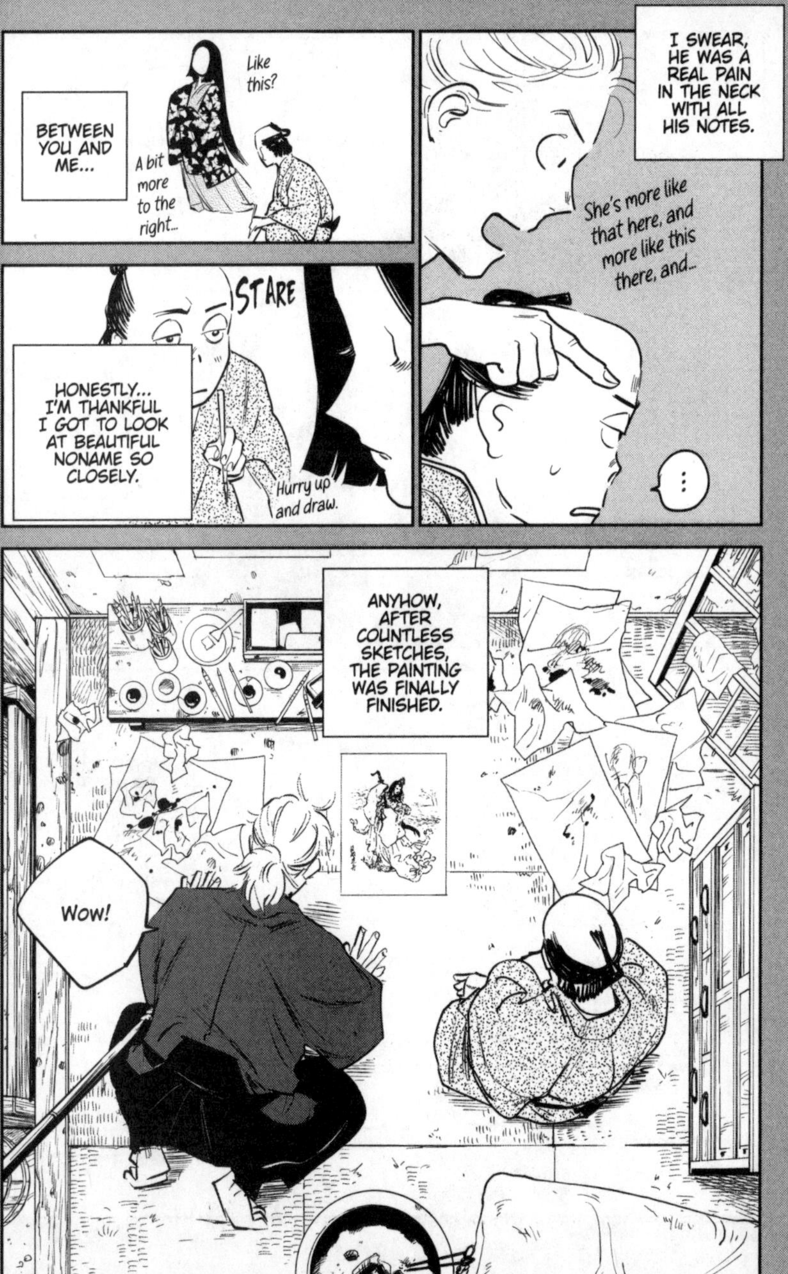
I SWEAR, HE WAS A REAL PAIN IN THE NECK WITH ALL HIS NOTES.
She's more like that here, and more like this there, and...
...
Like this?
BETWEEN YOU AND ME...
A bit more to the right...
STARE
HONESTLY... I'M THANKFUL I GOT TO LOOK AT BEAUTIFUL NONAME SO CLOSELY.
Hurry up and draw.
ANYHOW, AFTER COUNTLESS SKETCHES, THE PAINTING WAS FINALLY FINISHED.
WOW!

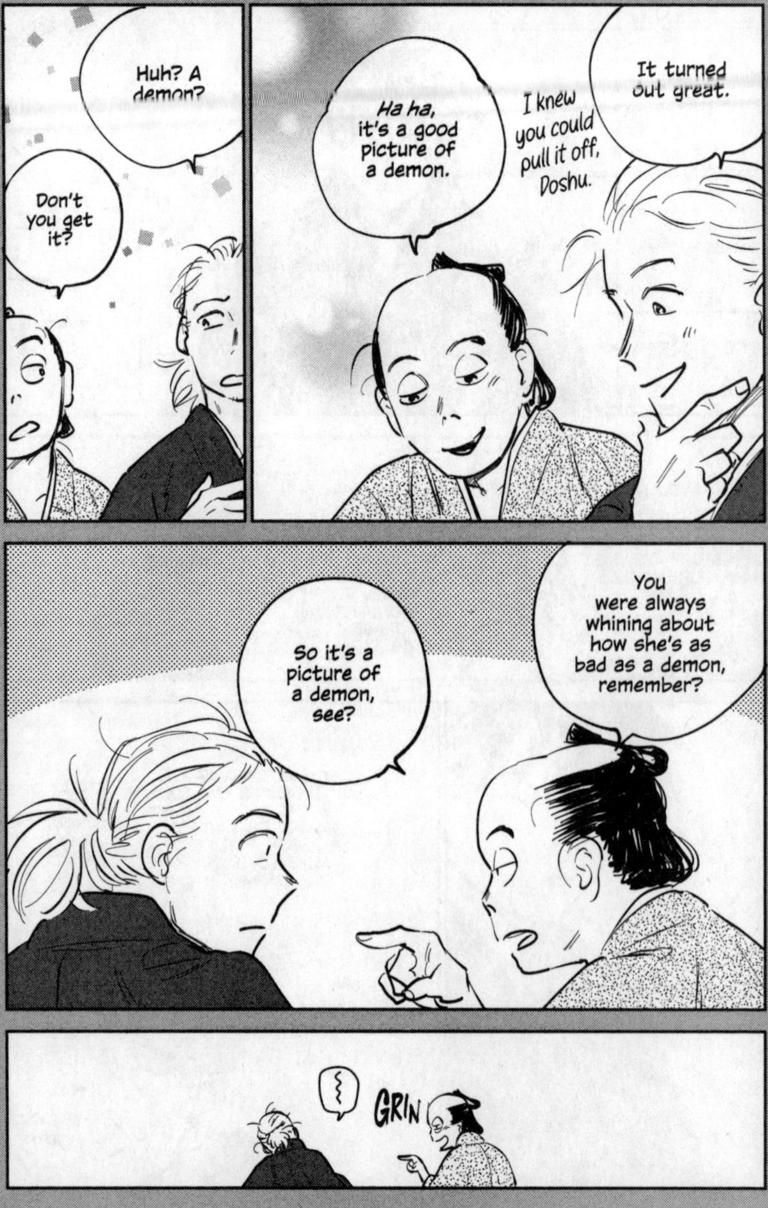
It turned out great.
I knew you could pull it off, Doshu.
Ha ha, it's a good picture of a demon.
Huh? A demon?
Don't you get it?
You were always whining about how she's as bad as a demon, remember?
So it's a picture of a demon, see?
GRIN

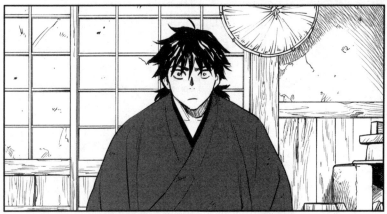

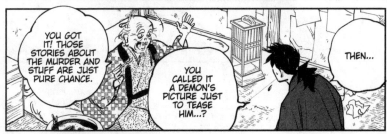

THEN...
YOU CALLED IT A DEMON'S PICTURE JUST TO TEASE HIM...?
YOU GOT IT! THOSE STORIES ABOUT THE MURDER AND STUFF ARE JUST PURE CHANCE.
I'M REALLY GOING SENILE THESE DAYS.
SO I MOANED ABOUT IT TO SENKENDOU. TOLD HIM IT'S KARMA FROM SELLING REPRINTS OF A DEMON PICTURE TO MAKE SOME QUICK MONEY.
Heh heh. It was funny, so I let him believe what he wanted.
...

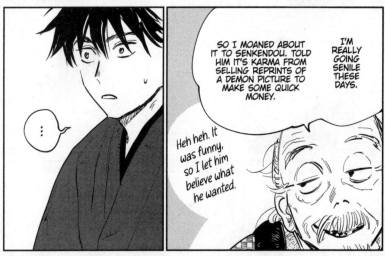

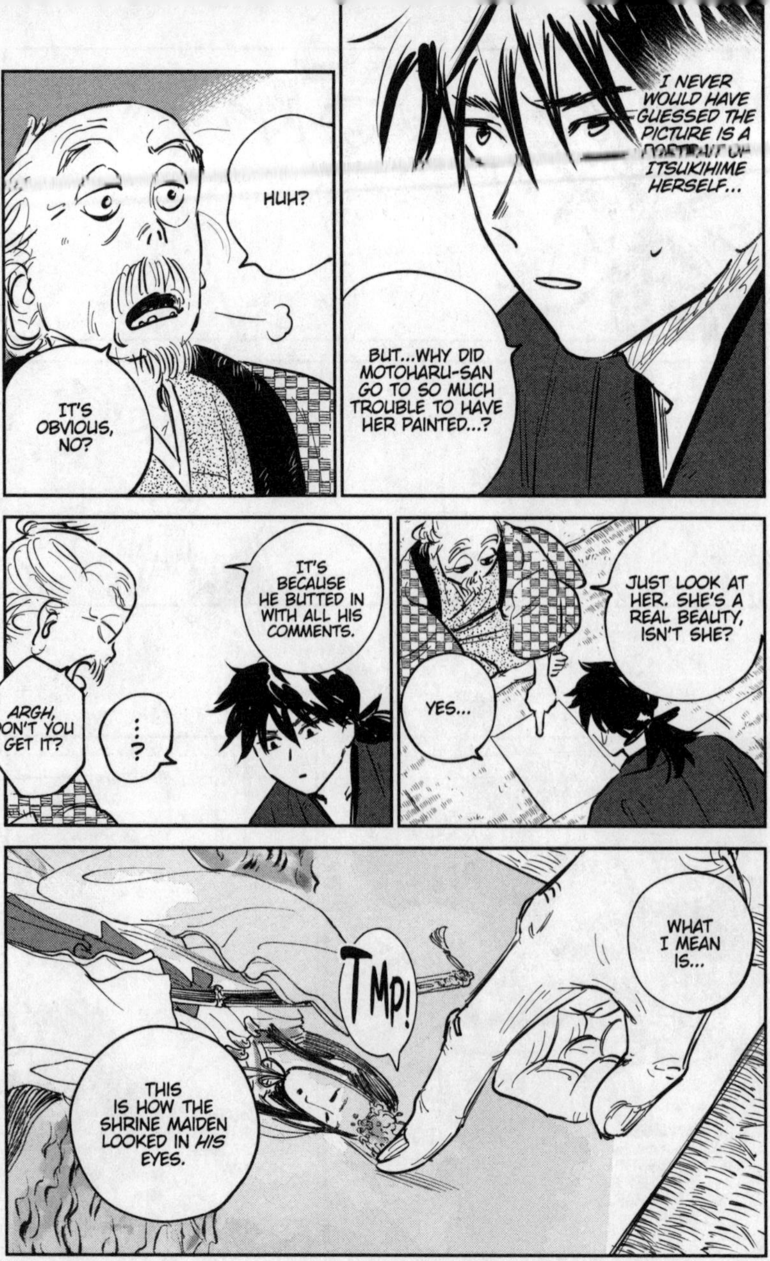
I NEVER WOULD HAVE GUESSED THE PICTURE IS A PORTRAIT OF ITSUKIHIME HERSELF...
BUT...WHY DID MOTOHARU-SAN GO TO SO MUCH TROUBLE TO HAVE HER PAINTED...?
HUH?
IT'S OBVIOUS, NO?
JUST LOOK AT HER. SHE'S A REAL BEAUTY, ISN'T SHE?
YES...
IT'S BECAUSE HE BUTTED IN WITH ALL HIS COMMENTS.
...?
ARGH, DON'T YOU GET IT?
WHAT I MEAN IS...
TMP!
THIS IS HOW THE SHRINE MAIDEN LOOKED IN *HIS* EYES.

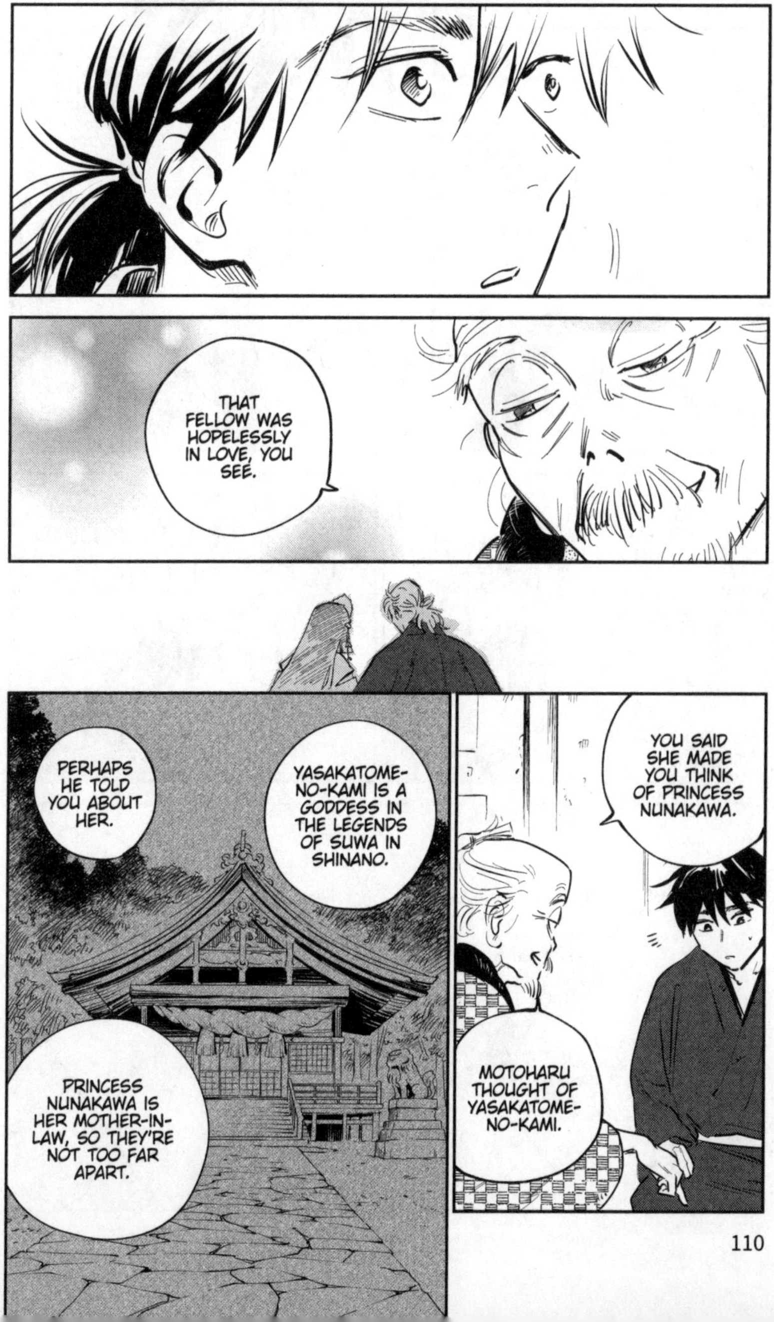
THAT FELLOW WAS HOPELESSLY IN LOVE, YOU SEE.
YOU SAID SHE MADE YOU THINK OF PRINCESS NUNAKAWA.
MOTOHARU THOUGHT OF YASAKATOME-NO-KAMI.
YASAKATOME-NO-KAMI IS A GODDESS IN THE LEGENDS OF SUWA IN SHINANO.
PERHAPS HE TOLD YOU ABOUT HER.
PRINCESS NUNAKAWA IS HER MOTHER-IN-LAW, SO THEY'RE NOT TOO FAR APART.

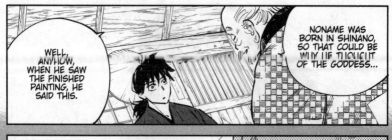

NONAME WAS BORN IN SHINANO, SO THAT COULD BE WHY HE THOUGHT OF THE GODDESS...
WELL, ANYHOW, WHEN HE SAW THE FINISHED PAINTING, HE SAID THIS.
She's almost like Yasakatome-no-kami... No...
She's at least another step more stunning than Yasaka.
So she better be called Kudanzaka!*
DU-DU N

*Yasaka means "eight hills;" Kudanzaka means "hill of nine steps."

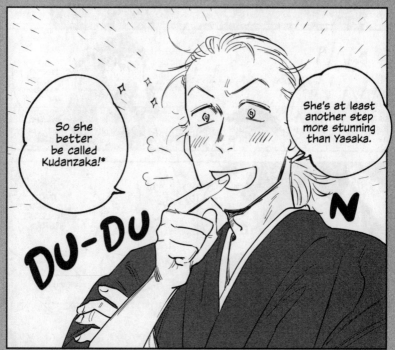

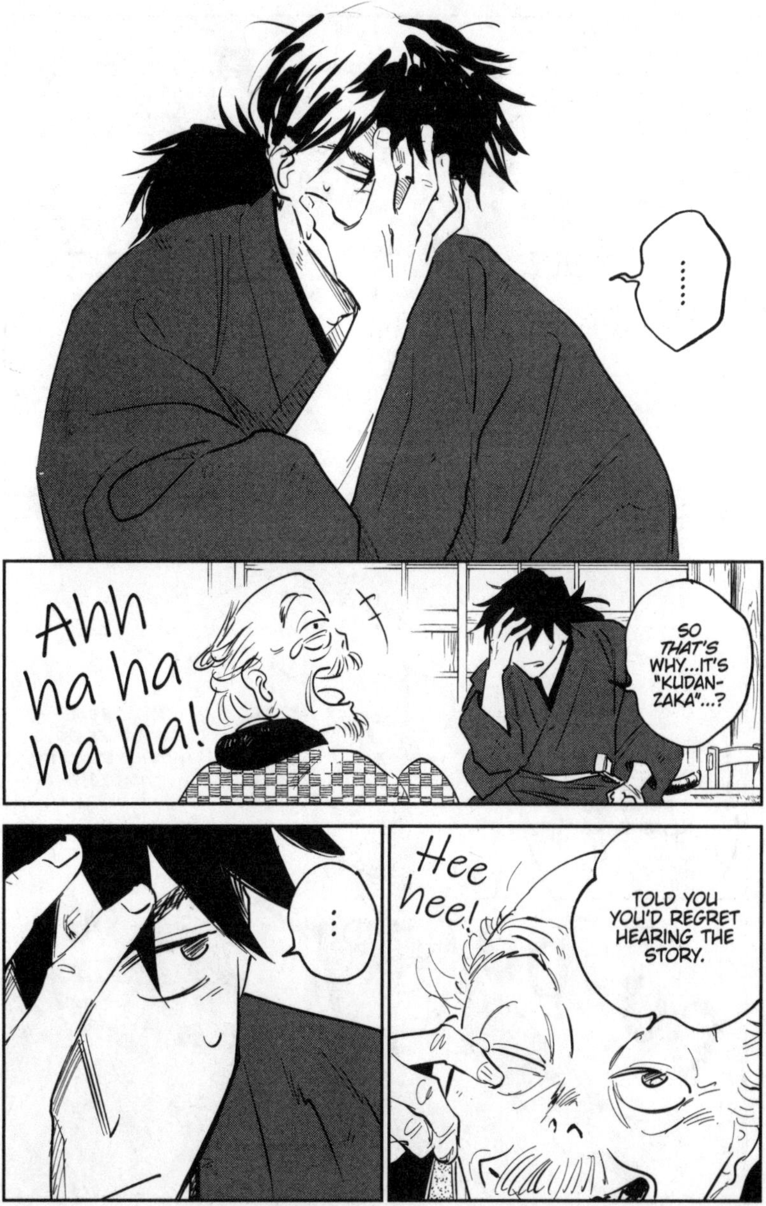
......
SO THAT'S WHY...IT'S "KUDAN-ZAKA"...?
Ahh ha ha ha ha!
TOLD YOU YOU'D REGRET HEARING THE STORY.
Hee hee!
...

*The words for "curse" and "being slow/unperceptive" are homonyms ("noroi").*
*The word for being so infatuated as to gush about one's lover ("noroke") derives from the latter "noroi."*

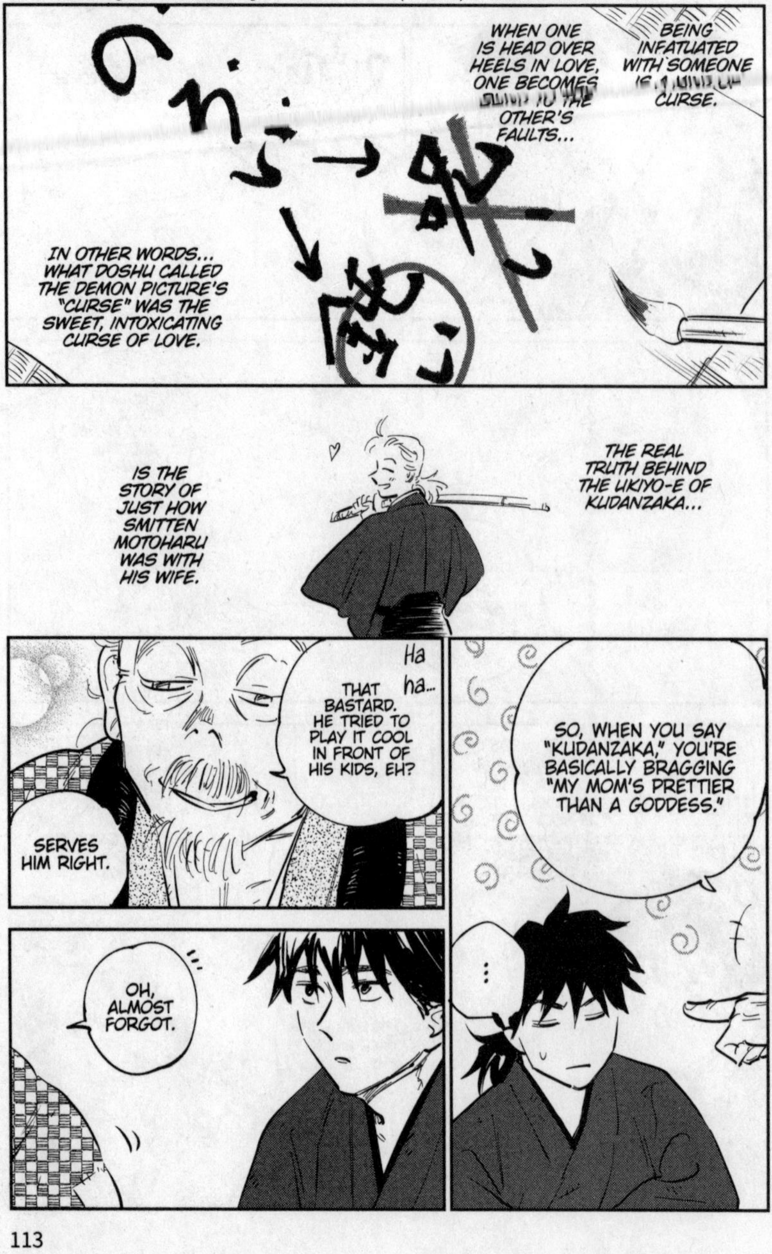

BEING INFATUATED WITH SOMEONE
CURSE.
WHEN ONE IS HEAD OVER HEELS IN LOVE, ONE BECOMES
OTHER'S FAULTS...
IN OTHER WORDS... WHAT DOSHU CALLED THE DEMON PICTURE'S "CURSE" WAS THE SWEET, INTOXICATING CURSE OF LOVE.
THE REAL TRUTH BEHIND THE UKIYO-E OF KUDANZAKA...
IS THE STORY OF JUST HOW SMITTEN MOTOHARU WAS WITH HIS WIFE.
SO, WHEN YOU SAY "KUDANZAKA," YOU'RE BASICALLY BRAGGING "MY MOM'S PRETTIER THAN A GODDESS."
Ha ha...
THAT BASTARD. HE TRIED TO PLAY IT COOL IN FRONT OF HIS KIDS, EH?
SERVES HIM RIGHT.
...
OH, ALMOST FORGOT.

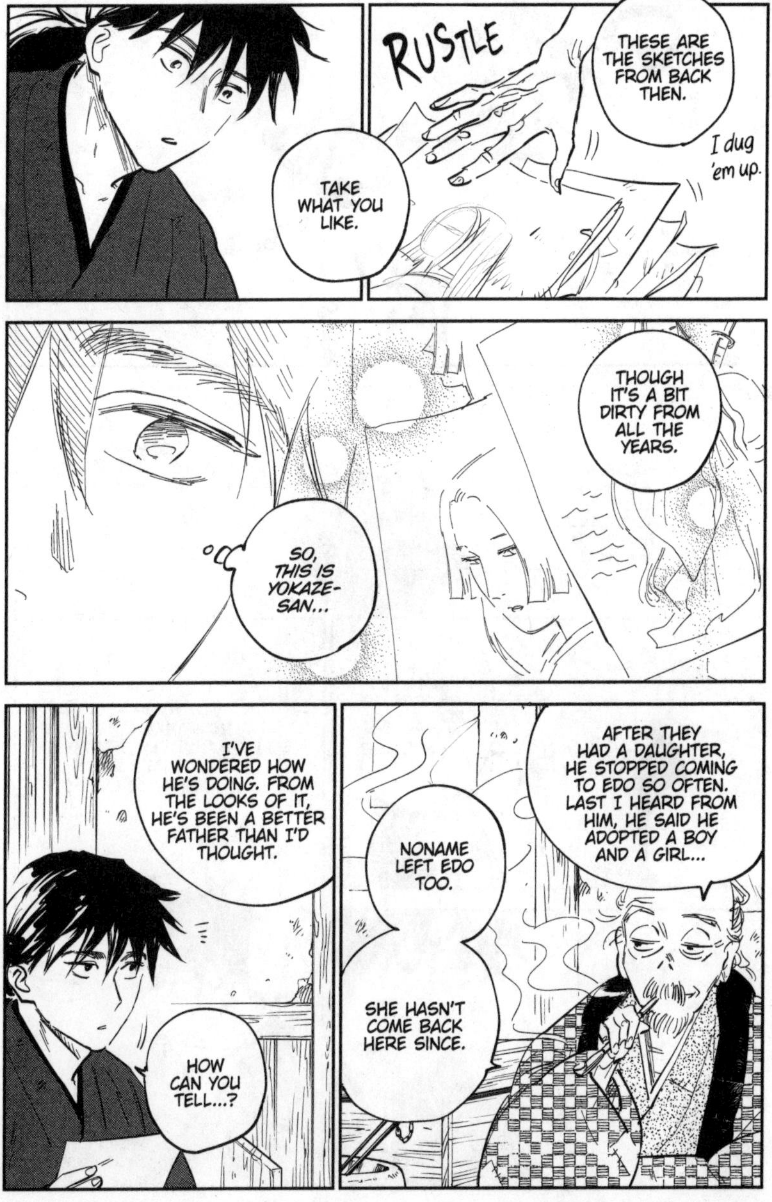
RUSTLE
THESE ARE THE SKETCHES FROM BACK THEN.
I dug 'em up.
TAKE WHAT YOU LIKE.
THOUGH IT'S A BIT DIRTY FROM ALL THE YEARS.
SO, THIS IS YOKAZE-SAN...
AFTER THEY HAD A DAUGHTER, HE STOPPED COMING TO EDO SO OFTEN. LAST I HEARD FROM HIM, HE SAID HE ADOPTED A BOY AND A GIRL...
NONAME LEFT EDO TOO.
SHE HASN'T COME BACK HERE SINCE.
I'VE WONDERED HOW HE'S DOING. FROM THE LOOKS OF IT, HE'S BEEN A BETTER FATHER THAN I'D THOUGHT.
HOW CAN YOU TELL...?

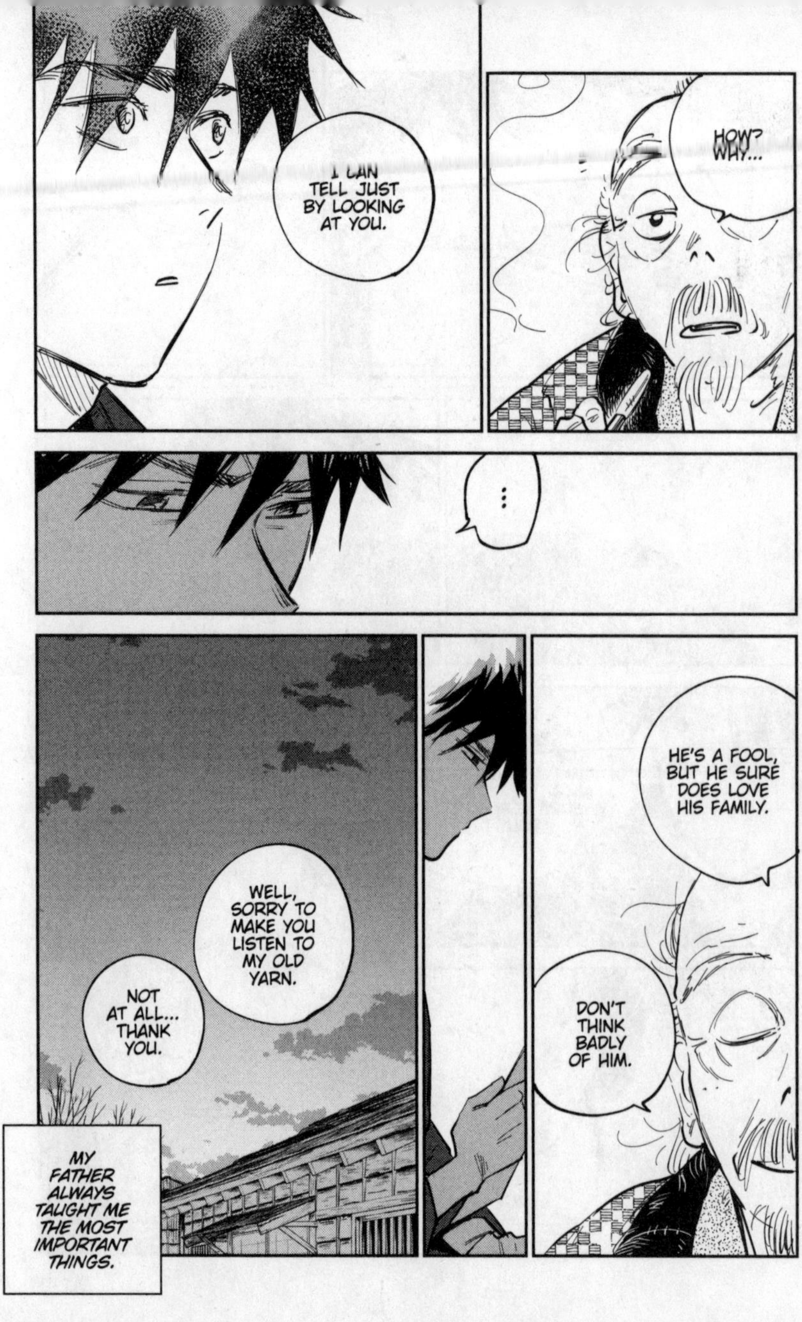
HOW? WHY...
I CAN TELL JUST BY LOOKING AT YOU.
...
HE'S A FOOL, BUT HE SURE DOES LOVE HIS FAMILY.
DON'T THINK BADLY OF HIM.
WELL, SORRY TO MAKE YOU LISTEN TO MY OLD YARN.
NOT AT ALL... THANK YOU.
MY FATHER ALWAYS TAUGHT ME THE MOST IMPORTANT THINGS.

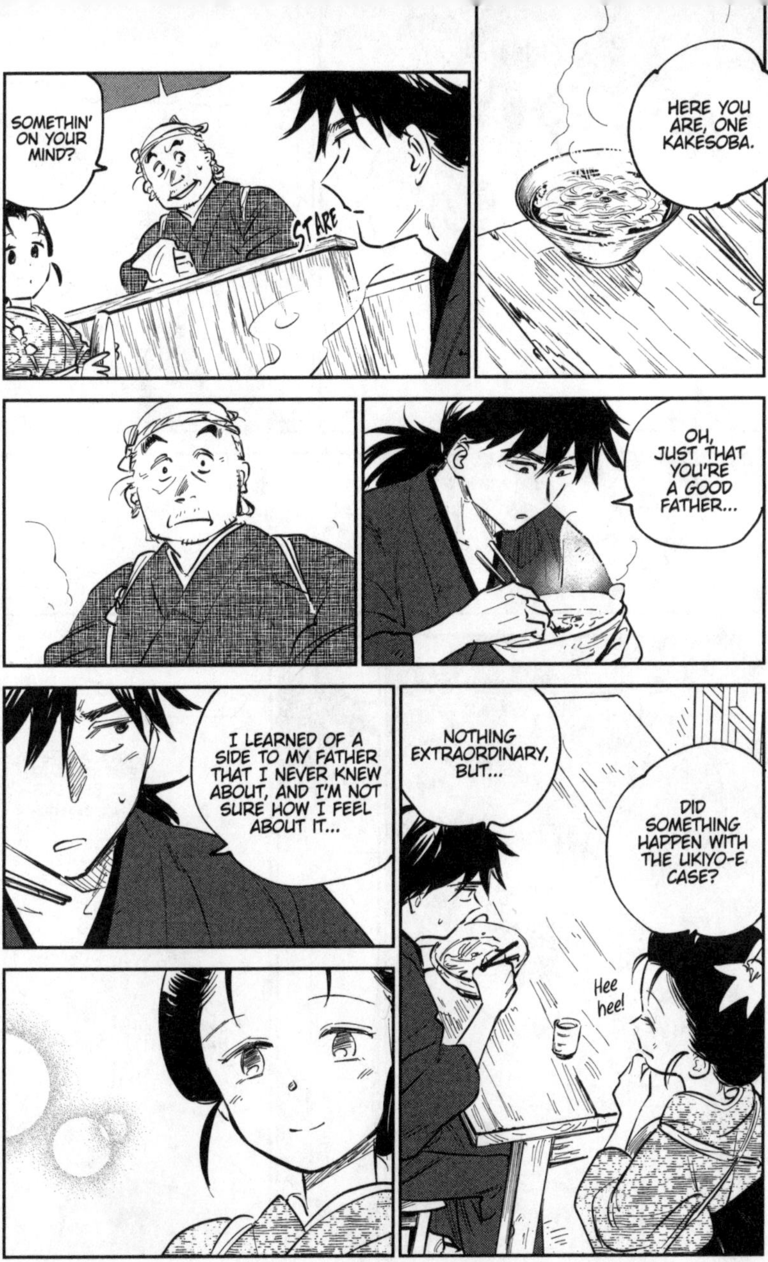
HERE YOU ARE, ONE KAKESOBA.
SOMETHIN' ON YOUR MIND?
STARE
OH, JUST THAT YOU'RE A GOOD FATHER...
DID SOMETHING HAPPEN WITH THE UKIYO-E CASE?
NOTHING EXTRAORDINARY, BUT...
Hee hee!
I LEARNED OF A SIDE TO MY FATHER THAT I NEVER KNEW ABOUT, AND I'M NOT SURE HOW I FEEL ABOUT IT...

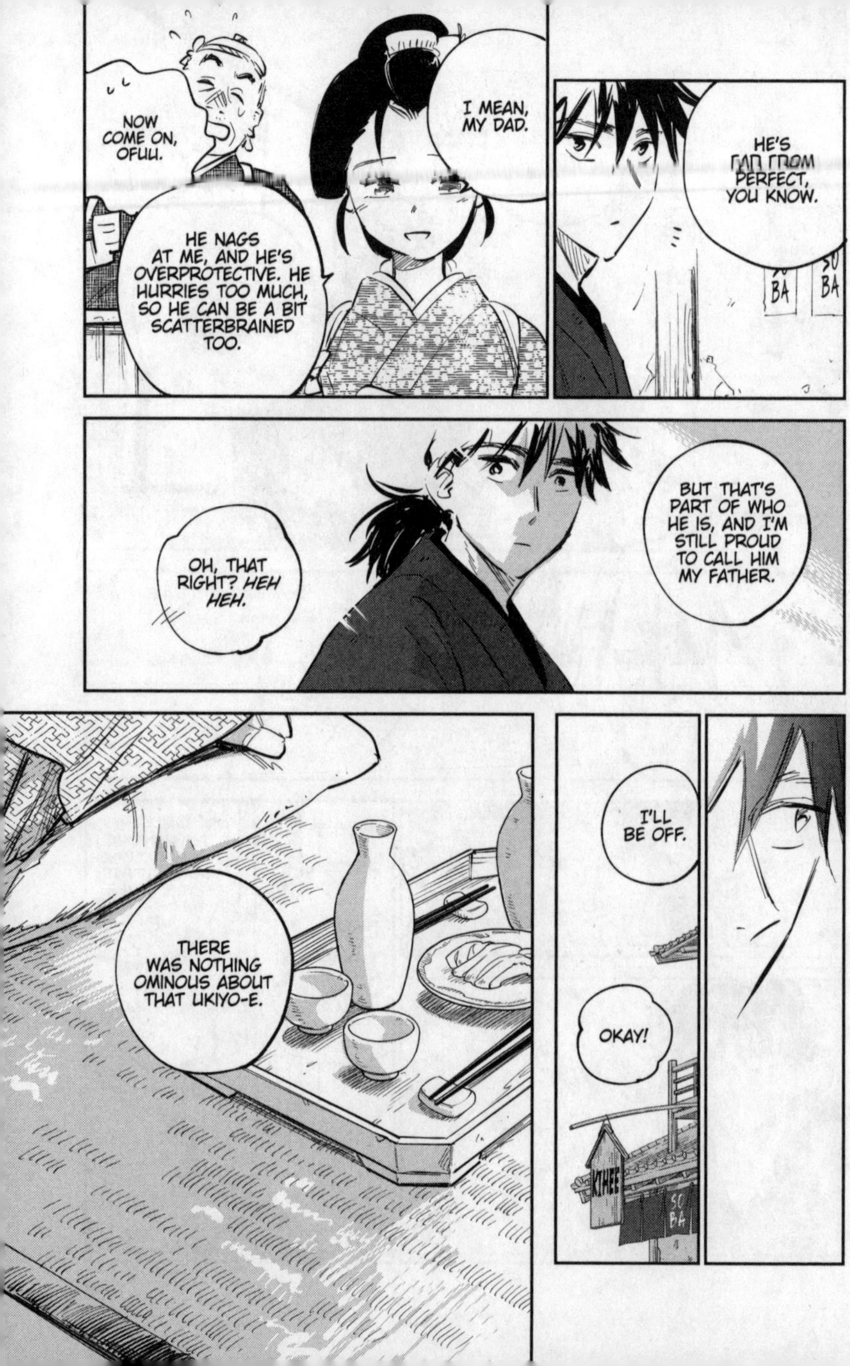
HE'S FAR FROM PERFECT, YOU KNOW.
SO BA
SO BA
I MEAN, MY DAD.
NOW COME ON, OFUU.
HE NAGS AT ME, AND HE'S OVERPROTECTIVE. HE HURRIES TOO MUCH, SO HE CAN BE A BIT SCATTERBRAINED TOO.
BUT THAT'S PART OF WHO HE IS, AND I'M STILL PROUD TO CALL HIM MY FATHER.
OH, THAT RIGHT? *HEH HEH.*
I'LL BE OFF.
OKAY!
KIHEE
SO BA
THERE WAS NOTHING OMINOUS ABOUT THAT UKIYO-E.

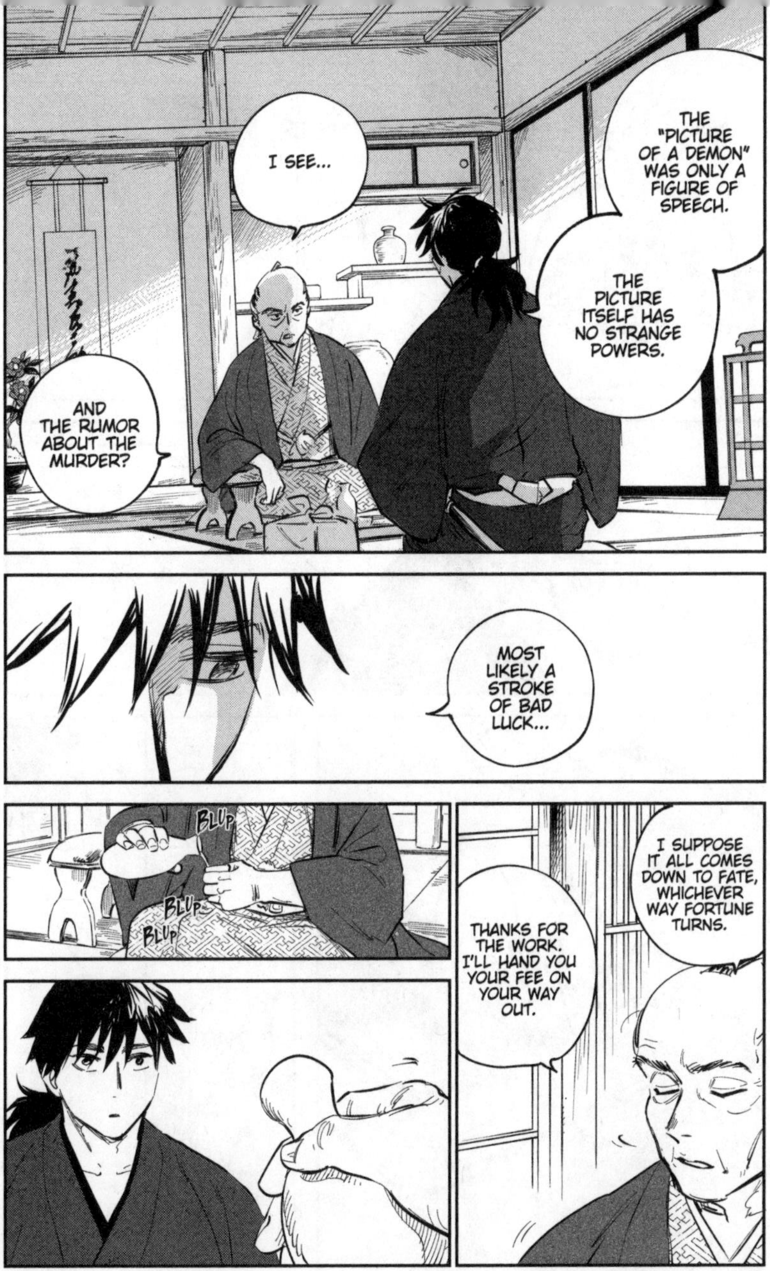
THE "PICTURE OF A DEMON" WAS ONLY A FIGURE OF SPEECH.
THE PICTURE ITSELF HAS NO STRANGE POWERS.
I SEE...
AND THE RUMOR ABOUT THE MURDER?
MOST LIKELY A STROKE OF BAD LUCK...
I SUPPOSE IT ALL COMES DOWN TO FATE, WHICHEVER WAY FORTUNE TURNS.
THANKS FOR THE WORK. I'LL HAND YOU YOUR FEE ON YOUR WAY OUT.
BLUP
BLUP
BLUP

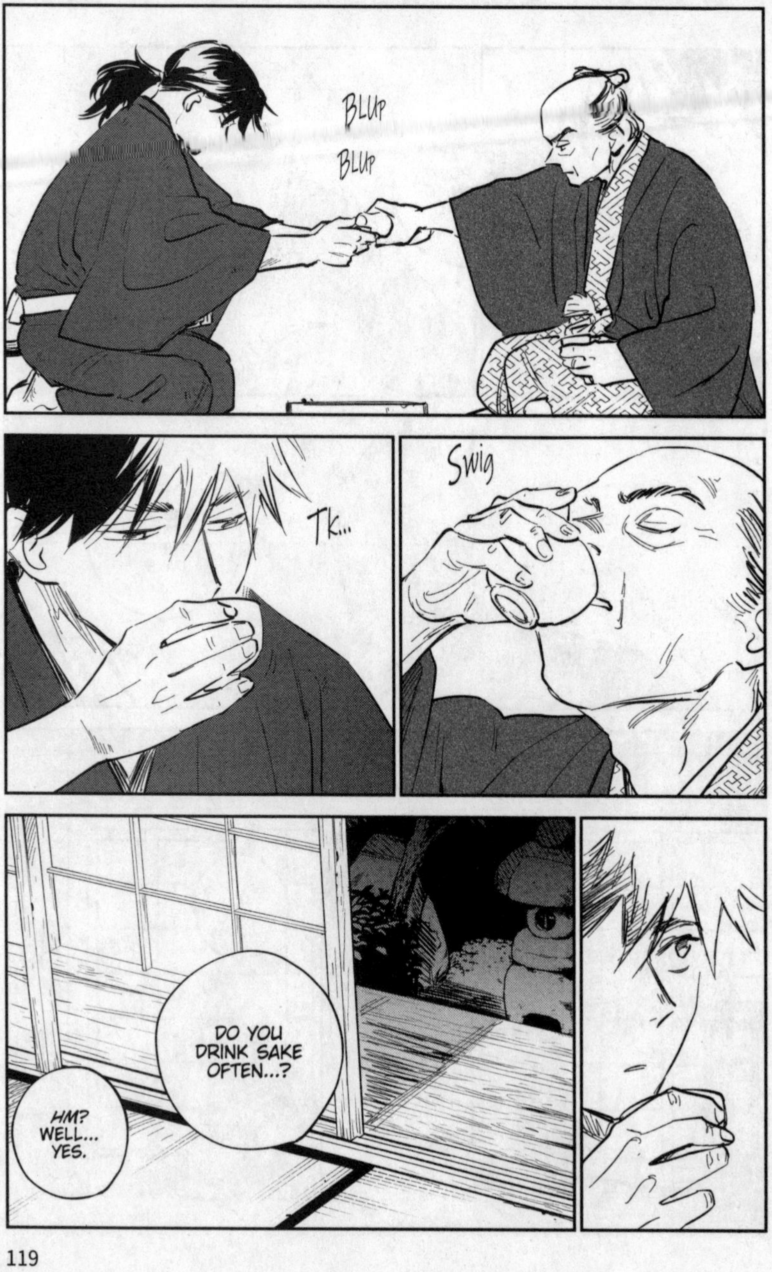
BLUP
BLUP
Swig
TK...
DO YOU DRINK SAKE OFTEN...?
HM? WELL... YES.

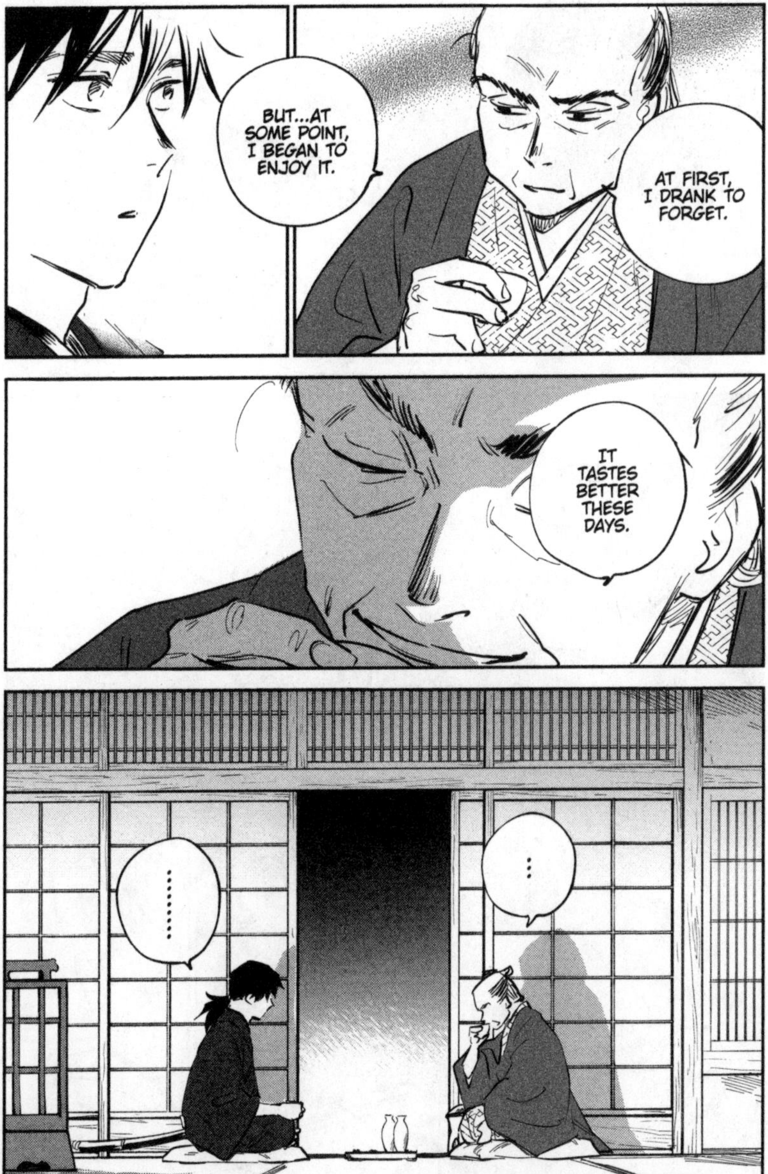
AT FIRST, I DRANK TO FORGET.
BUT...AT SOME POINT, I BEGAN TO ENJOY IT.
IT TASTES BETTER THESE DAYS.
...
........

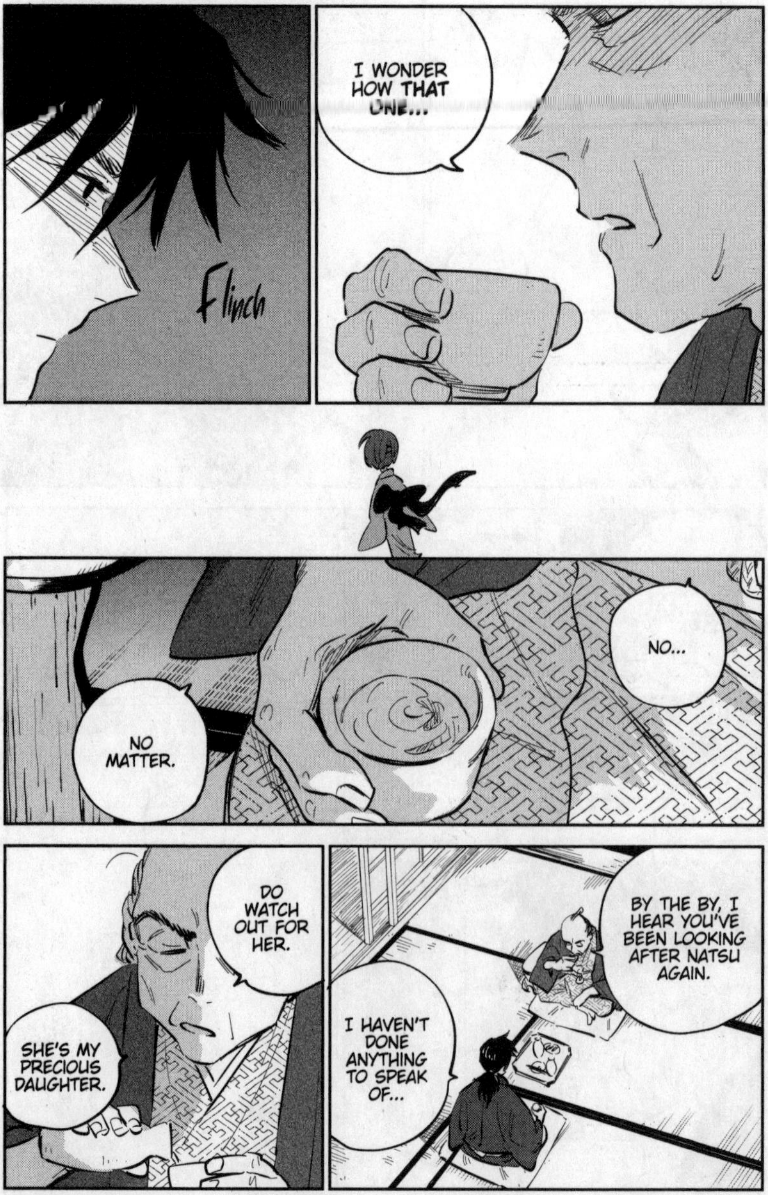
I WONDER HOW THAT ONE...
Flinch
NO...
NO MATTER.
BY THE BY, I HEAR YOU'VE BEEN LOOKING AFTER NATSU AGAIN.
I HAVEN'T DONE ANYTHING TO SPEAK OF...
DO WATCH OUT FOR HER.
SHE'S MY PRECIOUS DAUGHTER.

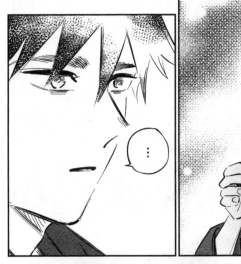

...

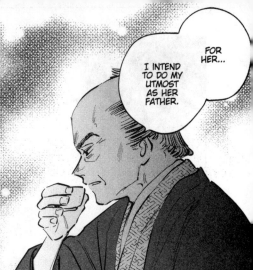

FOR HER...

I INTEND TO DO MY UTMOST AS HER FATHER.

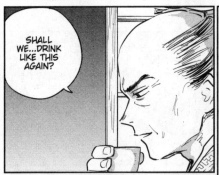

SHALL WE...DRINK LIKE THIS AGAIN?

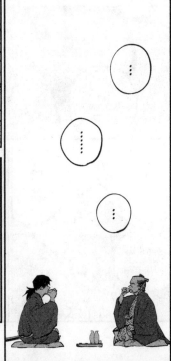

...

...

...

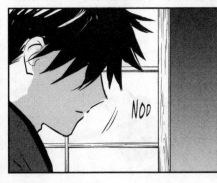

NOD

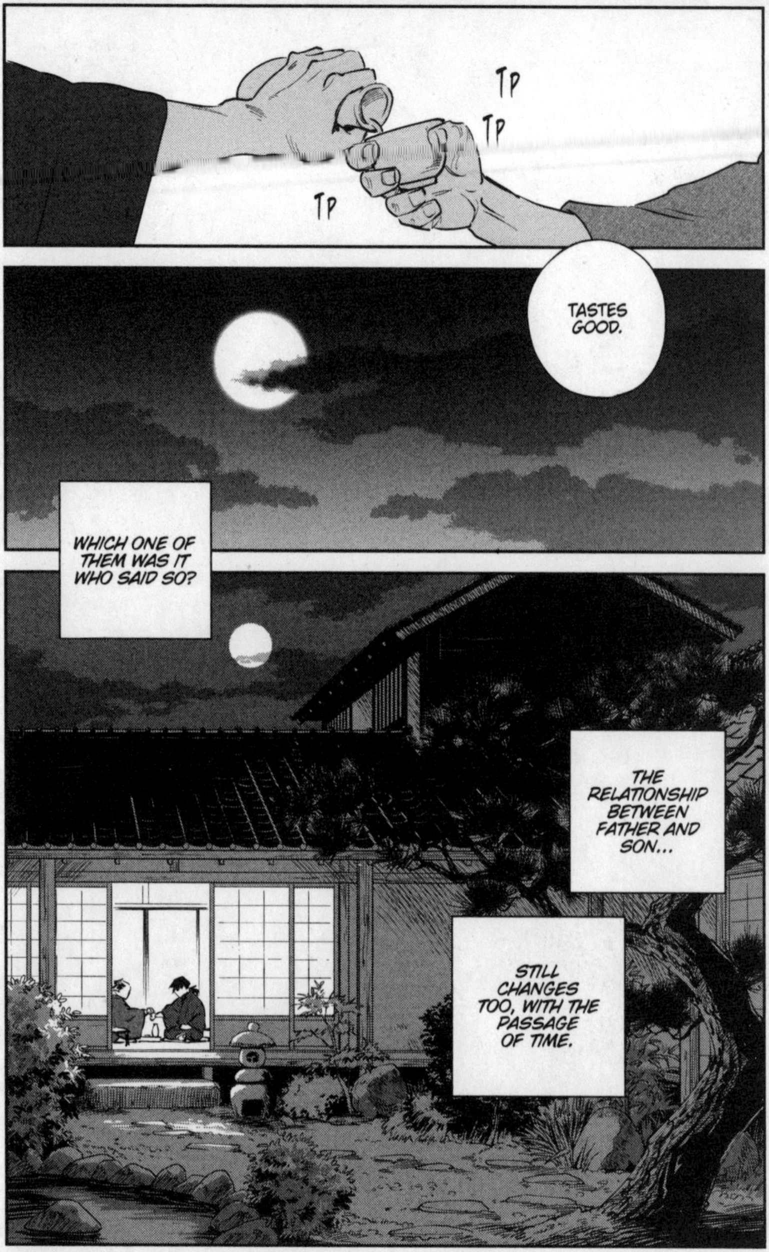
Tp
Tp
Tp
TASTES GOOD.
WHICH ONE OF THEM WAS IT WHO SAID SO?
THE RELATIONSHIP BETWEEN FATHER AND SON...
STILL CHANGES TOO, WITH THE PASSAGE OF TIME.

Sword
of the Demon
Hunter KIJIN
GENTŌSHŌ

# CHAPTER 24: UNDER THE CHERRY BLOSSOMS IN THE NIGHT

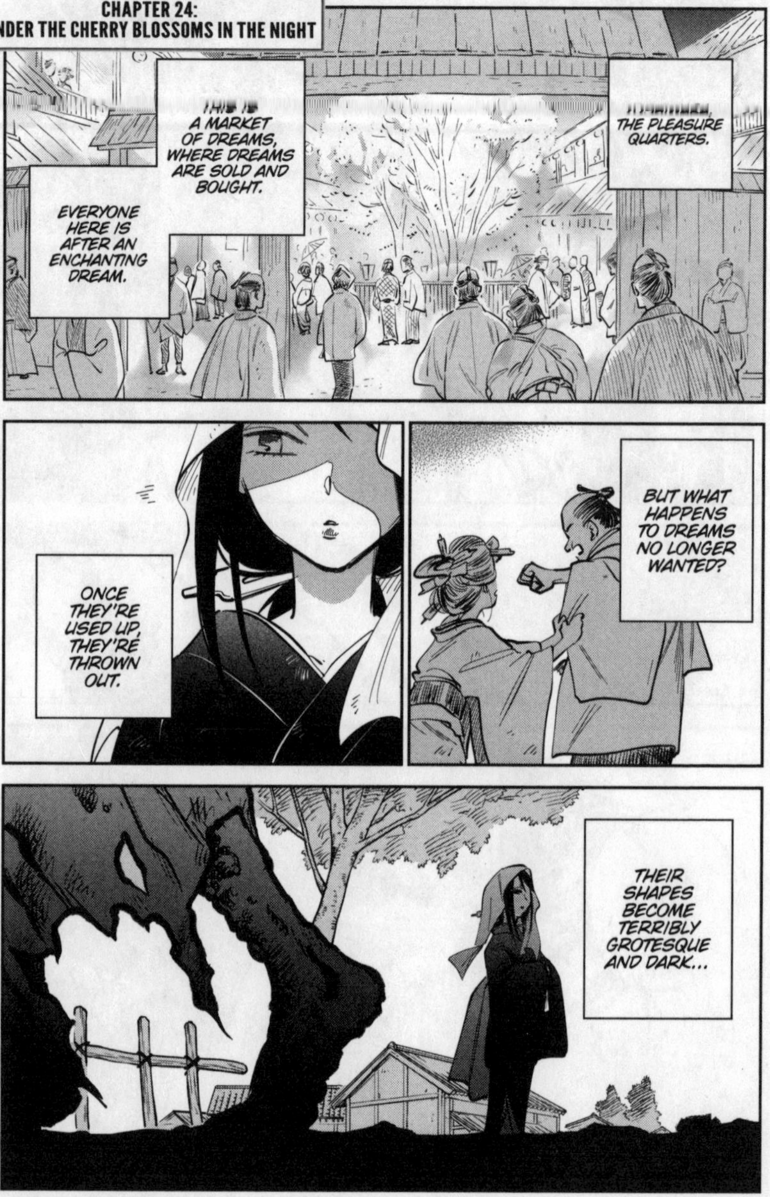

THE PLEASURE QUARTERS.
A MARKET OF DREAMS, WHERE DREAMS ARE SOLD AND BOUGHT.
EVERYONE HERE IS AFTER AN ENCHANTING DREAM.
BUT WHAT HAPPENS TO DREAMS NO LONGER WANTED?
ONCE THEY'RE USED UP, THEY'RE THROWN OUT.
THEIR SHAPES BECOME TERRIBLY GROTESQUE AND DARK...

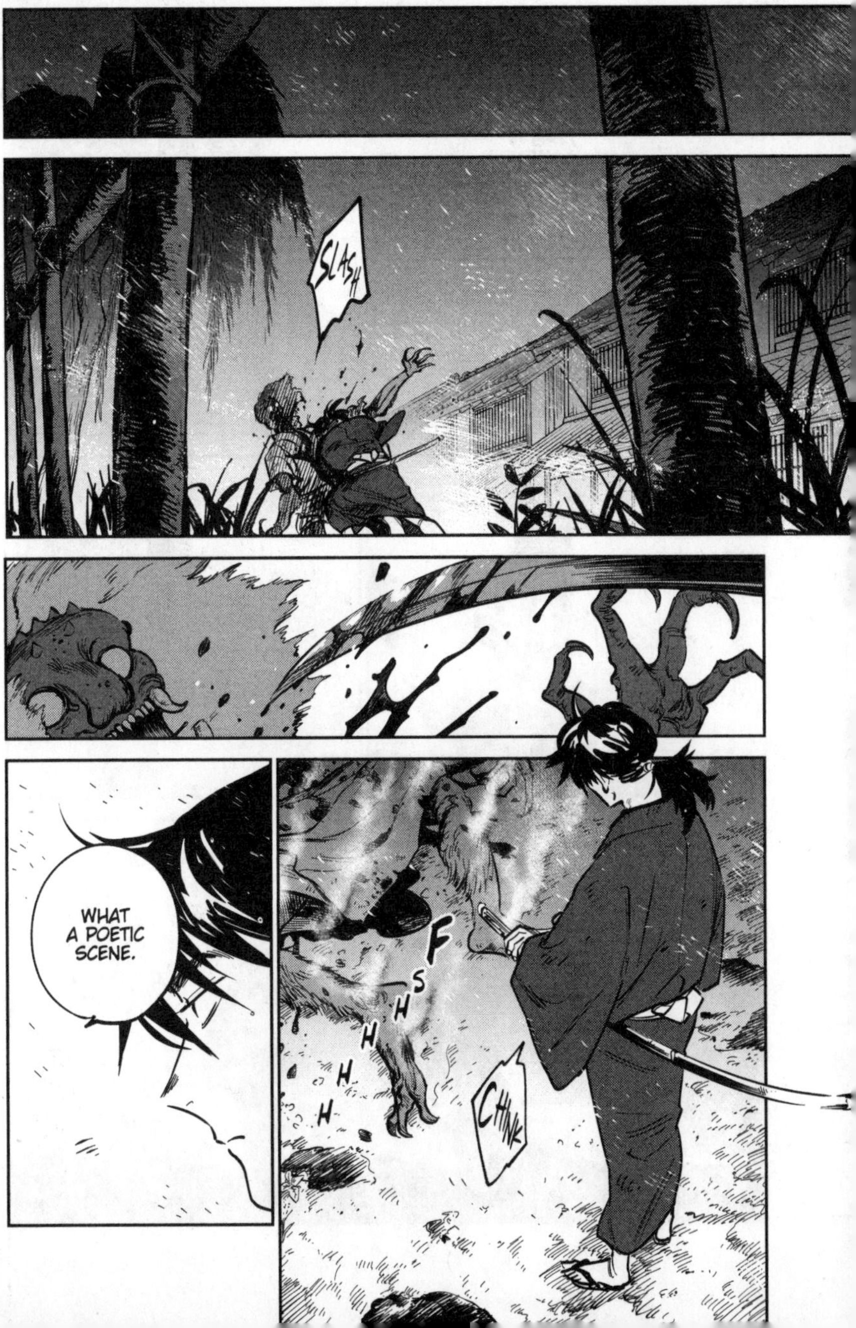
SLASH
FSHHHH
CHINK
WHAT A POETIC SCENE.

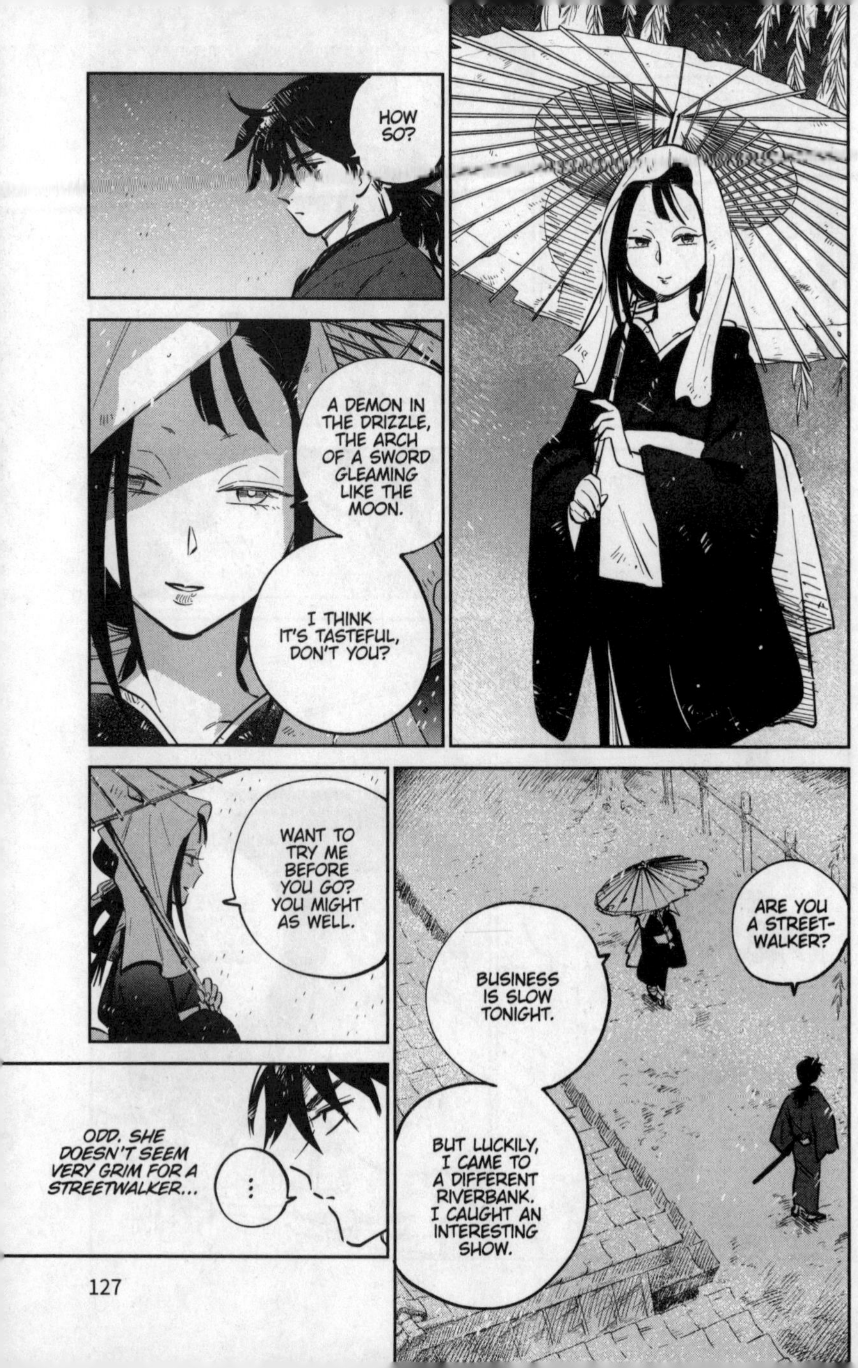
HOW SO?
A DEMON IN THE DRIZZLE, THE ARCH OF A SWORD GLEAMING LIKE THE MOON.
I THINK IT'S TASTEFUL, DON'T YOU?
ARE YOU A STREET-WALKER?
BUSINESS IS SLOW TONIGHT.
BUT LUCKILY, I CAME TO A DIFFERENT RIVERBANK. I CAUGHT AN INTERESTING SHOW.
WANT TO TRY ME BEFORE YOU GO? YOU MIGHT AS WELL.
...
ODD. SHE DOESN'T SEEM VERY GRIM FOR A STREETWALKER...

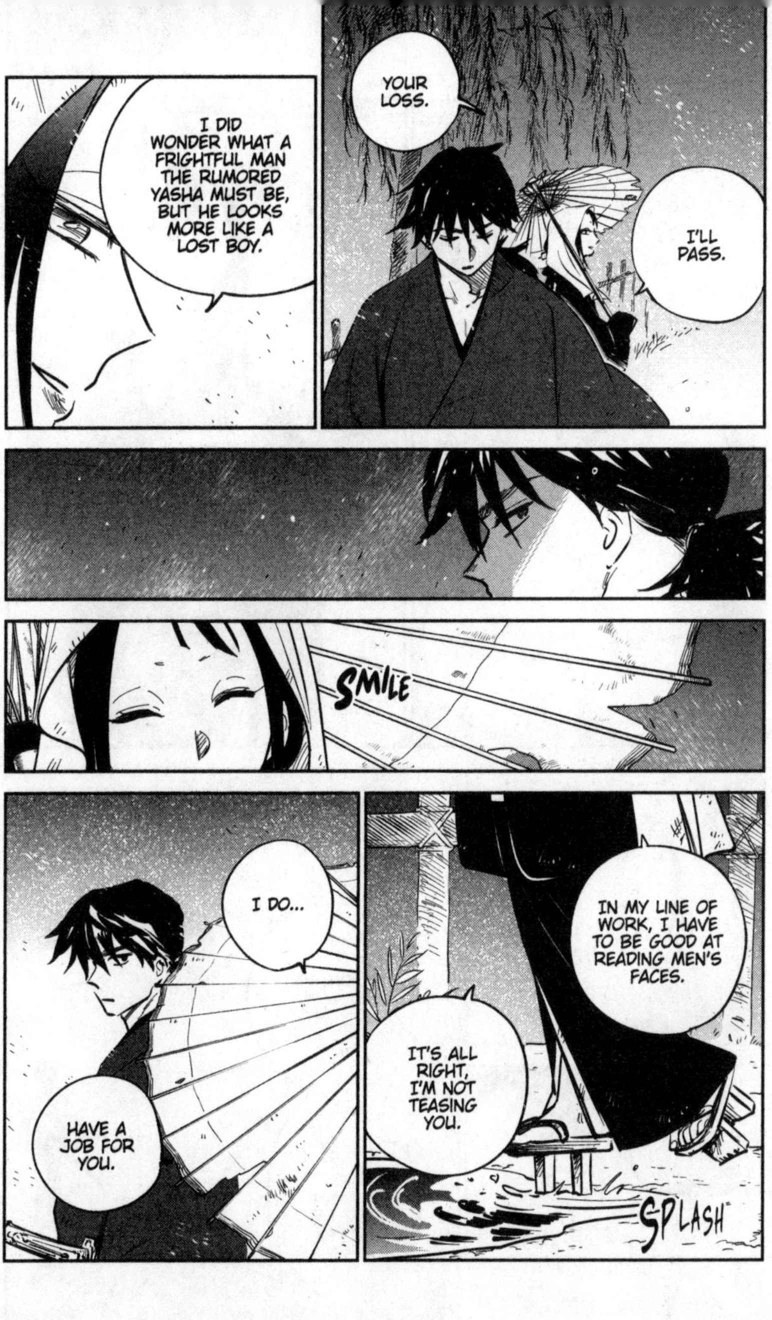
I'LL PASS.
YOUR LOSS.
I DID WONDER WHAT A FRIGHTFUL MAN THE RUMORED YASHA MUST BE, BUT HE LOOKS MORE LIKE A LOST BOY.
SMILE
IN MY LINE OF WORK, I HAVE TO BE GOOD AT READING MEN'S FACES.
IT'S ALL RIGHT, I'M NOT TEASING YOU.
SPLASH
I DO...
HAVE A JOB FOR YOU.

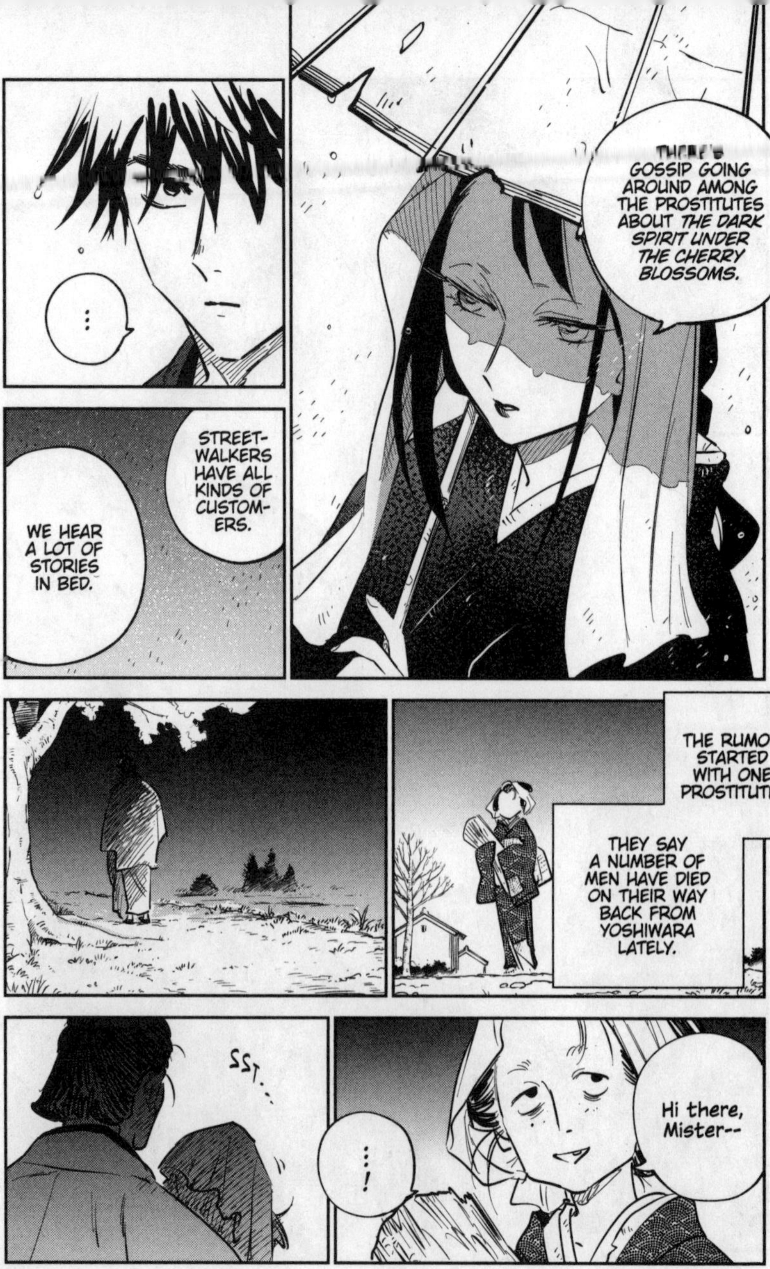
THERE'S GOSSIP GOING AROUND AMONG THE PROSTITUTES ABOUT *THE DARK SPIRIT UNDER THE CHERRY BLOSSOMS.*
...
STREET-WALKERS HAVE ALL KINDS OF CUSTOM-ERS.
WE HEAR A LOT OF STORIES IN BED.
THE RUMOR STARTED WITH ONE PROSTITUTE.
THEY SAY A NUMBER OF MEN HAVE DIED ON THEIR WAY BACK FROM YOSHIWARA LATELY.
Hi there, Mister--
...!
SST...

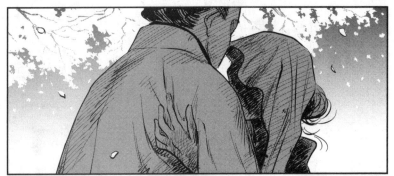

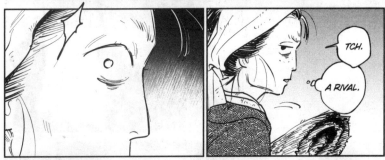

TCH.

A RIVAL.

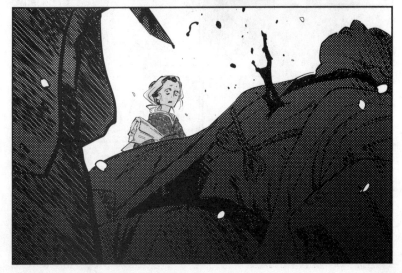

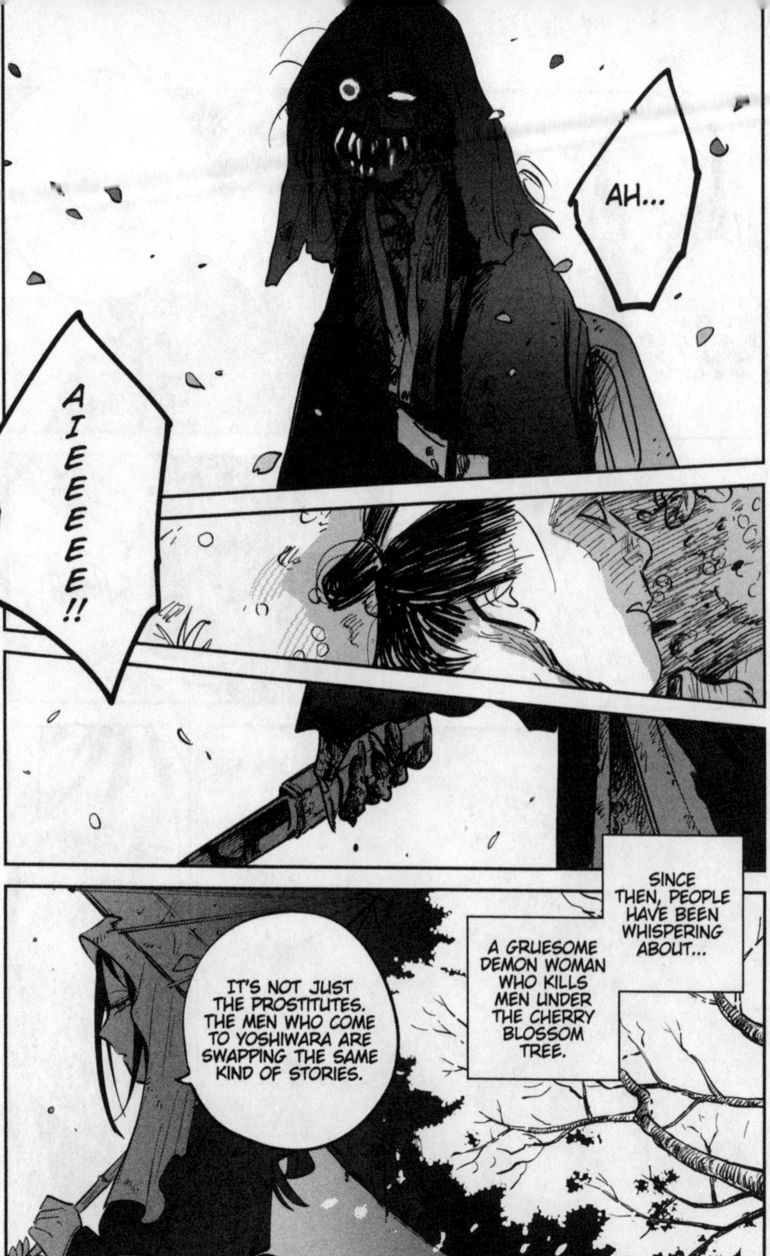
AH...
AIEEEEEE!!
SINCE THEN, PEOPLE HAVE BEEN WHISPERING ABOUT...
A GRUESOME DEMON WOMAN WHO KILLS MEN UNDER THE CHERRY BLOSSOM TREE.
IT'S NOT JUST THE PROSTITUTES. THE MEN WHO COME TO YOSHIWARA ARE SWAPPING THE SAME KIND OF STORIES.

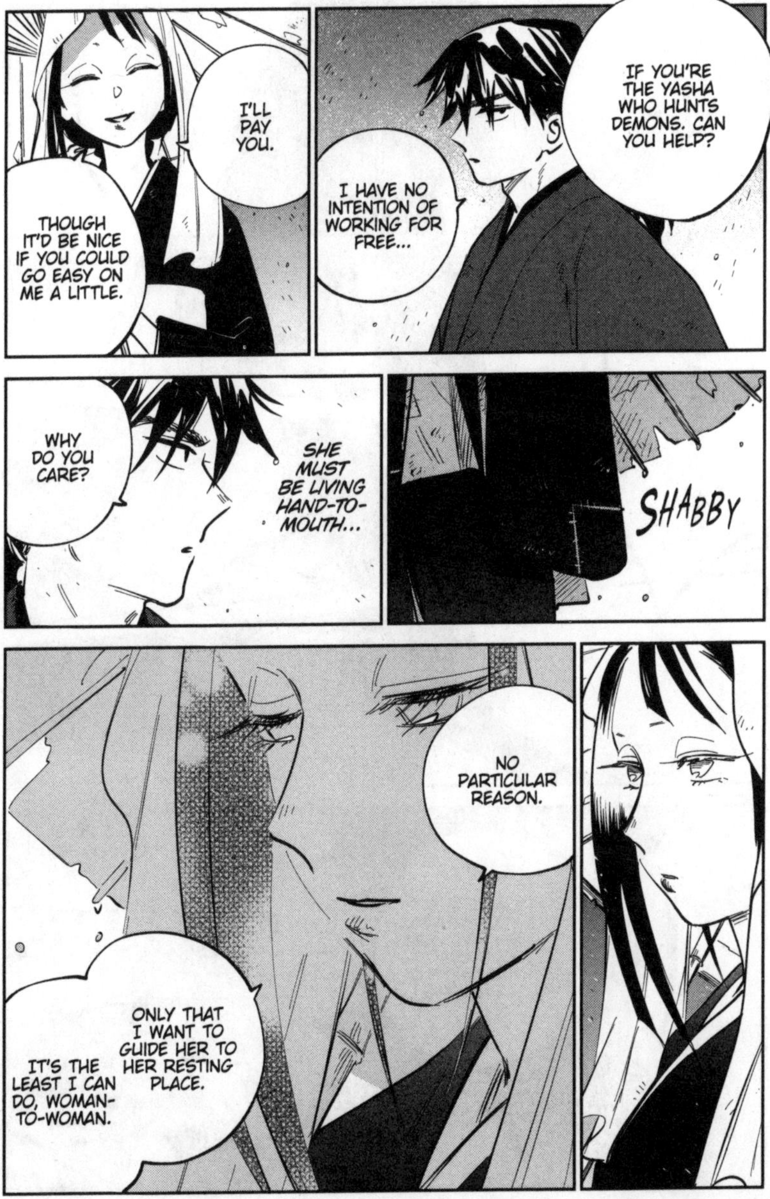
IF YOU'RE THE YASHA WHO HUNTS DEMONS. CAN YOU HELP?
I HAVE NO INTENTION OF WORKING FOR FREE...
I'LL PAY YOU.
THOUGH IT'D BE NICE IF YOU COULD GO EASY ON ME A LITTLE.
SHABBY
SHE MUST BE LIVING HAND-TO-MOUTH...
WHY DO YOU CARE?
NO PARTICULAR REASON.
ONLY THAT I WANT TO GUIDE HER TO HER RESTING PLACE.
IT'S THE LEAST I CAN DO, WOMAN-TO-WOMAN.

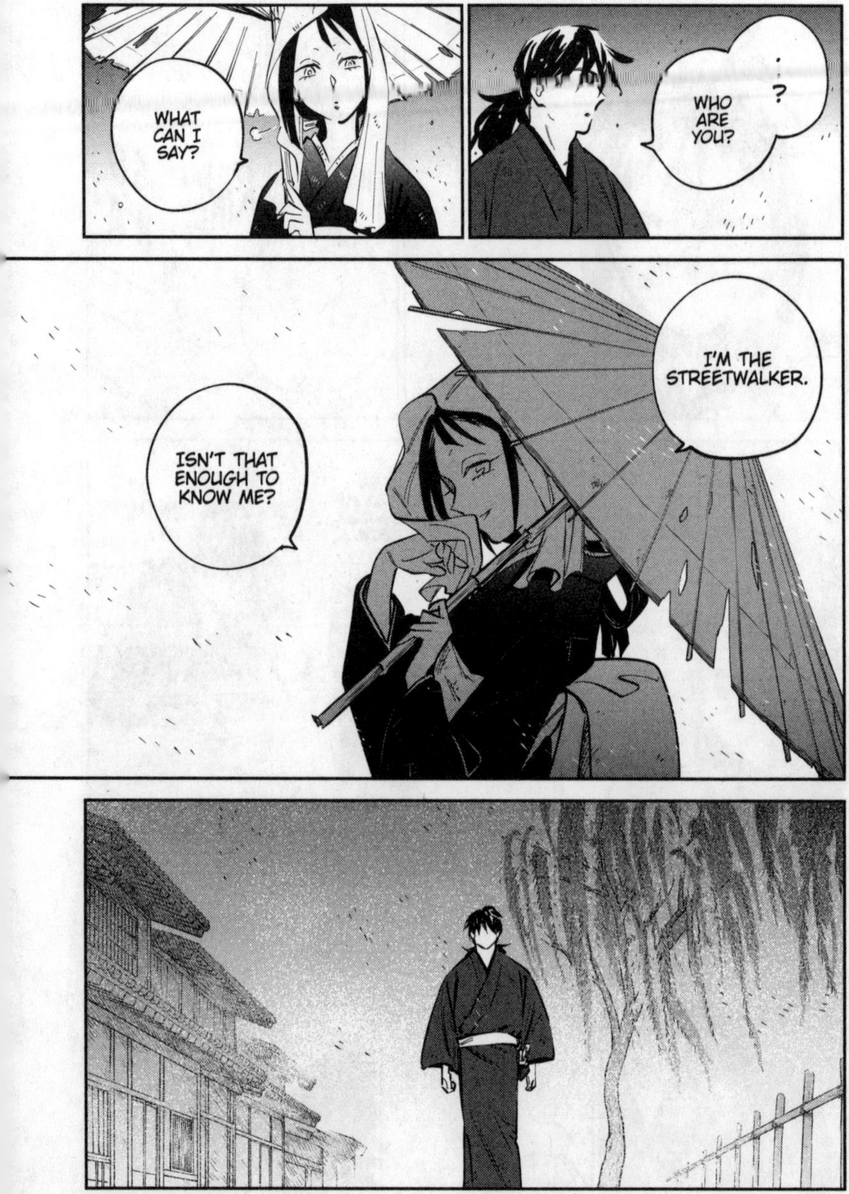
?
WHO ARE YOU?
WHAT CAN I SAY?
I'M THE STREETWALKER.
ISN'T THAT ENOUGH TO KNOW ME?

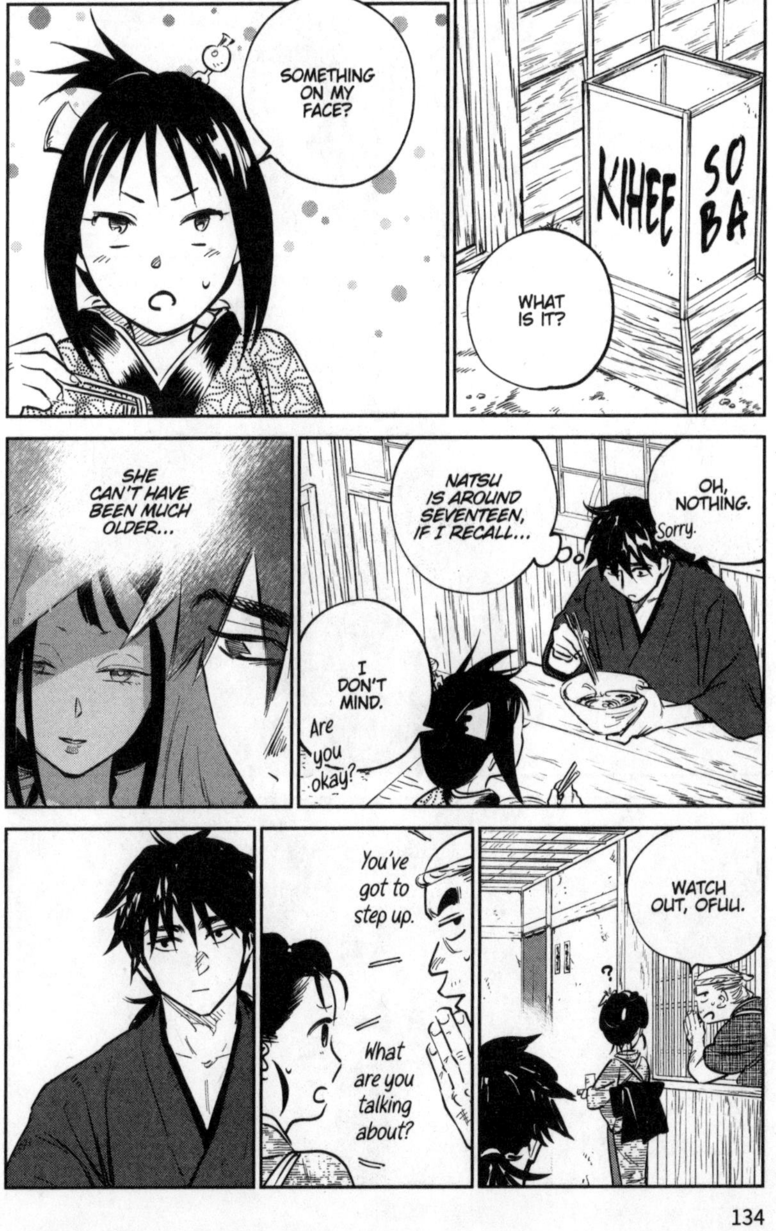
SO
BA
KIHEE
WHAT IS IT?
SOMETHING ON MY FACE?
OH, NOTHING.
Sorry.
NATSU IS AROUND SEVENTEEN, IF I RECALL...
I DON'T MIND.
Are you okay?
SHE CAN'T HAVE BEEN MUCH OLDER...
WATCH OUT, OFUU.
You've got to step up.
What are you talking about?

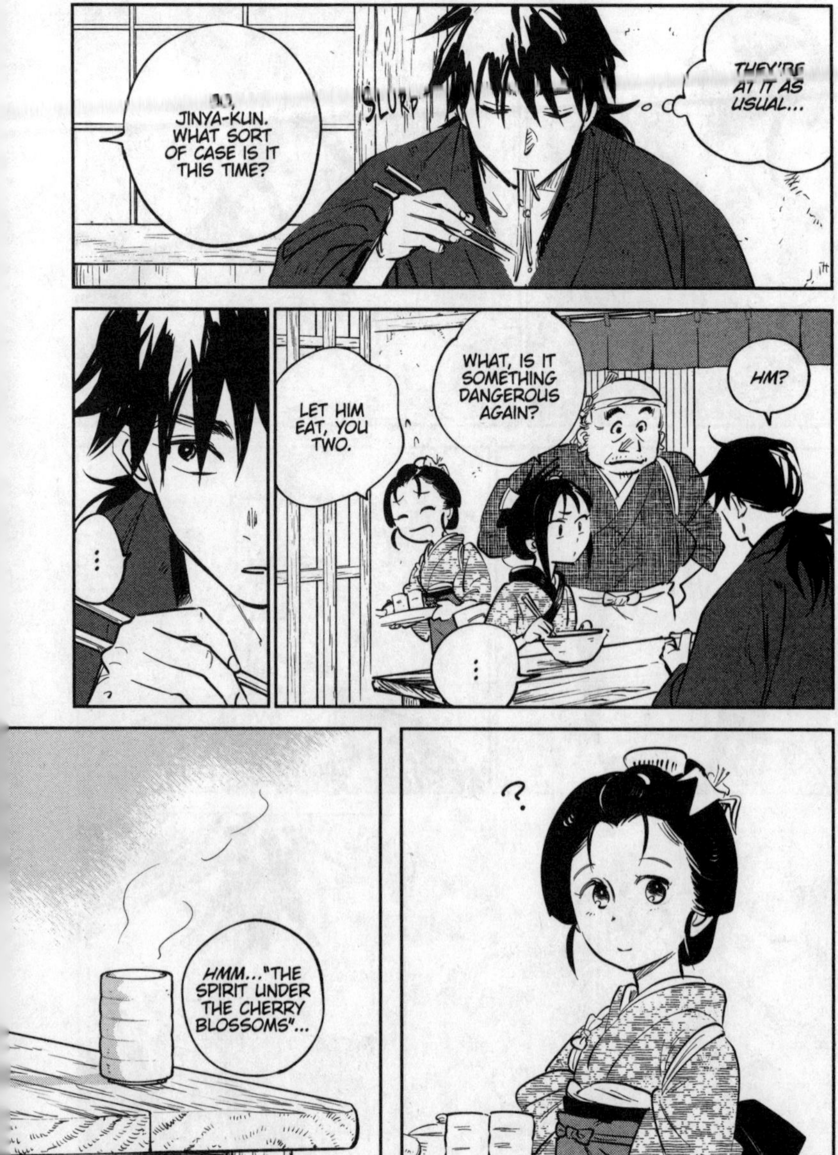
THEY'RE AT IT AS USUAL...
SLURP
SO, JINYA-KUN. WHAT SORT OF CASE IS IT THIS TIME?
HM?
WHAT, IS IT SOMETHING DANGEROUS AGAIN?
LET HIM EAT, YOU TWO.
...
...
?
HMM..."THE SPIRIT UNDER THE CHERRY BLOSSOMS"...

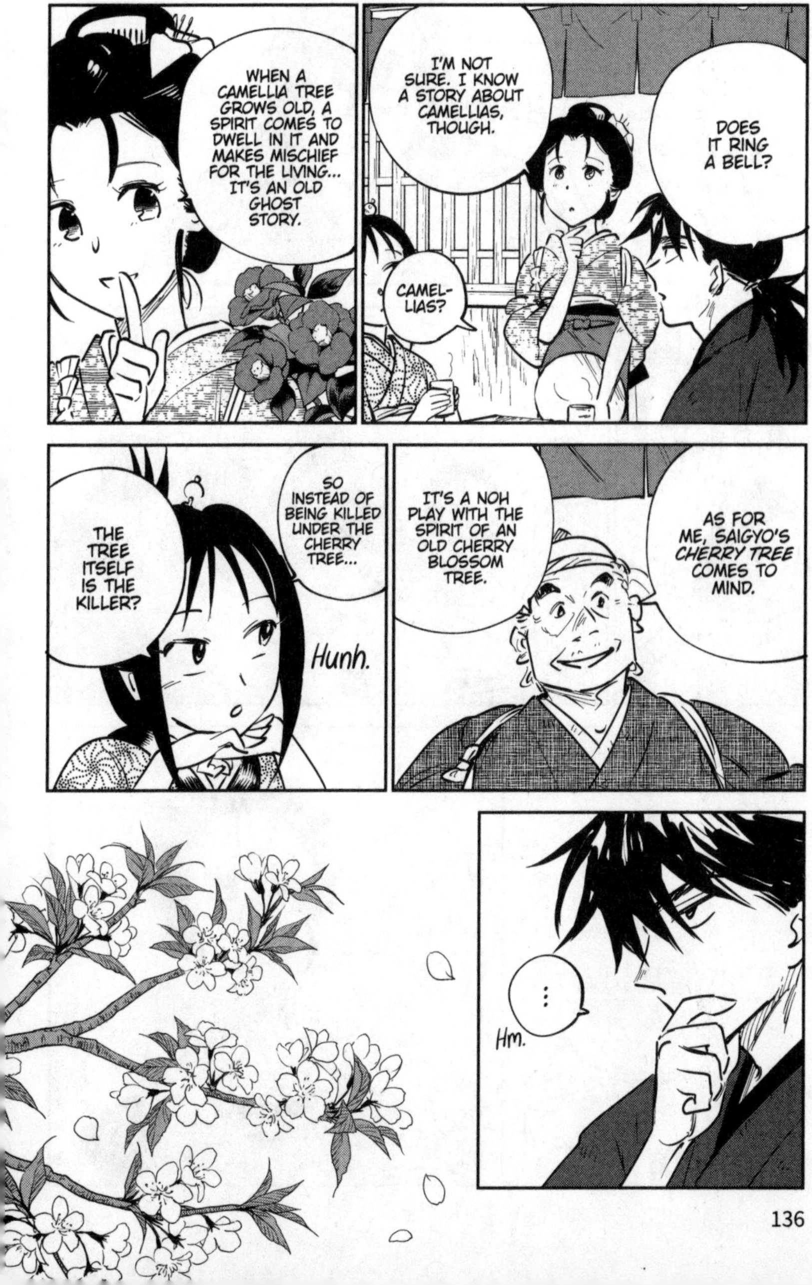
DOES IT RING A BELL?
I'M NOT SURE. I KNOW A STORY ABOUT CAMELLIAS, THOUGH.
CAMELLIAS?
WHEN A CAMELLIA TREE GROWS OLD, A SPIRIT COMES TO DWELL IN IT AND MAKES MISCHIEF FOR THE LIVING... IT'S AN OLD GHOST STORY.
AS FOR ME, SAIGYO'S *CHERRY TREE* COMES TO MIND.
IT'S A NOH PLAY WITH THE SPIRIT OF AN OLD CHERRY BLOSSOM TREE.
SO INSTEAD OF BEING KILLED UNDER THE CHERRY TREE...
THE TREE ITSELF IS THE KILLER?
Hunh.
...
Hm.

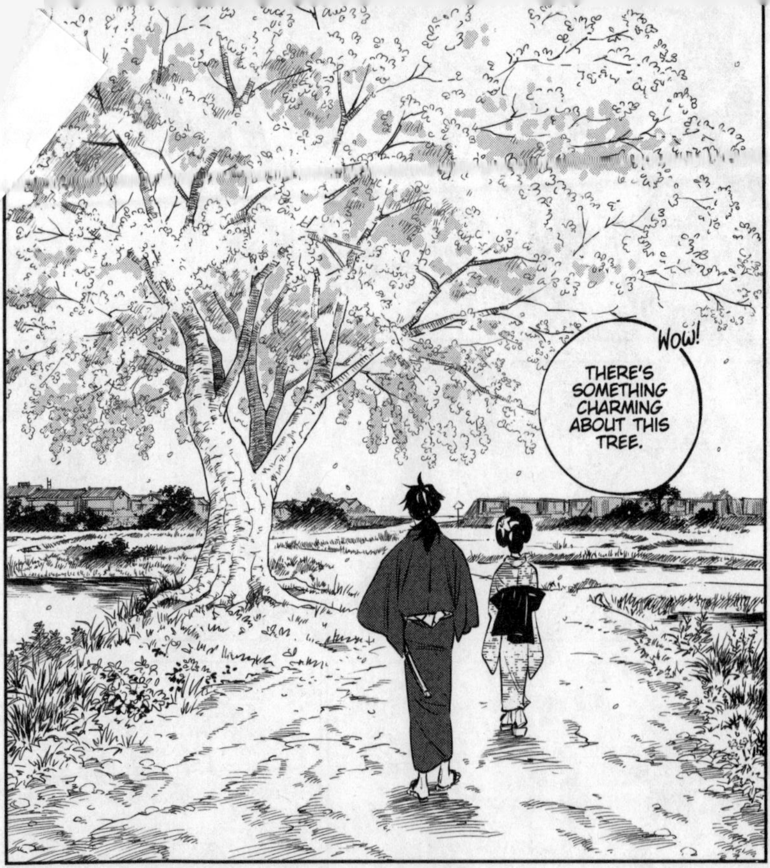
WOW!
THERE'S SOMETHING CHARMING ABOUT THIS TREE.

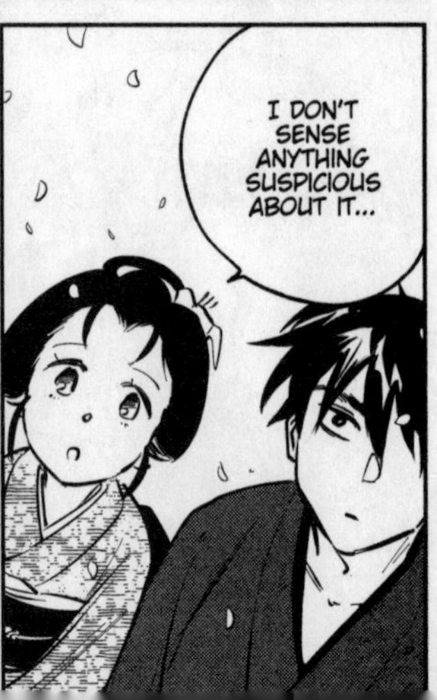
I DON'T SENSE ANYTHING SUSPICIOUS ABOUT IT...

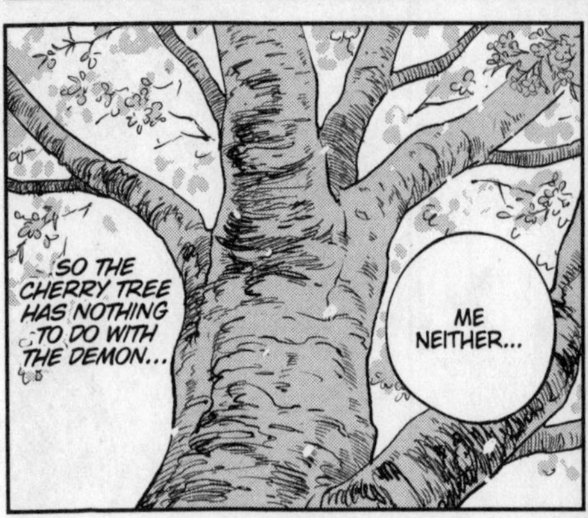
ME NEITHER...
SO THE CHERRY TREE HAS NOTHING TO DO WITH THE DEMON...

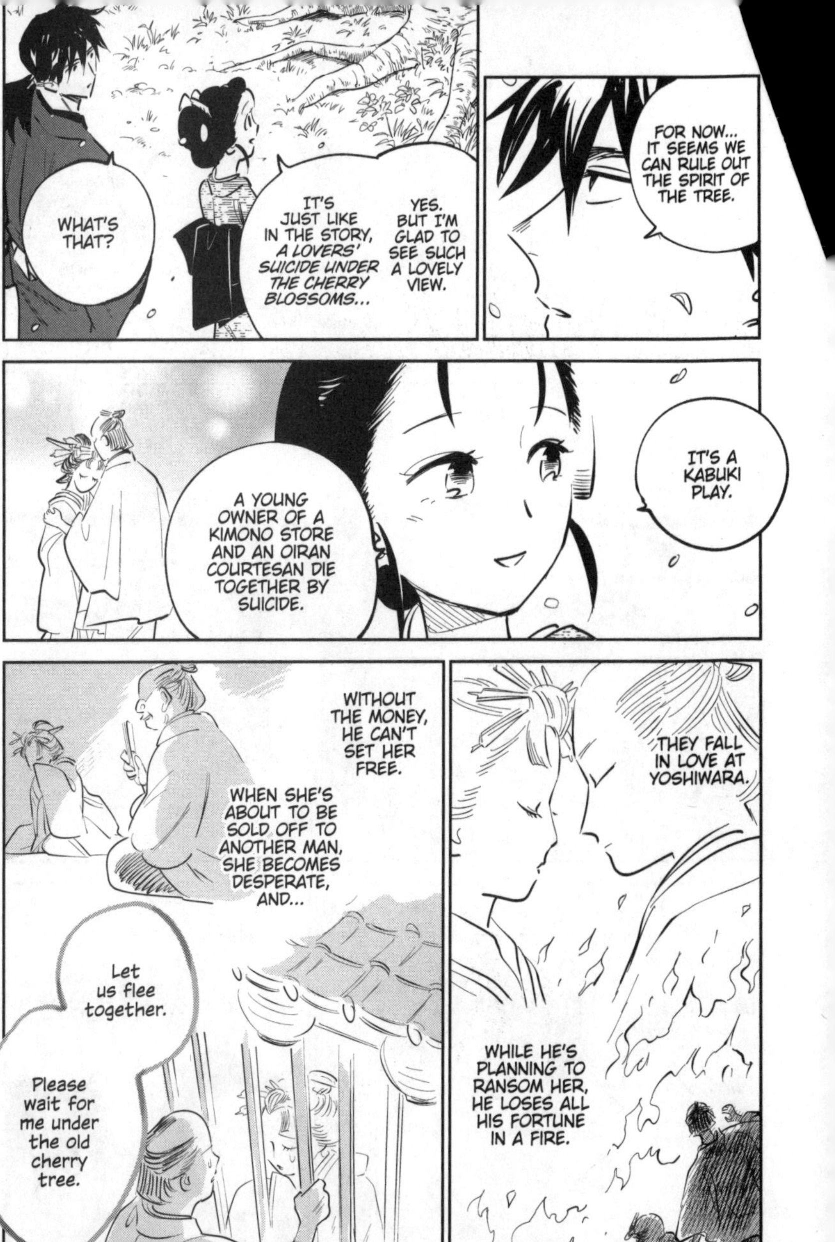
FOR NOW... IT SEEMS WE CAN RULE OUT THE SPIRIT OF THE TREE.
YES. BUT I'M GLAD TO SEE SUCH A LOVELY VIEW.
IT'S JUST LIKE IN THE STORY, *A LOVERS' SUICIDE UNDER THE CHERRY BLOSSOMS*...
WHAT'S THAT?
IT'S A KABUKI PLAY.
A YOUNG OWNER OF A KIMONO STORE AND AN OIRAN COURTESAN DIE TOGETHER BY SUICIDE.
THEY FALL IN LOVE AT YOSHIWARA.
WHILE HE'S PLANNING TO RANSOM HER, HE LOSES ALL HIS FORTUNE IN A FIRE.
WITHOUT THE MONEY, HE CAN'T SET HER FREE.
WHEN SHE'S ABOUT TO BE SOLD OFF TO ANOTHER MAN, SHE BECOMES DESPERATE, AND...
Let us flee together.
Please wait for me under the old cherry tree.

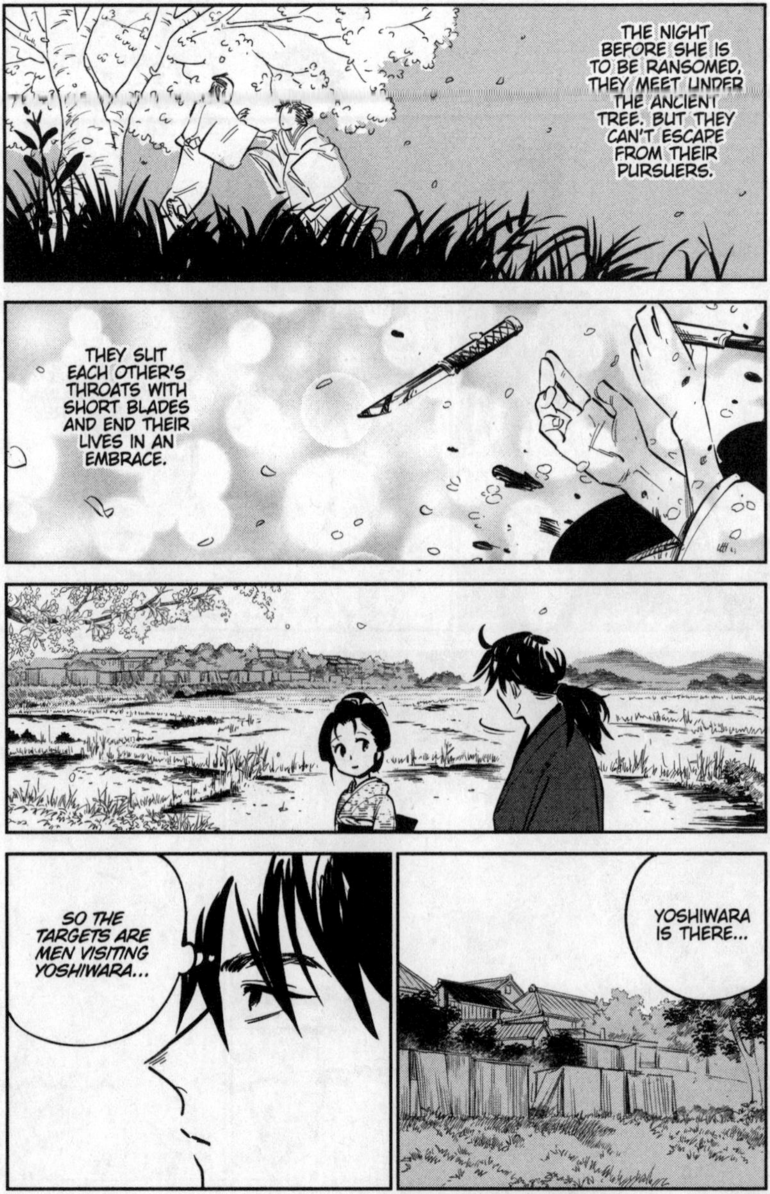
THE NIGHT BEFORE SHE IS TO BE RANSOMED, THEY MEET UNDER THE ANCIENT TREE. BUT THEY CAN'T ESCAPE FROM THEIR PURSUERS.
THEY SLIT EACH OTHER'S THROATS WITH SHORT BLADES AND END THEIR LIVES IN AN EMBRACE.
YOSHIWARA IS THERE...
SO THE TARGETS ARE MEN VISITING YOSHIWARA...

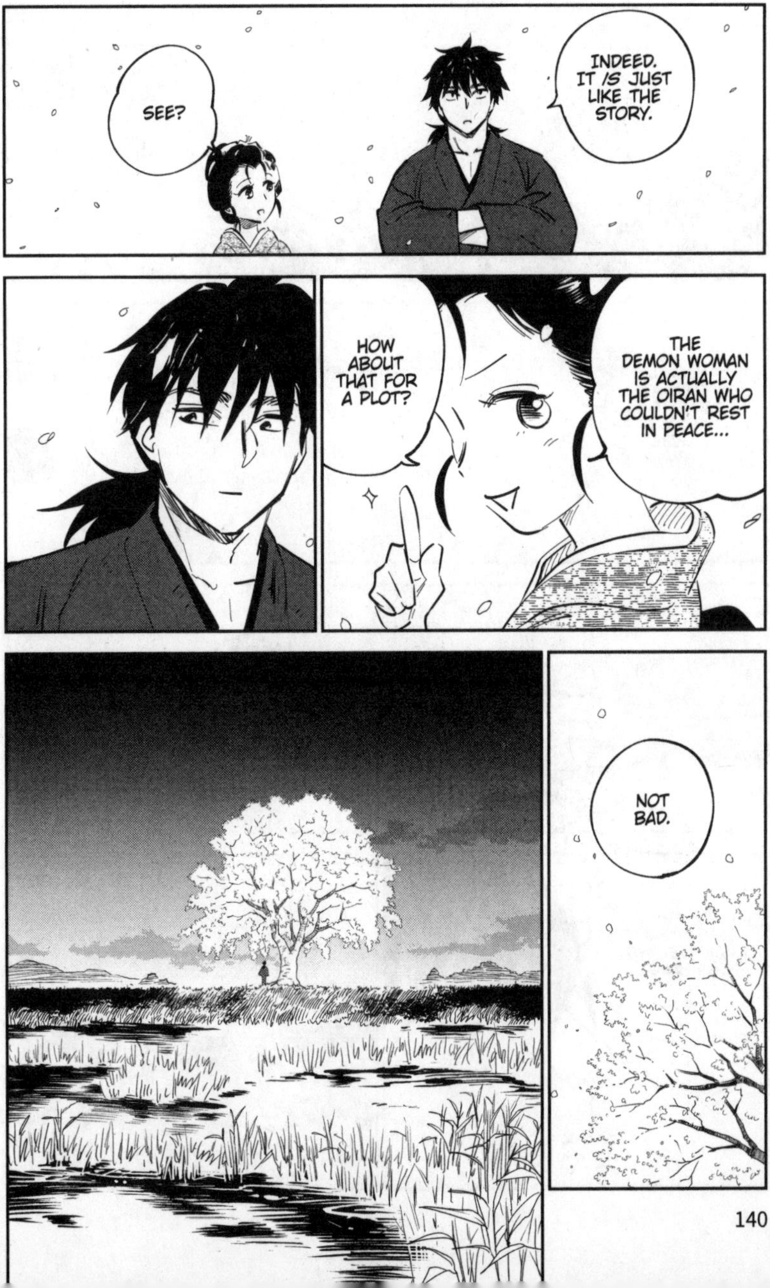
INDEED. IT *IS* JUST LIKE THE STORY.
SEE?
THE DEMON WOMAN IS ACTUALLY THE OIRAN WHO COULDN'T REST IN PEACE...
HOW ABOUT THAT FOR A PLOT?
NOT BAD.

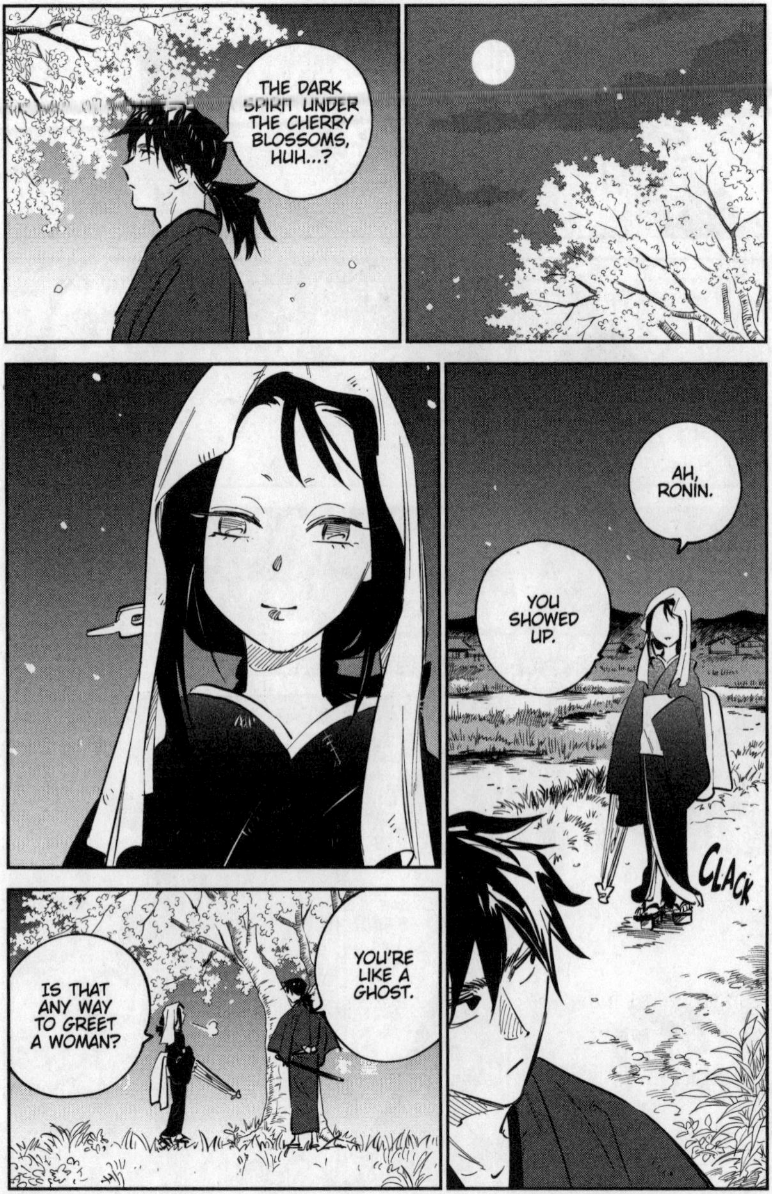
THE DARK SPIRIT UNDER THE CHERRY BLOSSOMS, HUH...?
AH, RONIN.
YOU SHOWED UP.
CLACK
YOU'RE LIKE A GHOST.
IS THAT ANY WAY TO GREET A WOMAN?

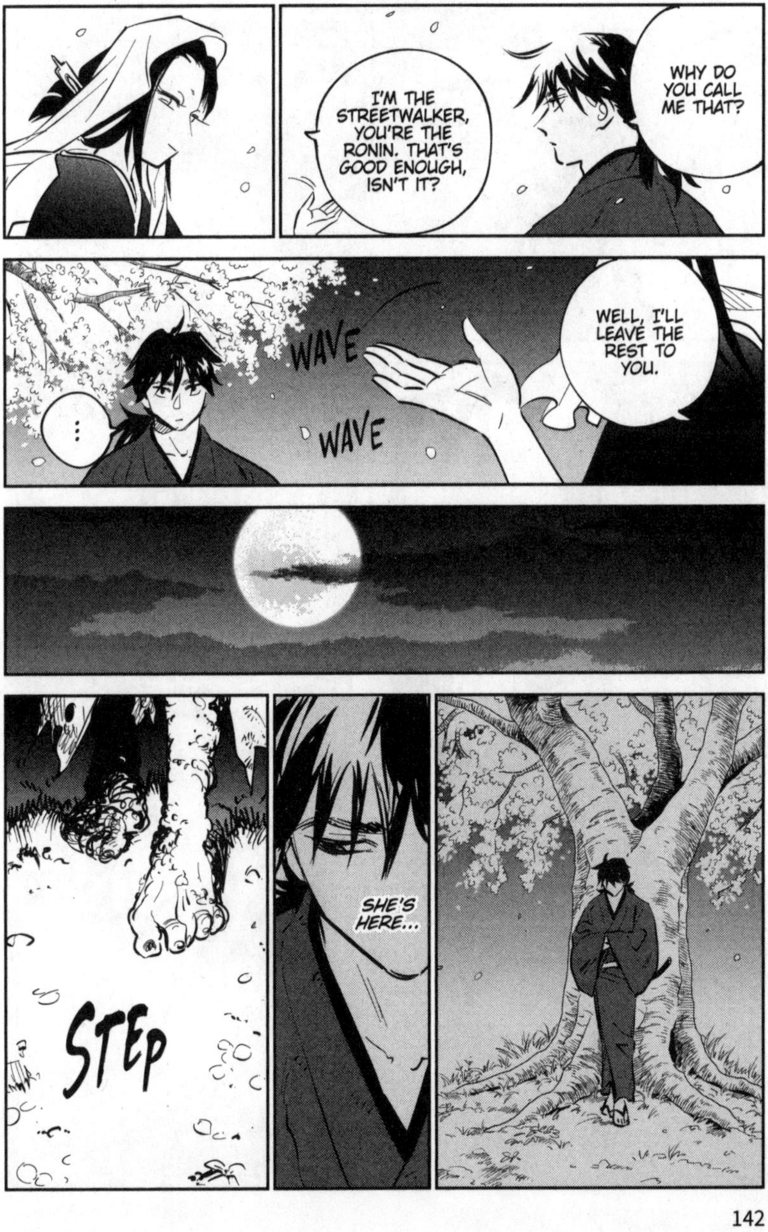
WHY DO YOU CALL ME THAT?
I'M THE STREETWALKER, YOU'RE THE RONIN. THAT'S GOOD ENOUGH, ISN'T IT?
WELL, I'LL LEAVE THE REST TO YOU.
WAVE
WAVE
...
SHE'S HERE...
STEP

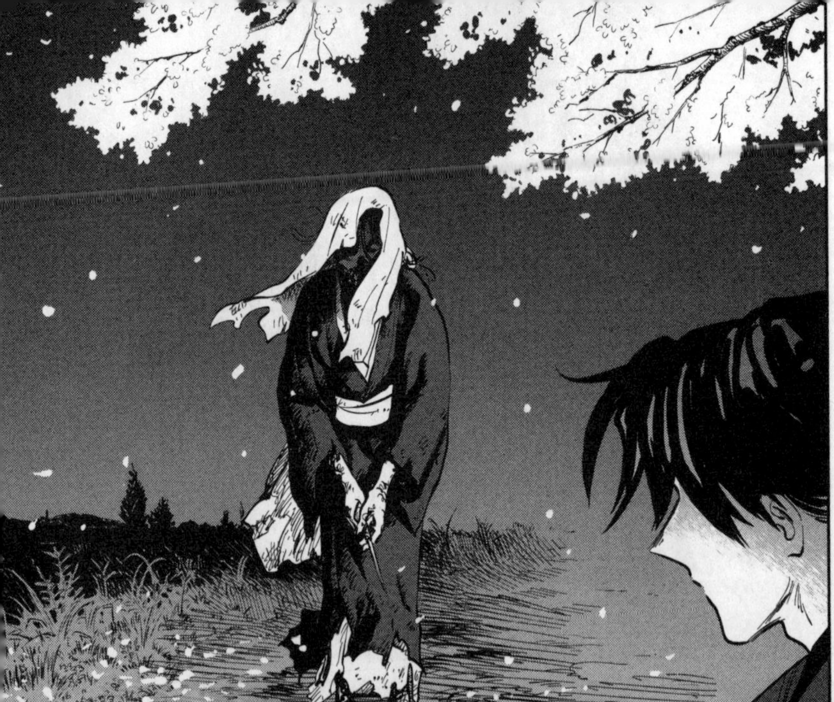
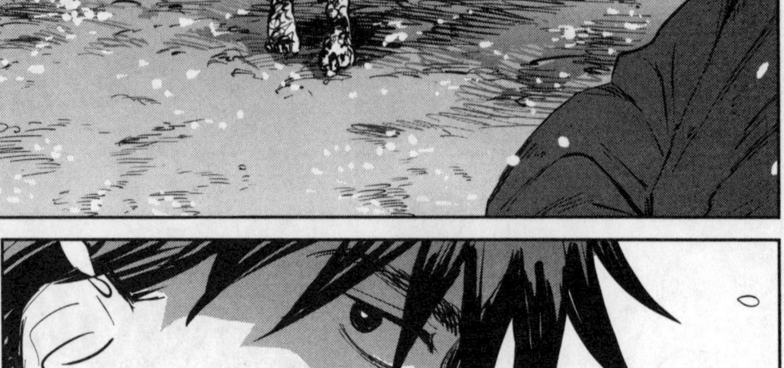

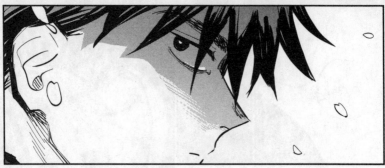

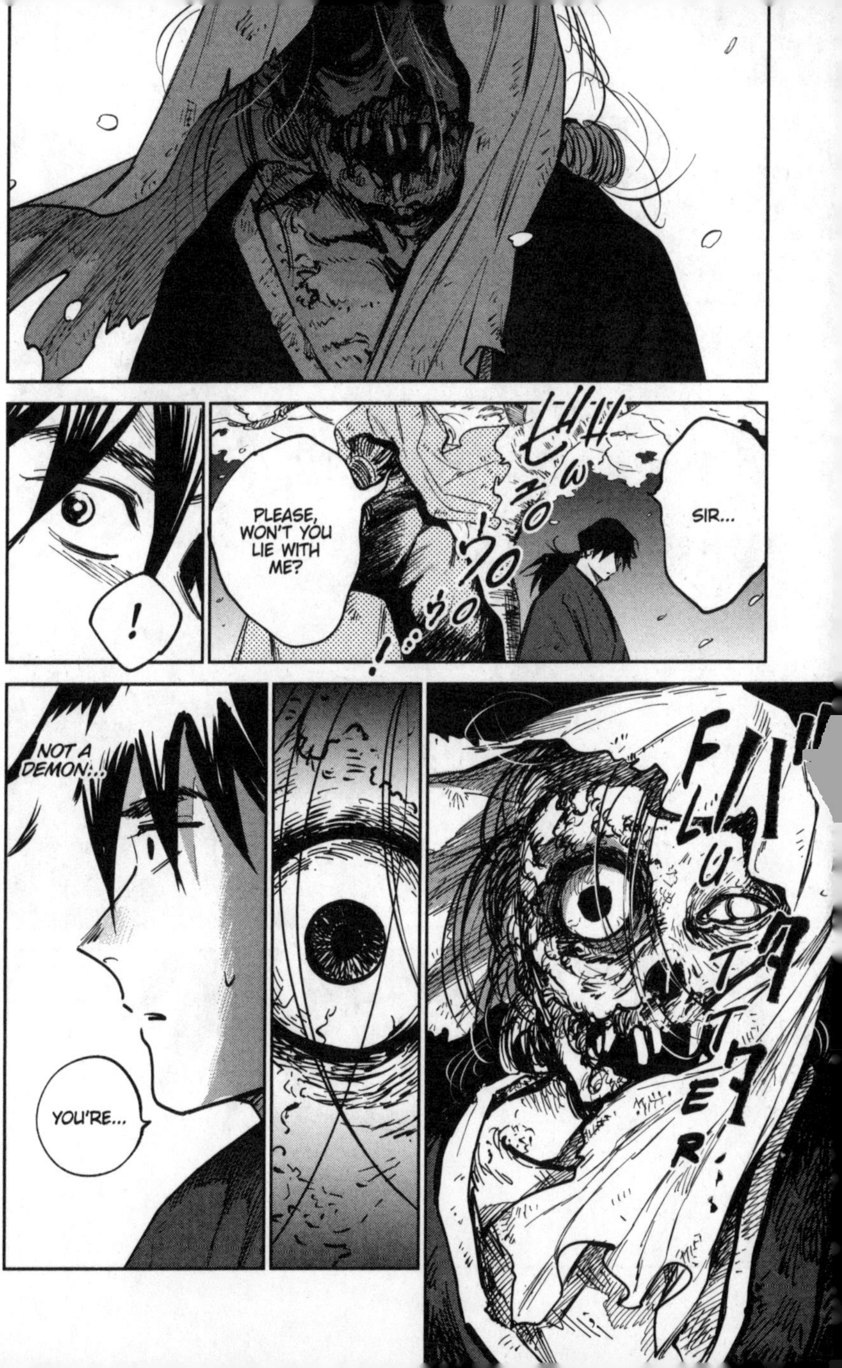
SIR...
PLEASE, WON'T YOU LIE WITH ME?
!
FLUTTER
NOT A DEMON...
YOU'RE...

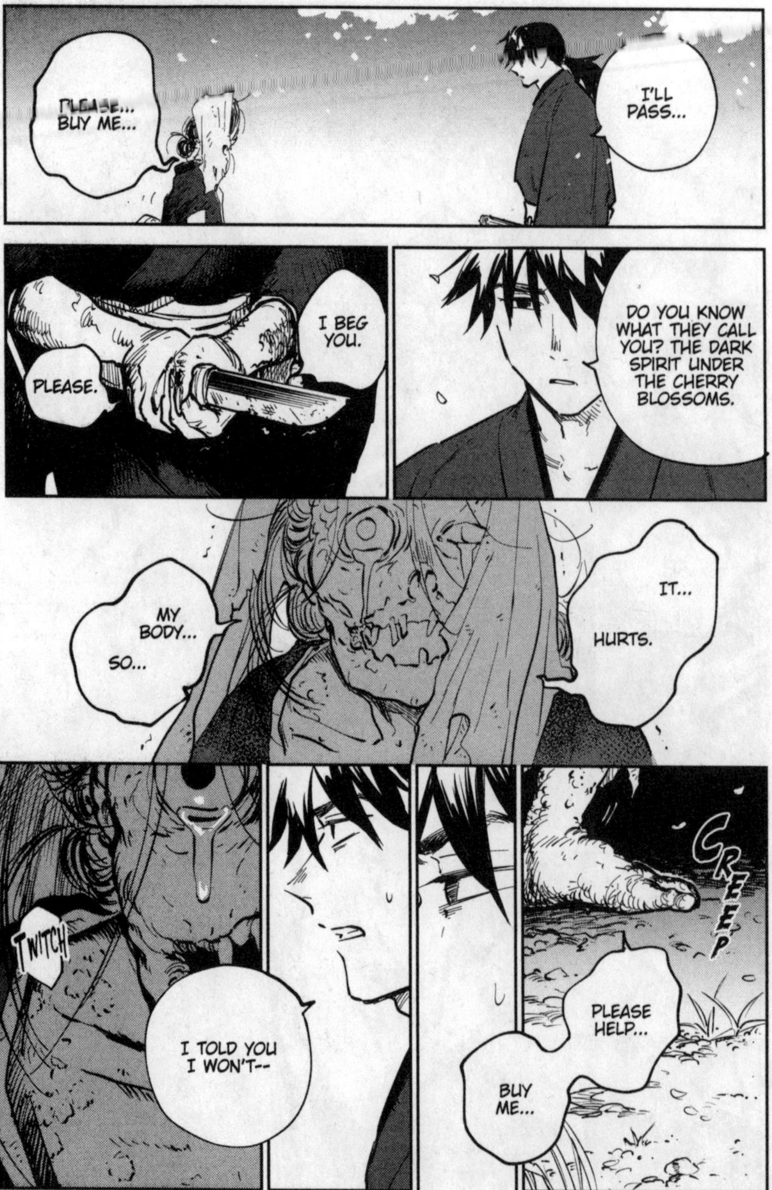
I'LL PASS...
PLEASE... BUY ME...
DO YOU KNOW WHAT THEY CALL YOU? THE DARK SPIRIT UNDER THE CHERRY BLOSSOMS.
I BEG YOU.
PLEASE.
IT... HURTS.
MY BODY... SO...
CREEP
PLEASE HELP...
BUY ME...
TWITCH
I TOLD YOU I WON'T--

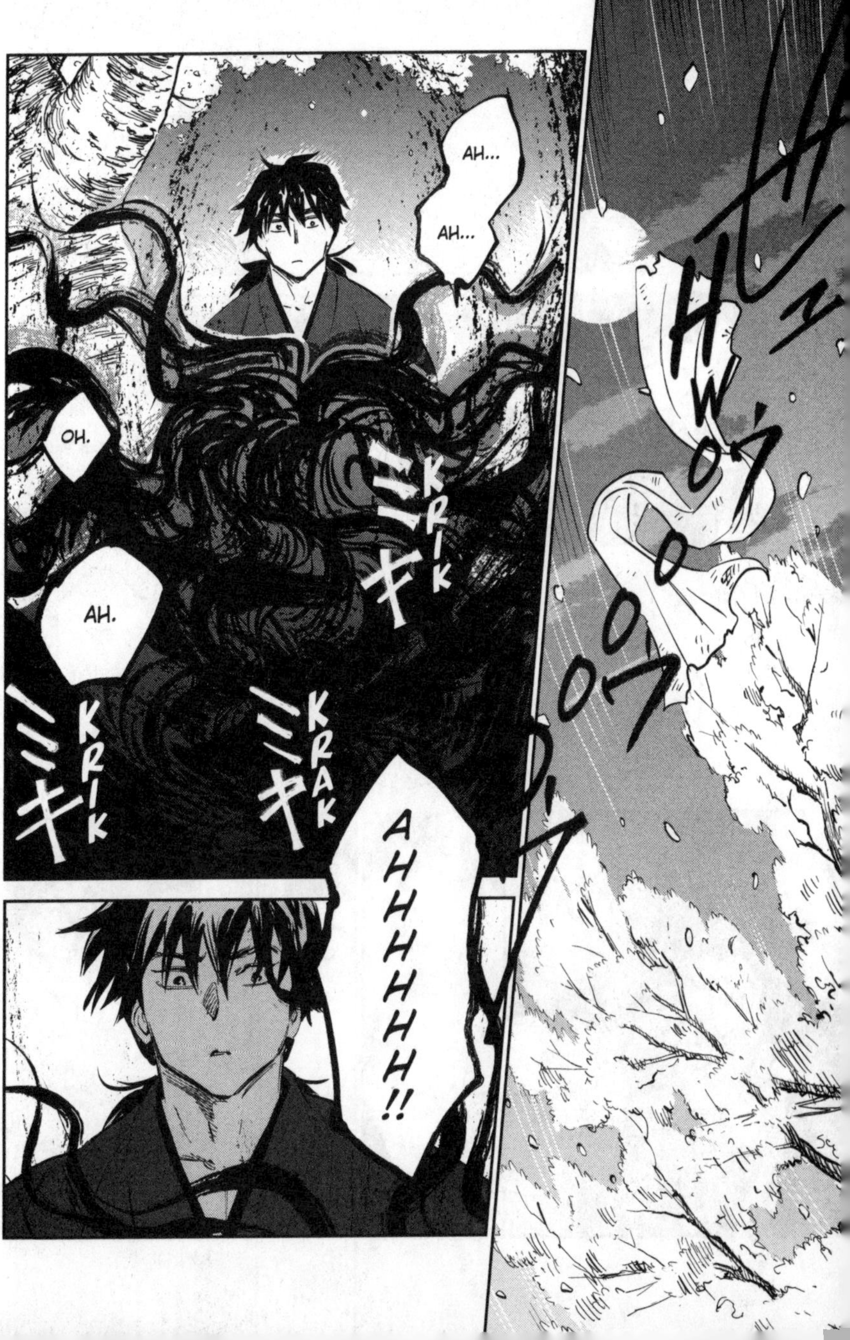
HWOOOOOO
AH...
AH...
OH.
KRIK
AH.
KRAK
KRIK
AHHHHHHH!!

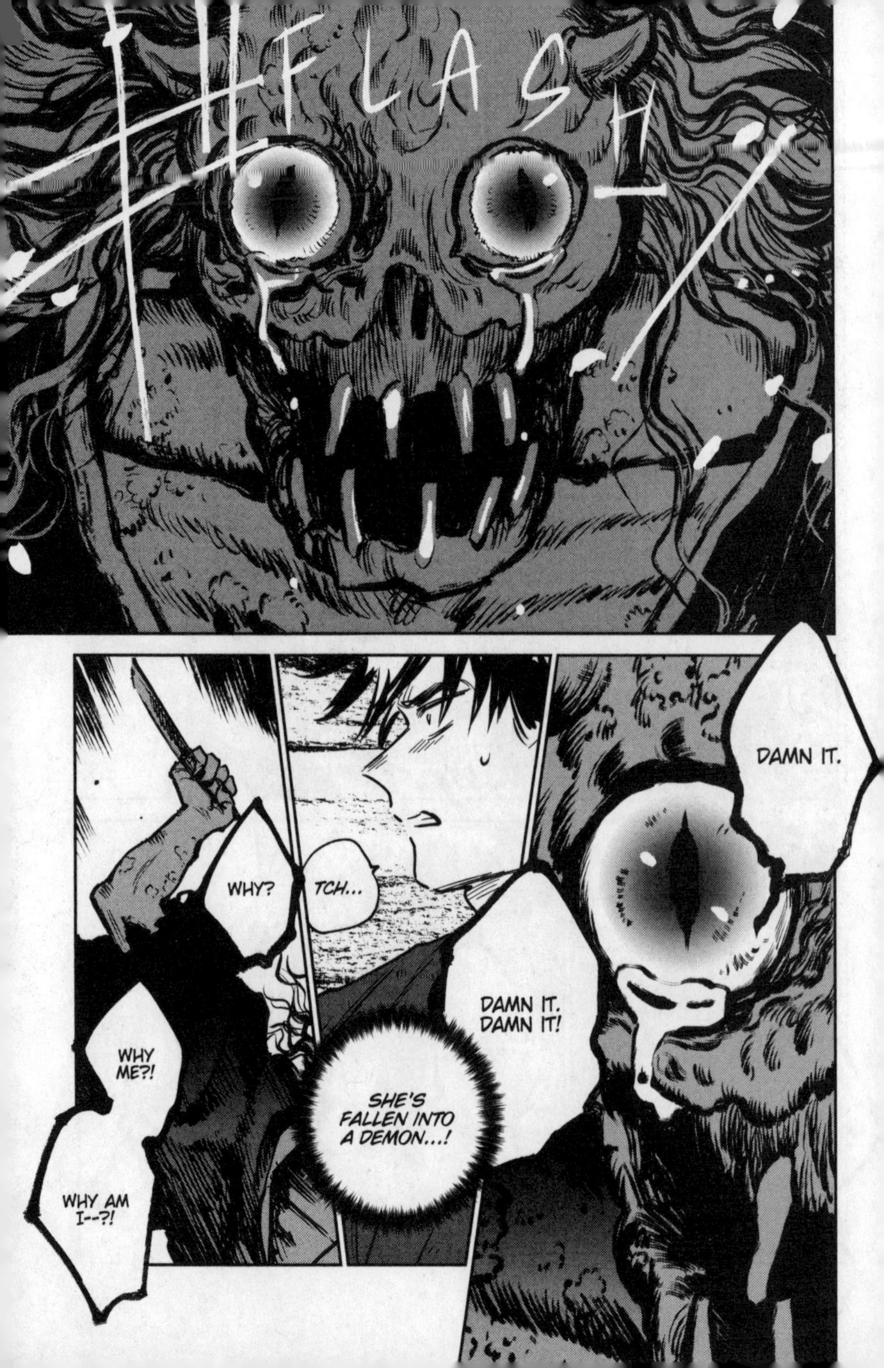
FLASH
DAMN IT.
DAMN IT. DAMN IT!
TCH...
SHE'S FALLEN INTO A DEMON...!
WHY?
WHY ME?!
WHY AM I--?!

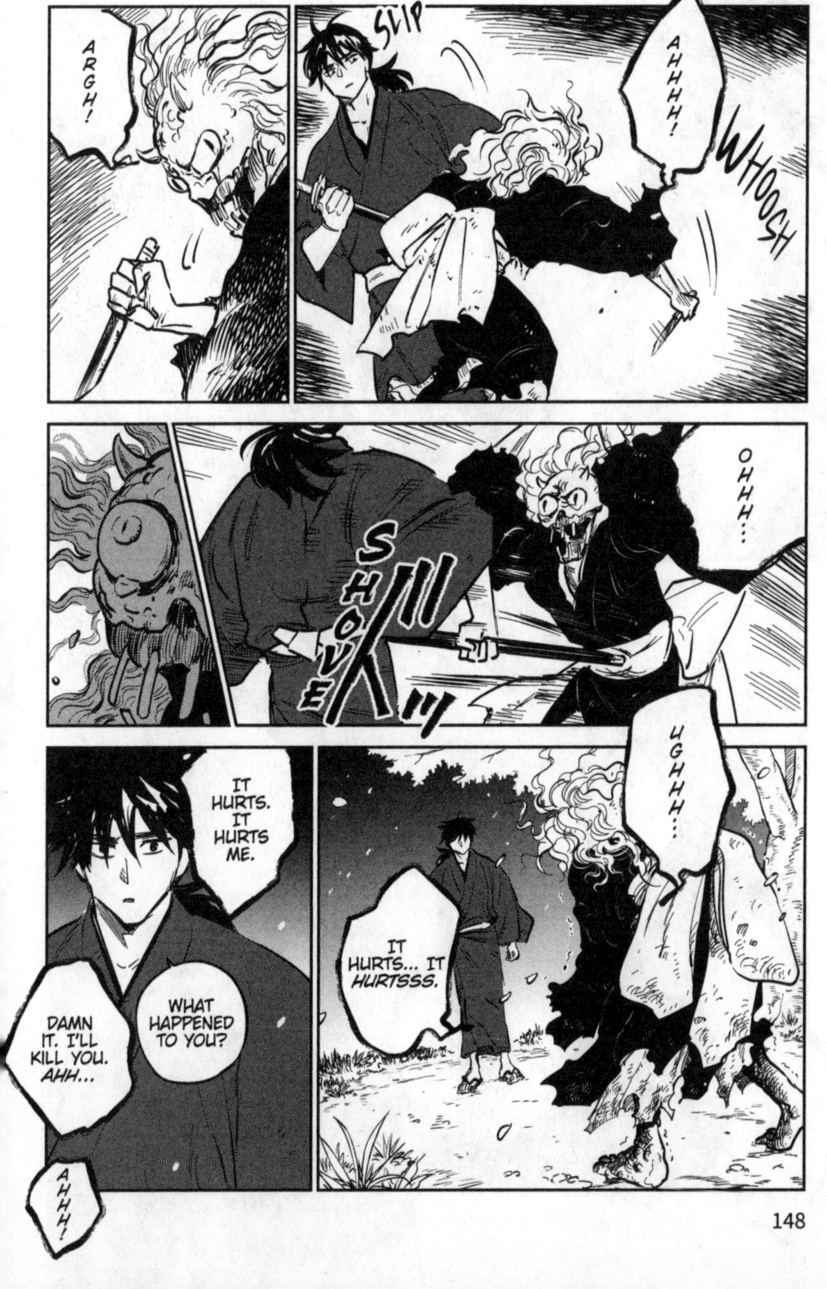
SLIP
AHHHH!
WHOOSH
ARGH!
OHHH...
SHOVE
UGHHH...
IT HURTS... IT HURTSSS.
IT HURTS. IT HURTS ME.
WHAT HAPPENED TO YOU?
DAMN IT. I'LL KILL YOU. AHH...
AHHH!

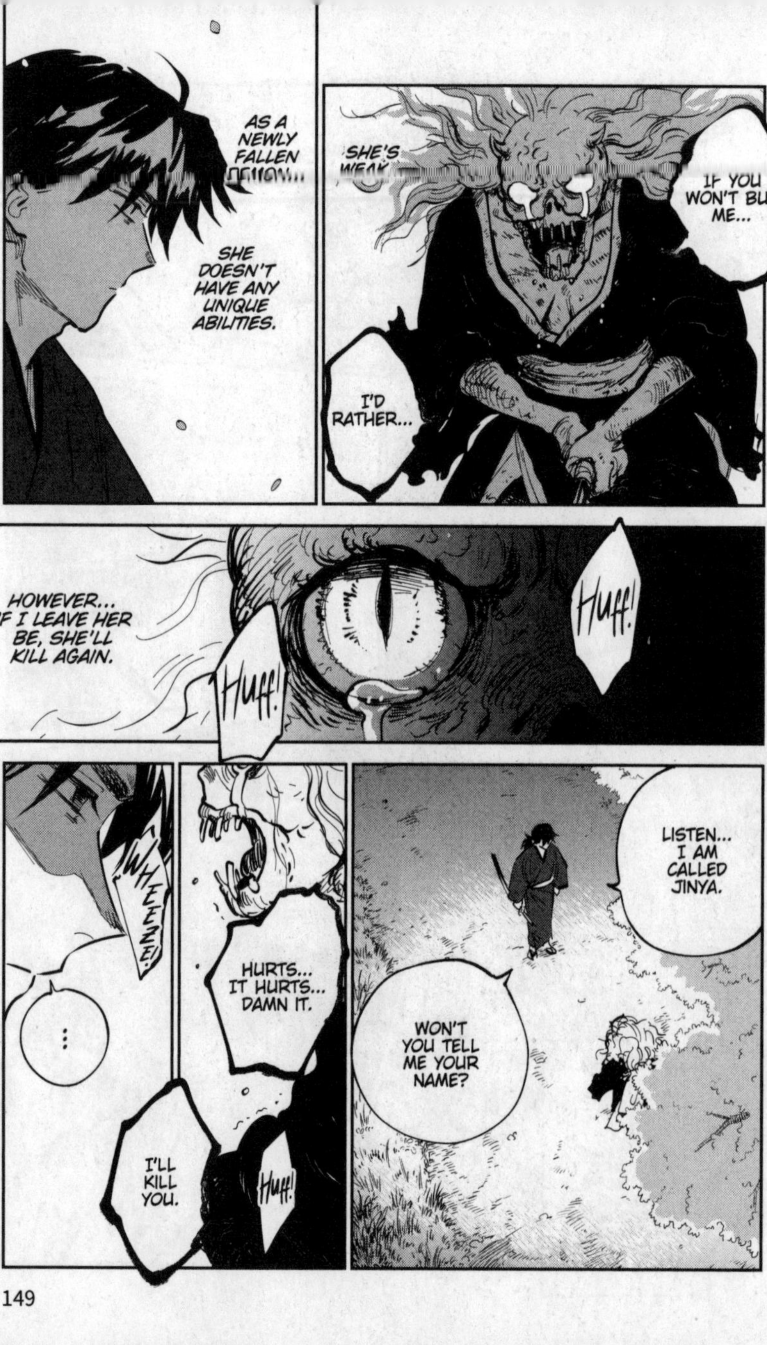
IF YOU WON'T BUY ME...
SHE'S
I'D RATHER...
AS A NEWLY FALLEN
SHE DOESN'T HAVE ANY UNIQUE ABILITIES.
Huff!
Huff!
HOWEVER... IF I LEAVE HER BE, SHE'LL KILL AGAIN.
LISTEN... I AM CALLED JINYA.
WON'T YOU TELL ME YOUR NAME?
HURTS... IT HURTS... DAMN IT.
Huff!
I'LL KILL YOU.
WHEEZE!
...

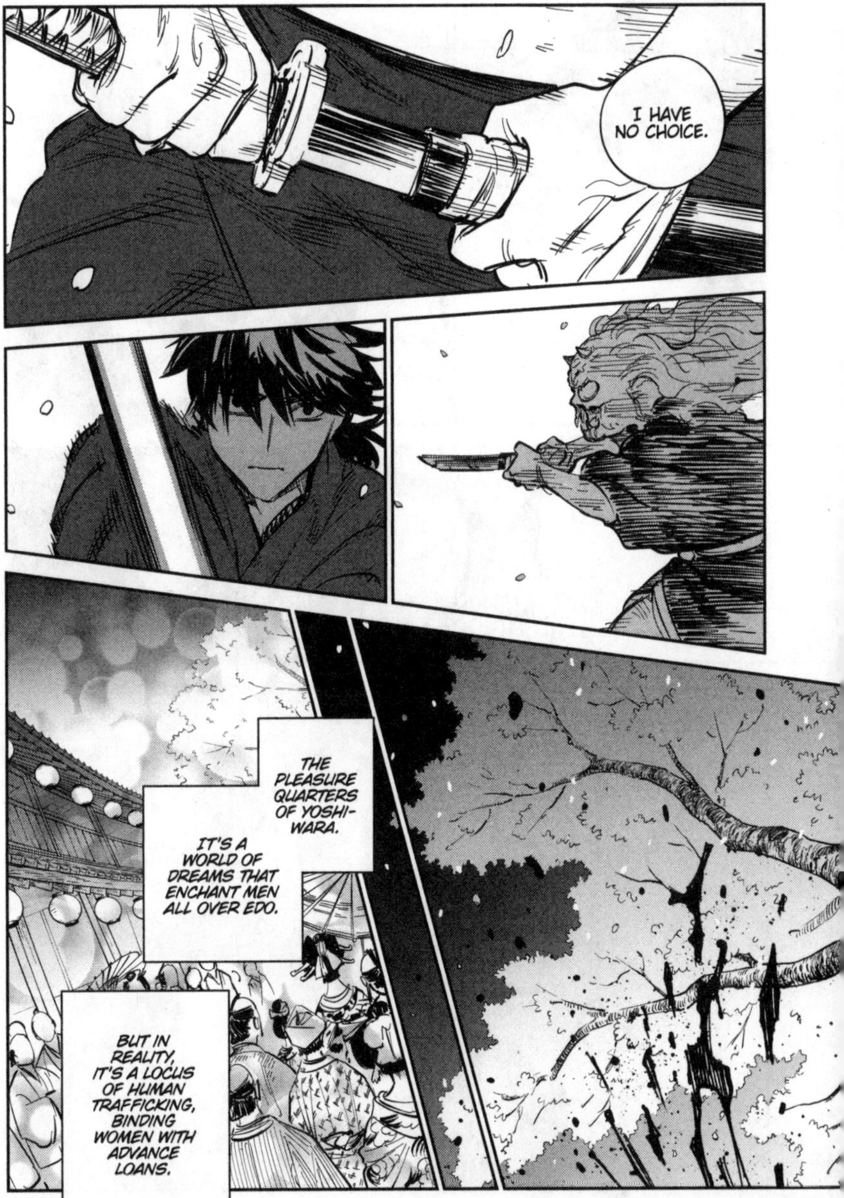
I HAVE NO CHOICE.
THE PLEASURE QUARTERS OF YOSHI-WARA.
IT'S A WORLD OF DREAMS THAT ENCHANT MEN ALL OVER EDO.
BUT IN REALITY, IT'S A LOCUS OF HUMAN TRAFFICKING, BINDING WOMEN WITH ADVANCE LOANS.

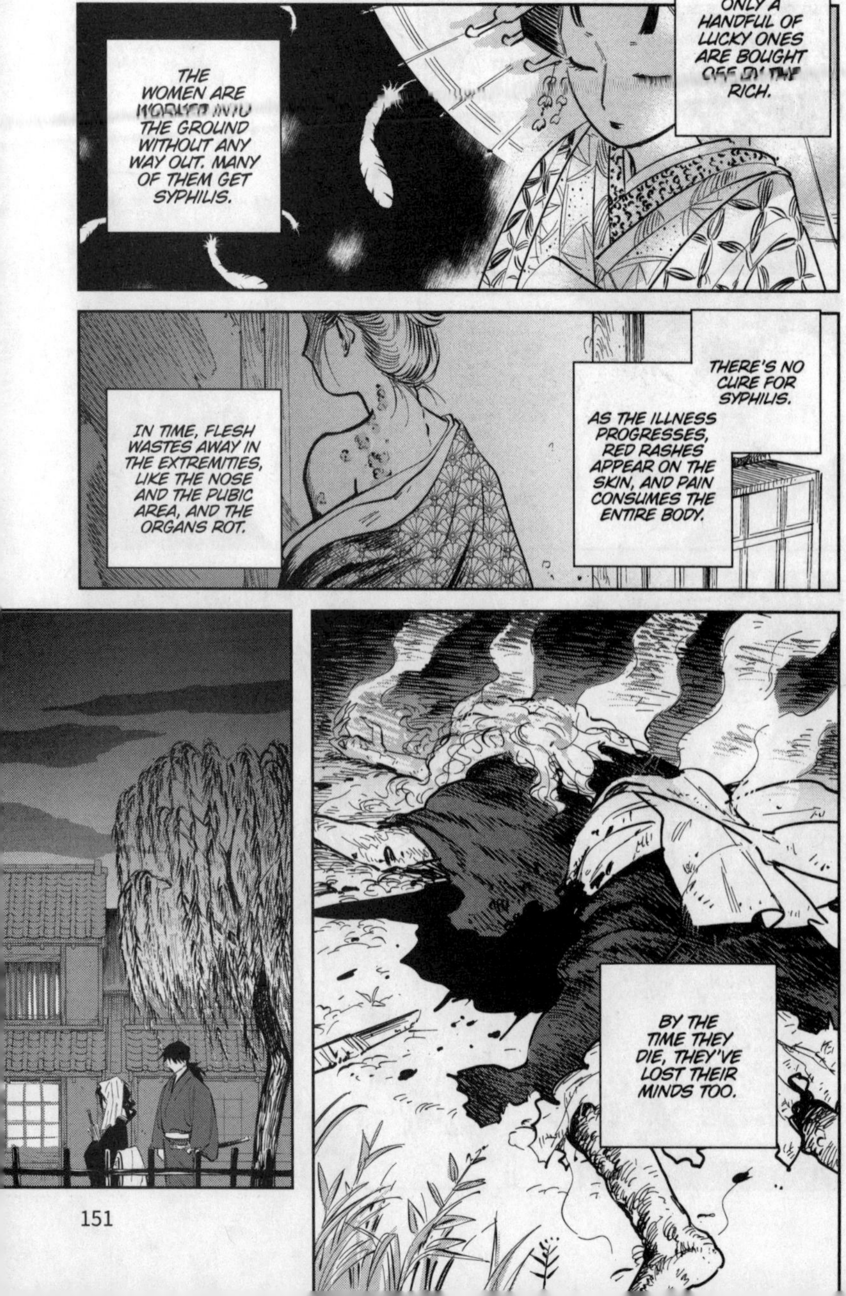
ONLY A HANDFUL OF LUCKY ONES ARE BOUGHT OFF BY THE RICH.
THE WOMEN ARE WORKED INTO THE GROUND WITHOUT ANY WAY OUT. MANY OF THEM GET SYPHILIS.
THERE'S NO CURE FOR SYPHILIS.
AS THE ILLNESS PROGRESSES, RED RASHES APPEAR ON THE SKIN, AND PAIN CONSUMES THE ENTIRE BODY.
IN TIME, FLESH WASTES AWAY IN THE EXTREMITIES, LIKE THE NOSE AND THE PUBIC AREA, AND THE ORGANS ROT.
BY THE TIME THEY DIE, THEY'VE LOST THEIR MINDS TOO.

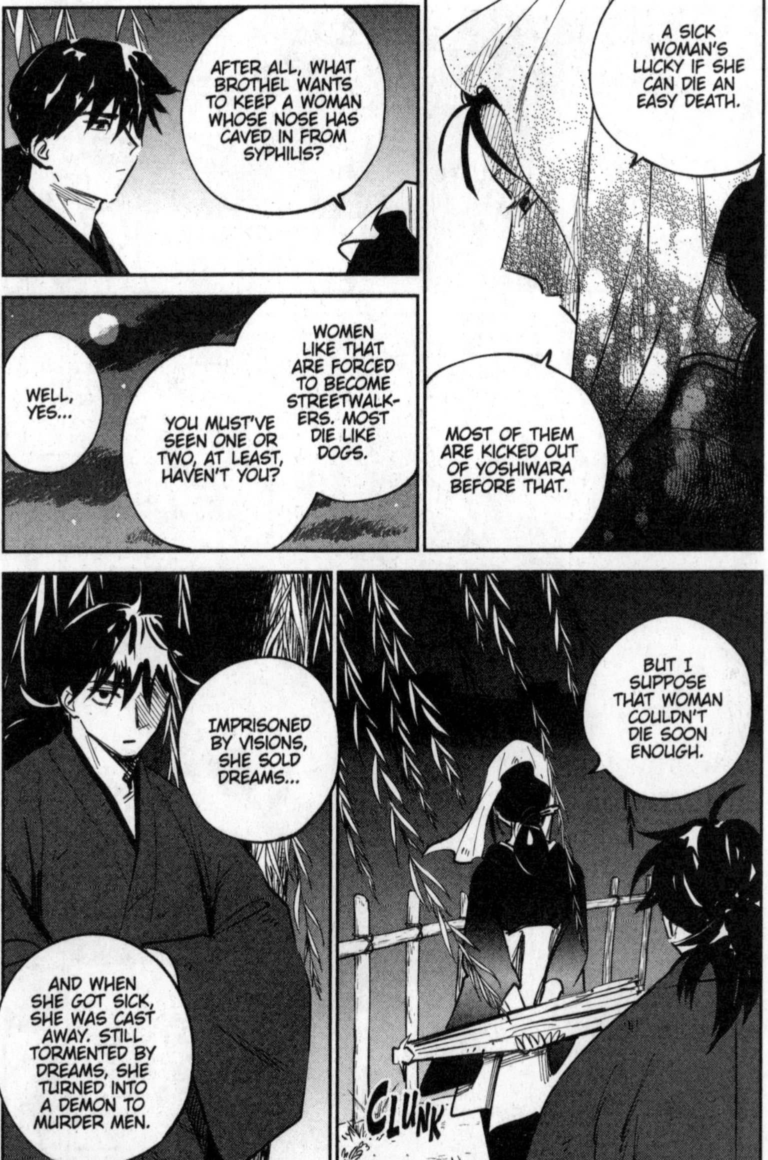
A SICK WOMAN'S LUCKY IF SHE CAN DIE AN EASY DEATH.
MOST OF THEM ARE KICKED OUT OF YOSHIWARA BEFORE THAT.
AFTER ALL, WHAT BROTHEL WANTS TO KEEP A WOMAN WHOSE NOSE HAS CAVED IN FROM SYPHILIS?
WOMEN LIKE THAT ARE FORCED TO BECOME STREETWALK-ERS. MOST DIE LIKE DOGS.
YOU MUST'VE SEEN ONE OR TWO, AT LEAST, HAVEN'T YOU?
WELL, YES...
BUT I SUPPOSE THAT WOMAN COULDN'T DIE SOON ENOUGH.
CLUNK
IMPRISONED BY VISIONS, SHE SOLD DREAMS...
AND WHEN SHE GOT SICK, SHE WAS CAST AWAY. STILL TORMENTED BY DREAMS, SHE TURNED INTO A DEMON TO MURDER MEN.

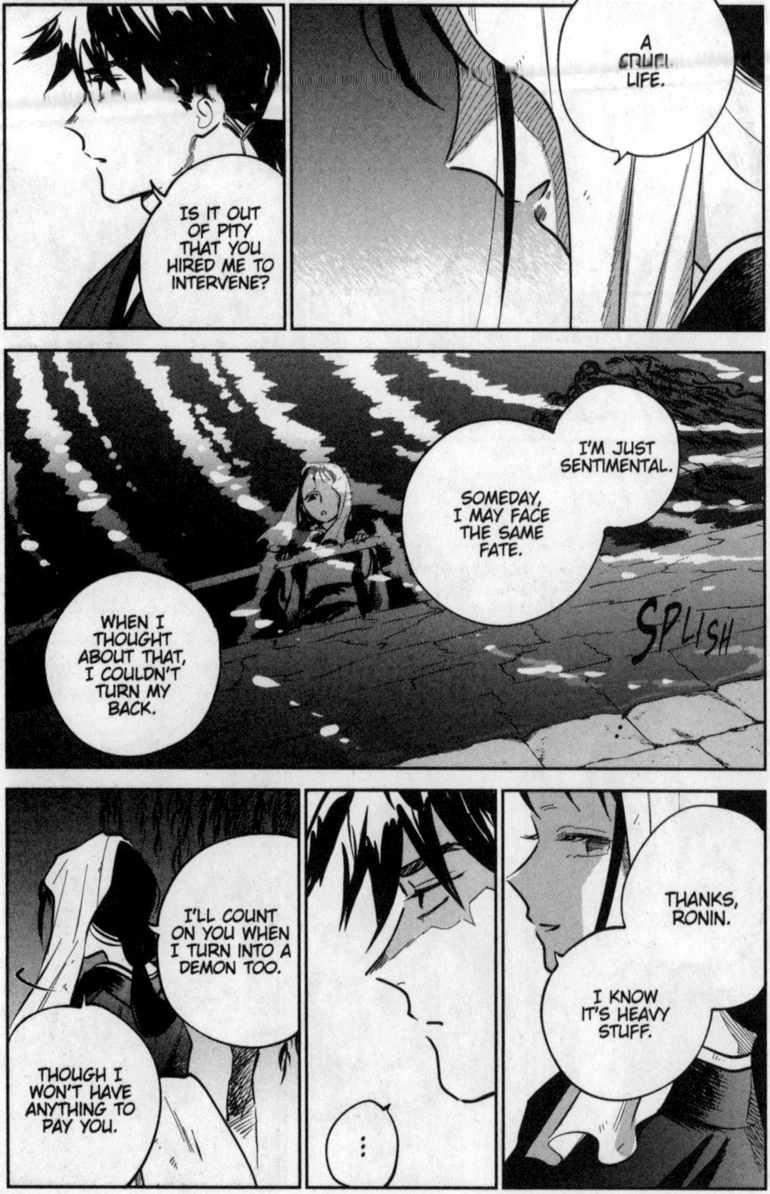
A CRUEL LIFE.
IS IT OUT OF PITY THAT YOU HIRED ME TO INTERVENE?
I'M JUST SENTIMENTAL.
SOMEDAY, I MAY FACE THE SAME FATE.
SPLISH
WHEN I THOUGHT ABOUT THAT, I COULDN'T TURN MY BACK.
THANKS, RONIN.
I KNOW IT'S HEAVY STUFF.
...
I'LL COUNT ON YOU WHEN I TURN INTO A DEMON TOO.
THOUGH I WON'T HAVE ANYTHING TO PAY YOU.

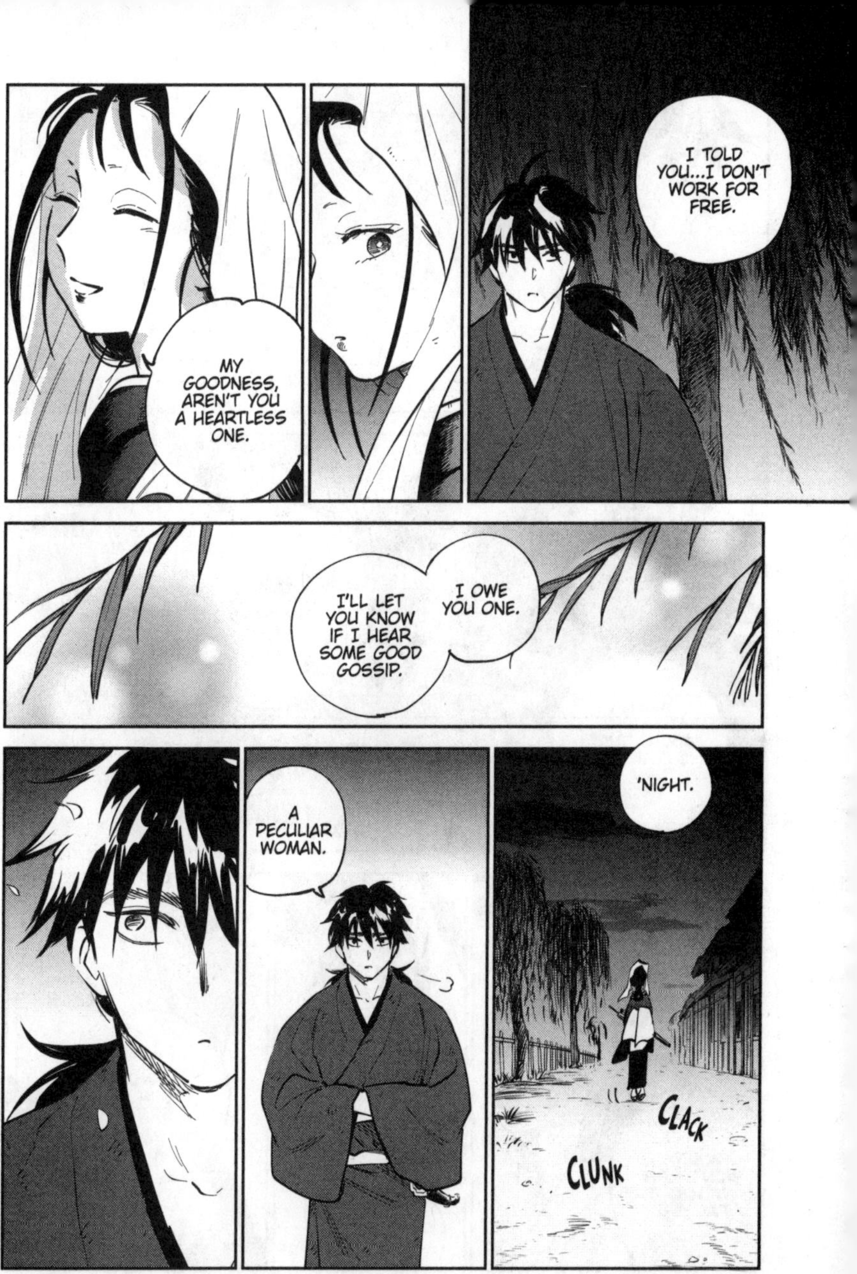
I TOLD YOU...I DON'T WORK FOR FREE.
MY GOODNESS, AREN'T YOU A HEARTLESS ONE.
I OWE YOU ONE.
I'LL LET YOU KNOW IF I HEAR SOME GOOD GOSSIP.
'NIGHT.
CLACK
CLUNK
A PECULIAR WOMAN.

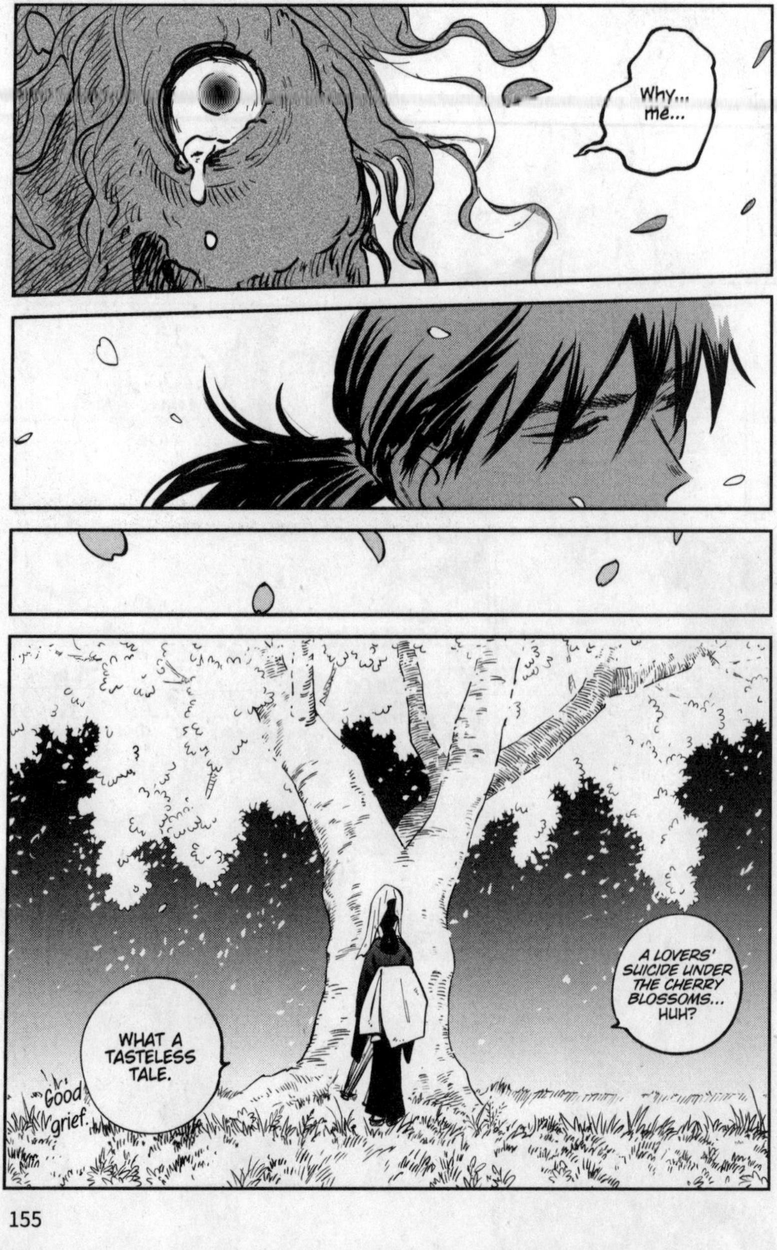
Why... me...
A LOVERS' SUICIDE UNDER THE CHERRY BLOSSOMS... HUH?
WHAT A TASTELESS TALE.
Good grief.

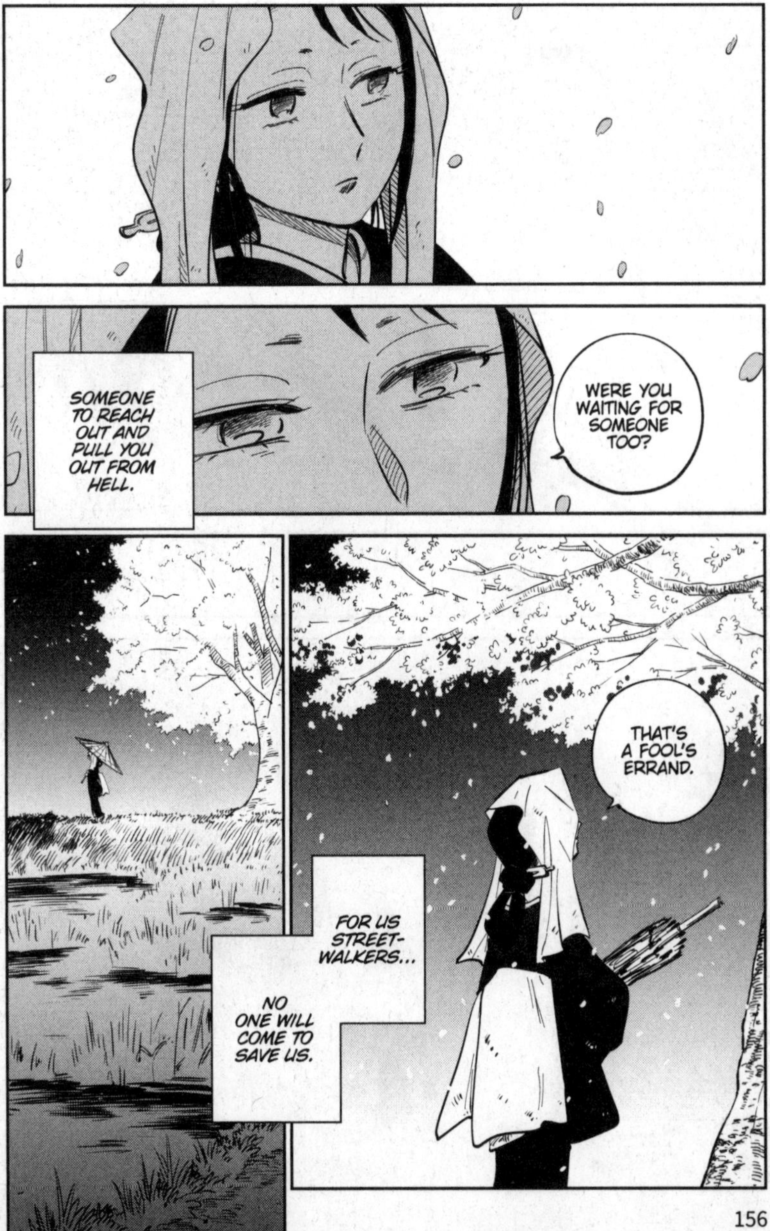
WERE YOU WAITING FOR SOMEONE TOO?
SOMEONE TO REACH OUT AND PULL YOU OUT FROM HELL.
THAT'S A FOOL'S ERRAND.
FOR US STREET-WALKERS...
NO ONE WILL COME TO SAVE US.

KIJIN GENTŌSHŌ
VOLUME 6:
COMING SOON!

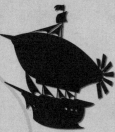
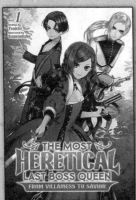
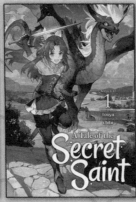
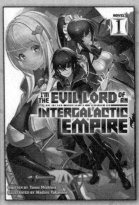
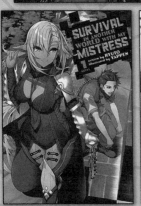
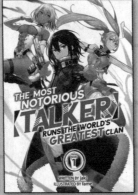
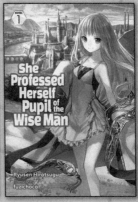

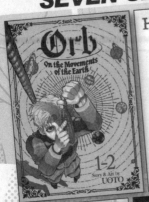
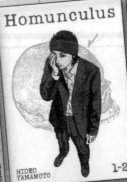
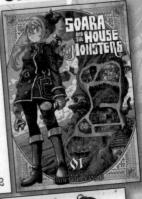
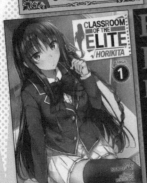
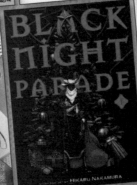
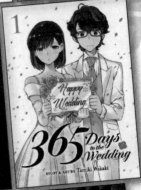
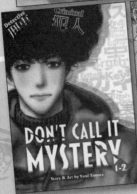
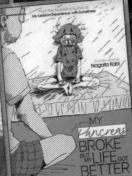
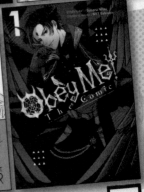

MW00779036

# Sword of the Demon Hunter

**SWORD OF THE DEMON HUNTER: KIJIN GENTŌSHŌ VOL. 5**
**STORY BY MOTOO NAKANISHI**
**ART BY YU SATOMI**

Translation: **Yui Kajita**
Lettering: **Kai Kyou**
Logo Design: **H. Qi**
Cover Design: **Mariel Dágá**
Copy Editor: **Leighanna DeRouen**
Proofreader: **Krista Grandy**
Quality Control: **Dave Murray**
Production Designer: **George Panella**
Editor: **Kristiina Korpus**

**Seven Seas Entertainment, Inc.** | President: **Jason DeAngelis** | Vice President: **Adam Arnold** Publisher: **Lianne Sentar** | Licensing Managers: **Y. Takahashi & Lena LeRay** | Editor-In-Chief: **Julie Davis** | Managing Editors: **Jack Sullivan & Shanti Whitesides** | Production Manager: **John Ramirez** | Assistant Production Manager: **Jinky Besa** | Prepress Technicians: **Salvador Chan Jr., Melanie Ujimori, & Jules Valera** | Digital Manager: **CK Russell** | Sales & Marketing Manager: **Lauren Hill** | Marketing Associate: **Leanna Cruz** | Administrative Associate: **Danya Adair** | Inventory & Logistics Manager: **Marsha Reid**

ISBN: 979-8-89160-198-7
Printed in Canada
First Printing: September 2024
10 9 8 7 6 5 4 3 2 1